Outdoor recreation and the urban environment

In the last few decades, the provision for leisure in urban areas has increased significantly. Changes in working practices and urban lifestyles have meant people have more time for leisure than ever before. But how well has the recent growth of outdoor recreation been accommodated in a rapidly changing environment? How should we shape the future for outdoor recreation in our towns and cities?

These are the kinds of issues Stephen Williams addresses in this volume. He looks at how people interact with the resources currently available and offers a critical review of the policies through which recreational opportunities in towns and cities are currently being developed. He calls for a more flexible approach to the way in which the urban environment is evaluated, developed and managed. A range of urban areas are discussed, from public open spaces to seldom covered areas such as private gardens and the street. Offering international examples of good practice, this volume will be of interest to students and researchers in leisure, recreation and urban planning.

Stephen Williams is Principal Lecturer in Geography at Staffordshire University.

Outdoor recreation and the urban environment

Stephen Williams

London and New York

First published 1995
by Routledge
11 New Fetter Lane, London EC4P 4EE

Simultaneously published in the USA and Canada
by Routledge
29 West 35th Street, New York, NY 10001

Typeset in Times by
Michael Mepham, Frome, Somerset

Printed and bound in Great Britain by
Mackays of Chatham PLC, Chatham, Kent

British Library Cataloguing in Publication Data
A catalogue record for this book is available from the British
Library

Library of Congress Cataloguing in Publication Data
A catalogue record for this book has been requested

ISBN 0–415–09632–4 (hbk)
ISBN 0–415–09633–2 (pbk)

Contents

Figures

Tables

Acknowledgements

I would like to acknowledge assistance from a number of individuals and organisations in the preparation of this text. The award of a sabbatical semester by the Division of Geography at Staffordshire University was of particular value and sincere thanks are extended to those colleagues who rearranged their teaching commitments to accommodate my leave of absence. Amongst those who took an interest in the development of this text, I must single out Professor George Kay who kindly spent time in reading and advising on drafts of the early parts of the book. Owen Tucker, the cartographer in the Division of Geography, prepared the diagrams and I am grateful to him for his careful translation of my rough sketches into finished illustrations. The maps were prepared by myself with considerable (professional) assistance from my wife, Jane.

Finally, I acknowledge the permission of the following to use or reproduce material: Mintel International Group Ltd. (Figure 2.6); Sports Council (Figures 2.7–2.10 and 8.1); Ordnance Survey (Figures 4.1–4.3); Liverpool University Press (Figure 4.7); Geographical Association (Figures 4.8, 4.9); Van Nostrand Reinhold Ltd. (Figure 5.3) and Plenum Publishing Ltd. (Figure 5.7).

Stephen Williams

Introduction

From some perspectives, the development of urban recreation could be seen to have reached a crossroads. There is no doubt that in the period since the end of the Second World War, the provision for leisure in urban areas has increased significantly and that through changes in working practice, higher real incomes and greater mobility, people are generally better placed to take advantage of those opportunities. Over the same timescale, the nature of urban places has changed too. The pressures of urban population growth which fuelled the spread of suburbia have dissipated but have been replaced by changes in urban lifestyles which have continued to create physical expansion and relocation of functions to the urban periphery. At the same time, attention has been focused upon processes of restructuring such as inner city renewal, and recently, policies for urban enhancement (for example 'green city' policies and traffic calming) have begun to attract attention. Superficially, such physical restructuring of towns and cities creates new opportunities to develop provision for recreation, yet it is also apparent that the potential benefits of such processes are easily undermined or negated by other changes within the urban environment. In particular, the socio-economic context of urban life has not always developed in a way that is conducive to recreation activity, especially activity out of doors. Urban poverty, unemployment, social stress, racial tensions, rising crime and, most of all, increases in the fear of crime, can be seen as potentially powerful impediments to widespread use of urban environments by people at leisure.

The years of post-war recovery in the 1950s, the prosperity and enlightenment of the 1960s, the uncertainties of the 1970s and the often contradictory tensions of growth and decline which characterised the 1980s, can therefore be construed as having led to the point at which a relatively large number of comparatively affluent and leisured people reside in urban environments which in physical, economic and social terms are increasingly fragile and potentially unstable. As a society (or perhaps a set of societies), we enjoy more leisure time and have more disposable income available for recreational use than ever before. Despite the growing trend in urban–rural migration that has become prominent over the same timescale, the majority of the population, at least within the western world, still reside in towns and cities. Yet the extent to which those urban places will provide a forum within which public outdoor recreation will flourish depends very much upon how planners and those in positions of power and influence face up to the challenge of urban restructuring – physical, economic and social – that is being posed by contemporary processes of urban change.

That is one possible interpretation of the context within which the discussions that follow might be located. It is a primary objective of this text to argue that if, collectively, we do not give careful consideration to the ways in which people use the urban environment for recreation and to how that environment might be recast to facilitate those activities, then the capacity of urban areas to attract and sustain recreational usage will be frustrated by other processes of change. In particular, decay within the physical fabric of cities and the fragmentation of urban economy and society pose a major challenge to successful development of outdoor recreation in towns and cities.

This text arises directly from the needs and interests generated by the teaching of leisure studies on undergraduate degree programmes, and it strives to address the range of issues that confront the student seeking to examine the ways in which people use different environments for their pleasure. An important objective of the study is to explore the nature and extent of outdoor recreational activity within urban places, to establish what people like to do, how they interact with different resources and indeed, how those resources are actually perceived and appraised.

Although recreation is often characterised as discretionary use of free time, in reality people are limited in the way in which they recreate by a host of personal and external constraints. As we will see, notions of discretion and flexibility of choice in how time may be used for recreation are perhaps too simplistic. In the specific case of outdoor activity, patterns of provision (whether from the public, private or voluntary sectors) will frequently pose constraints on patterns and timings of recreational actions that are additional to those felt personally by the individual and which arise through their own particular circumstances. Critical examination of the policy through which development of recreational opportunity in towns and cities is pursued must also form a key focus for attention within this study.

Consideration of the wide range of activities that urban populations pursue in a recreational fashion, set alongside an assessment of the extent and character of provision, leads to the basic thesis of the book – that outdoor recreational activity is far more extensive and varied than is formally recognised and that, in consequence, evaluation of recreational environments in towns and cities needs to be more flexible, and policy responses more imaginative. If basic elements in the urban fabric – residential neighbourhoods, housing areas, streets and routeways, town centres – were to be planned in a more creative and less stereotypical fashion, the range of environments that would welcome and facilitate recreational use, rather than accept it grudgingly or exclude it altogether, could be significantly extended.

In attempting to address both the general thesis and the more specific aims of the book, my approach draws upon several complementary perspectives (geography, sociology, economics and land planning) to try to provide an integrated synthesis of our present understanding of urban outdoor recreation patterns and needs. The chapter headings perhaps betray the author's academic background in geography (with its preoccupations with spatial structures and the ties between people and places), but the chapters reflect a multi-disciplinary perspective. Within the modest compass of the book, the focus of discussions is largely the United Kingdom, but not exclusively so. There is much to be learnt from examining research findings and examples of good practice in provision from overseas, particularly in Europe and in North America, and wherever possible, such material will be incorporated.

The selection of a specific focus upon *outdoor* recreation and *urban* environments is a conscious decision, taken because this was perceived as a relatively neglected area of study. A great deal of scholarly and practical research has illuminated in considerable detail the uses made of rural areas for leisure and recreation, but the same cannot be said of the urban experience. In the latter area, much valuable work has been completed on the social context of leisure (particularly by sociologists) and from a spatial/planning perspective certain types of resource have been well covered, most notably open space. Elsewhere the understanding is much more fragmentary. This book aims to redress some of these imbalances.

Chapter 1

Recreational resources and urban places

THE CONCEPT OF OUTDOOR RECREATION

'Recreation' can mean many things to many people. It is a word which is recognised, is in common usage, yet is seldom clearly defined. For some it may be used interchangeably with the concept of 'leisure', for others it has a more specific connotation which defines and distinguishes a distinctive behavioural area.

However, conventionally, 'recreation' has tended to be seen as a sub-area of 'leisure'. Patmore (1983) summarises the matter both succinctly and clearly. Leisure, he states, may be used in three distinct contexts. First, it may be conceived in terms of time, leisure normally being that period of the day which remains after routine commitments to work, domestic chores and other obligations have been discharged. Secondly, it may be seen as an attitude of mind; in other words a reflection of an individual's perception of whether he or she is 'at leisure'. Finally, leisure may be associated with activity, and it is in this latter context that the concept of recreation emerges most clearly. Recreations may have a range of functions: they may be relaxing or energetic; they may foster social, cultural, intellectual or creative developments for individuals or for groups; they may be recuperative; they may revitalise or *re-create* the participant, and normally they perform several of these functions simultaneously. But primarily, recreation is about activity in which participants have chosen to engage. This is the sense in which the term 'recreation' is intended and will be deployed within this present discussion – as active use of free time within an individual's lifestyle.

But simple statements seldom tell the whole story. At one level we must acknowledge that the recognition of what actually constitutes recreational activity will vary from person to person and that that variation is, in turn, a reflection of the more complex structure of the 'recreation experience', an experience which is only partly dependent upon the activity itself.

The focus within this book is upon the outdoor environment of towns and cities. For some readers that might suggest a preoccupation with a particular and rather limited range of individual activities (for example casual recreations of the type encountered in urban parks, formal sports and team games and perhaps children's play). But in practice, distinctions between indoor and outdoor recreations are tenuous since there are very few activities which are precluded from the outdoor environment by the nature of the activity itself. Individual perceptions and preferences as much as physical opportunity or constraint dictate where most recreational events take place.

Similarly, it is difficult to draw up lists of recreational and non-recreational activities since it is readily evident that for some people a particular event would be conceived as a duty or a chore (and therefore non-recreational in character if we deploy the definitional criteria outlined above) whilst others might see precisely the same activity in quite a different light. Gardening, car maintenance and DIY are all examples of activities which float between the recreational and non-recreational ends of the spectrum, according to personal inclination or even the specific circumstance in which the event is set. An activity like gardening, for example, may on one day require a set of unattractive tasks to be performed that the participant will treat as a chore and from which little pleasure or recreational benefit will be derived. Yet on another occasion a quite different set of garden tasks might be willingly confronted and enjoyed in a leisurely way.

So, although we may happily define recreation as active use of available leisure time, the practical implications are varied because of the nature of activity itself and the manner in which individuals will appraise opportunity. It therefore seems appropriate in approaching the subject of outdoor recreation in urban environments to think broadly and flexibly about both the range of possible recreations that might occur out of doors in a town or city and the different environments in which these could take place.

The nature of the recreation experience also demands consideration. A great deal of research into recreational patterns (whether in town or country) has tended to focus upon activities, almost in isolation. The General Household Survey, for example, which forms a common starting point for many analyses of what people do with their leisure time, follows precisely such a path in listing popular recreations and their associated levels of participation. But this type of analysis, although useful as a start point, provides us with only part of the picture and as Figure 1.1 implies, it is more revealing to consider a recreational experience as composed of two basic, interrelated elements, the activity and the context, the benefit derived from engagement here being seen as a combination of the activity itself and a wider benefit drawn from the context.

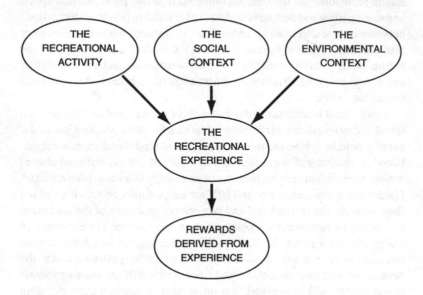

Figure 1.1 Principal elements in the recreational experience

Recreational activity is normally seen as discretionary use of time, so the individual presumably perceives a benefit (or reward) to be gained through participation. In the specific case of outdoor recreation that element of reward may be stronger since participation will usually require the physical removal of the participant from the home or the workplace in order to engage in the activity in question. There is thus an additional cost in effort, time and/or money which must be a part of the decision to participate.

Figure 1.1 suggests that the reward may be acquired through the twin channels of activity and context, which make up the experience. The recreational activity will bestow a benefit upon the participant that will be directly derived through the pursuit of the activity itself. This may be a physical, emotional or psychological reward associated with actually doing something, and commonly it will be a combination of these elements. A soccer player, for example, will enjoy the benefit of physical exercise, the development of skills associated with the game and the challenge of a competitive sport. Alternatively, someone reading a novel in the back garden will experience a different set of benefits – perhaps relaxation, education or entertainment. Traditionally, recreation research has drawn a distinction between the active and passive pursuits (see, for an early example, Burton, 1967). This is certainly relevant, although it might be more useful to think in terms of a continuum which ranges from the highly active to the purely passive, rather than a simple dichotomy, but either way the nature of the benefit from the activity will vary according to this basic attribute.

Part of the reward, however, stems not from the activity itself but from the context in which it takes place. Two experiential contexts appear particularly important to outdoor recreation; the environmental and the social. In the majority of instances, whether it be a stroll in the park, a ball game with the children, an active team game or leisurely window shopping, the recreational event is enhanced or devalued by the nature of the environment in which the activity is located. The quality of the built environment, the space it affords, its design, layout, interest, cleanliness and safety, its capacity to excite or relax, to provide sounds and smells, all will have an impact upon the quality of the recreation experience, simply because most forms of outdoor activity are dependent upon inter-action between individuals (or groups) and that environment. We may derive the physical benefits of, say, walking, from exercise on a treadmill. But few would choose the option when the experience can be enhanced by the addition of an aesthetic dimension gained from walking through a park or past pleasant front gardens in a leafy suburb.

The social environment within urban areas is also directly relevant to the study of recreation because most forms of recreation are overtly social in nature. Although some activity is driven by a quest for a measure of temporary isolation from others, a great deal is centred upon interpersonal relationships with relatives, friends or neighbours. Family outings, trips to facilities or attractions, children's play, even sporting participation, tend to have a social dimension which cannot be overlooked. Indeed, some sociologists have recognised recreation as one of the mechanisms through which social bonding of intimate family and friends is developed and maintained (Kelly, 1983; Stokowski and Lee, 1991), although the precise nature of the relationship is not always consistent or clear.

In seeking to understand patterns of outdoor recreation in the urban environment we must look beyond the activity itself and into the wider context of recreational events and the meanings and values they hold for the participants.

OUTDOOR RECREATION IN URBAN AREAS

Towns and cities are major recreational areas – a plain assertion which may be supported on the basis of three simple and interrelated observations. First, most of us live within urban areas. In 1981 in England and Wales, approximately 76 per cent of the population resided in towns and larger metropolitan areas (Central Statistical Office, 1994) and although the precise share of the population that is urban by residence will vary from country to country, the numerical dominance of urban over rural populations is consistent throughout the developed world. It is true that the emerging problems of many urban areas, when allied to certain attitudinal changes on the part of sections of the urban population, have encouraged migration from urban to peri-urban or rural locations but this has not prevented the continuing spatial expansion of urban areas that has been such a prominent feature of urbanism in the twentieth century.

Secondly, urban populations engage in most of their leisure activities within the same urban area in which they live. The geographical patterns of residence are translated very readily into a pattern of recreation that is focused upon the urban environment, purely by the fact that most people spend the majority of their leisure time in, or close to, the home. Patmore (1983: 87) highlights an interesting paradox when he comments that 'the greatest changes in recreation habits in the last fifty years have taken place in two opposing directions'. On the one hand, increased mobility has facilitated an extension of recreation activities well away from the home and often beyond the bounds of the urban area (although for most, such trips are intermittent and account for only a small share of the total leisure time that is available). Conversely, leisure that is centred within and around the home has taken on greater significance and, as we shall see in subsequent chapters, the domestic garden and the street outside the domestic front door have both a considerable utility and a potential as locations for outdoor recreation. Studies by, amongst others, the BBC (1978); Glyptis and Chambers (1982) and Glyptis et al. (1987) show that on average more than half of all leisure time is spent at home. At an individual level there is, of course, some variation, but whilst some groups (for example, young adults) may spend proportionately less time at home than aggregate figures suggest, by the same token others – for example the very young and the mothers in whose care they tend to be lodged and, at the other extreme, the elderly – spend a great deal more time in the domestic environment.

While the growth of in-home entertainment, which was a prominent feature of the changing leisure patterns of the 1980s, has been quite well documented (see, for example, Glyptis *et al.*, 1987; Roberts, 1989; Leisure Consultants,1990a, 1990b), the importance of outdoor space at home and in the immediate neighbourhood is relatively neglected. Initially, the growing emphasis upon in-home leisure (as reflected, for instance, in the burgeoning market for television sets and home videos) might suggest a diminution in the role of the outdoor environment, but estimates show that over 26 million people in the UK count themselves as gardeners of one sort or another (see Table 1.1), by far the most significant of the active recreations, although one which is often overlooked in surveys of popular activity.

Table 1.1 The major recreations in the UK – 1990

Activity	% participating in the 4 weeks before survey	% participating in the 12 months before survey
Watching TV	99	
Visiting/entertaining friends	96	
Listening to radio	89	
Listening to records/tapes	76	
Reading books	62	
Gardening	48	
DIY	43	
Walking	41	65
Dressmaking/knitting	23	
Swimming (indoors)	12	36
Swimming (outdoors)	4	22
Snooker/pool/billiards	14	22
Keep fit/yoga	12	19
Cycling	9	17
Darts	7	13
Golf	5	12
Running/jogging	5	9
Weight training	5	9
Soccer (outdoors)	4	7
Soccer (indoors)	2	4
Ten-pin bowling	4	11
Badminton	3	9
Squash	3	6
Lawn bowls	1	4
Carpet bowls	1	3

Source: OPCS (1992)

Thirdly, the significance of the urban environment as a location and setting for recreation is emphasised when we consider what people actually like to do with their leisure time. The data in Table 1.1, derived from the General Household Survey for 1990 (OPCS, 1992), illustrate the major activities cited by respondents. The practical difficulty of distinguishing between activity pursued in the rural as opposed to the urban environment is to be noted and there is no clear distinction between the role of outdoor and indoor environments. But several points remain relevant to this discussion.

The activity profile re-emphasises the importance of the domestic environment, with the top seven recreations in the listing all likely to be largely or entirely conducted in or around the home. These activities are, by and large, the types of event around which the leisure lifestyles of probably a majority of the population are centred.

A significant number of the activities are associated with built provision, particularly of the type that is afforded at the modern sports and leisure centre or, in some instances, by commercial leisure providers. Indoor swimming, the cue sports, keep-fit and similar types of aerobic activity, weight training, indoor soccer, ten-pin bowling, badminton, squash and carpet bowls are all examples of recreations that would normally be associated with indoor activity and usually (because of the population thresholds that are necessary to support provision of this character) in an urban location.

The General Household Survey does not include information relating to popular usage of entertainments, nor does it make direct reference to open space such as parks and gardens. However, the Central Statistical Office annual review of social trends does provide some insight into how significant these other recreational resources might be (Central Statistical Office, 1992) and selected reference to individual case studies can add further illumination.

Table 1.2 lists in rank order the most popular leisure purposes for day trips over at least 20 miles as identified by the Central Statistical Office. The distance element deployed within the survey definition is an unwelcome complication since it makes it harder to ascertain a probable balance between inter-urban, intra-urban and urban–rural journeys. But the data are still useful in helping to paint a broad picture in which an urban focus for much of the activity (for example visits to friends and relations, recreational shopping, visits to cinemas and theatres, participation or spectating at sporting events and trips to parks and gardens), is likely to be present.

There is, of course, a seasonal rhythm to such excursions. The summer

Table 1.2 Leisure day visits of between 20 and 40 miles (1988–89)

Object of visit	No. of trips (millions)
Visiting friends or relations	144
Sightseeing	66
Shopping (not routine)	64
Restaurant	27
Theatre, opera, cinema, etc.	25
Playing outdoor sport	23
Walking, hiking, climbing, etc.	22
Watching outdoor sport	21
Swimming, sunbathing	20
Pub	18
Parks and gardens	14
Playing indoor sport	14
Zoo, aquarium, safari park, etc.	13
Theme park	9
Museum, gallery	9
Picnicking	8
Castle or ancient monument	8
Fishing	7
Stately home	6
Cathedral or church	4

Source: CSO (1993)

months not only see a higher overall level of outdoor activity, but also a spatially more extensive range of destinations. Data from the 1993 UK Day Visitors Survey (Anon, 1994) tells us that during the year under review, 59 per cent of respondents made trips to the countryside and 41 per cent took outings to seaside resorts or the coast, but 80 per cent of respondents had visited an urban place, and of the estimated 2,200 million visits made, the majority (64 per cent) were located in a town or city.

General studies of recreational patterns within individual cities or urban areas are not especially common, the tendency within research being to deal with particular activities or resources. However, work conducted on Stoke-on-Trent by Williams and Jackson (1985, 1986, 1987) does provide such an overview and a more recent study by Kay (1991) of Broxtowe (Nottinghamshire) is also useful.

The general findings from the Stoke survey lend weight to the view that most recreation is conducted within the urban area in which the population resides, and normally close to home. The most popular recreations included those that are often social in character, visits to pubs and clubs being especially common. Parks and open spaces were used widely, entertainments and formal sports facilities rather less so, although it is important to note the role played by urban environments as locations for traditional sport, especially the popular team games such as soccer, rugby, hockey and cricket (Table 1.3). Trips outside the city were much more occasional in nature although widely encountered within the population as a whole.

Table 1.3 Major recreational activities amongst adults in Stoke-on-Trent

Activity	Percentage participating
Visiting parks and open spaces	72
Visiting pubs and working clubs	58
Swimming	35
Visiting cinemas	26
Playing sport, including	26
badminton	5
soccer	3
bowls	2
golf	1
rugby	1
Visiting theatres	21
Visiting discos, clubs, etc.	12
Jogging	9
Playing bingo	5

Source: Williams and Jackson (1985, 1986)

The study of Broxtowe had a more overt focus upon outdoor recreation and this is reflected in the information presented. Respondents here identified walking as the most popular recreation, followed, at some distance and in rank order by cycling, football, swimming, golf, tennis and fishing, amongst a lengthy and varied listing (Table 1.4). (Some of the differences between Tables 1.3 and 1.4 are a reflection of different sampling procedures in the two studies.)

However, all these surveys tend to suffer from certain common problems which may ultimately distort the picture of recreation patterns that are presented. Kay appends to his data a most important caveat in noting the tendency for respondents in unprompted interviews to overlook the commonplace outdoor recreations, with the resulting risk that they are grossly under-recorded. Thus, in the Broxtowe survey, motoring, trips to the countryside and gardening were hardly mentioned, not because they are unimportant – there is, after all, a substantial body of evidence to the

Table 1.4 Major recreational activities amongst adults in Broxtowe

Activity	Percentage participating
Walking	67
Cycling	19
Football	18
Swimming	16
Golf	14
Tennis	10
Fishing	8
Cricket	6
Running	6
Bowling	6
Riding	4
Sailing	4
Gardening	3
Hockey	3
Climbing	3
Netball	2
Rugby	2
Camping/caravanning	2
Wind-surfing	2
Bird-watching	1

Source: Kay (1991)

contrary – but simply because they are routine or because they are not always perceived as recreations. This observation has major implications, particularly for policymakers. If the tendency is to overlook the commonplace, to recognise only certain activities as being recreational and only some environments as being appropriate for such events, then we limit significantly the capacity of the urban environment to support the true range of pursuits which actually exist within the population, particularly those latent demands that are frustrated by constraints the present environment imposes on recreational choices. In practice, recreational use of city space is far wider than would be suggested by an examination of only those facilities with a clear recreational role, and could be wider still if policy and practice were more favourably disposed towards the types of change in the urban fabric that would realise this potential.

A second common failing is to overlook the capacity for multiple use of time. This is a complication which may very easily blur apparently clear-cut distinctions between leisure and other uses of time and may also lead to a failure to take into account the way in which the recreation experience may be broadened by the juxtaposition of more than one activity. For example, pleasure motoring and sightseeing are normally cited separately in surveys of popular recreations when, in practice, they often take place simultaneously and the participant's satisfaction with the experience is largely derived from the mutual dependence of the two activities. Or a routine domestic chore such as washing dishes may be enhanced by the recreational opportunity to observe wild birds within the garden.

It is also important to emphasise the fluctuating nature of the interplay of the indoor and outdoor recreational environments which is concealed within aggregate descriptions of activity. This may work in several ways. At one level we see the visual penetration of the outdoors into the home. We fit 'picture' windows to our houses to enable a view of the garden to enhance the living room. One of the major growth areas in home improvement in recent years has been the construction of conservatories, which are often intended as a leisure room and are always placed physically at the interface of the two environments and designed to permit a blending of the two. At a second level, there may be a spill-over effect in which internal functions are temporarily removed to the outdoors. These may be domestic functions but are more likely to be social/recreational activities: entertaining around the barbecue, listening to the radio, reading or knitting in a deckchair on the patio rather than in an armchair in the lounge, playing with children or pets. Such flexibility is rarely reflected in standard surveys of recreational habits amongst urban populations but awareness and understanding of these processes are essential to any wider appreciation of the character of recreation within urban areas.

We have therefore, in our towns and cities, a primary recreation environment that is used extensively by a majority of the population for a wide cross-section of recreations – from the high levels of activity associated with competitive sports to the passivity of casual recreations around the home. But it is not a straightforward environment to interpret, its recreational utility varies considerably according to context and perception and there is much that is subconscious in the way that urban populations use their environment for outdoor recreation and the benefits they derive from the experience.

THE URBAN SETTING

The urban domain is complex – towns and cities present an outwardly confusing mosaic of land uses into which recreational provision must fit and over which recreational activity must be superimposed. Patterns of opportunity are in most cases the product of lengthy periods of urban evolution in which physical growth, economic development and social change have combined to produce an environment that is dynamic, competitive and diverse.

Detailed analysis of this process is unwarranted in a text of this character but to assist readers who may be unfamiliar with the subject, a brief summary of key themes or processes which have shaped urban development and some guidance to further reading on this often fascinating topic may be helpful. Six processes are worth highlighting.

1 Perhaps the most conspicuous aspect of recent urbanism has been the physical expansion of built-up areas and associated concentrations of population into industrial towns and cities. Since, say, 1800, urban places have developed from compact and densely settled areas with low overall populations to, in the modern post-industrial city, extended areas of highly populated but relatively low-density occupation, with residual zones of higher-density occupation in older, inner areas. Lawless and Brown (1986) provide a valuable review of overall processes. For a full account of suburban development, particularly its stylistic progress, see Edwards (1981) and for an interesting case study of London's suburban expansion see A.A. Jackson (1991).

2 A second process has been the increase in the degree of social segregation. Early industrial cities were often socially mixed at a local level (see, for example, Pooley, 1977; Ward, 1980) but through time, distinctive social areas within cities have tended to develop and a social patterning to most contemporary cities is readily evident (Davies and Herbert, 1993). The growth of such areas has been encouraged by a number of factors including mobility, preference and the purchasing powers of different groups and the ability of some to exert influence over emergent municipal authority (Cooke, 1990).

3 Municipal regulation of development has tended to increase through time. Initially, by-law legislation such as the 1875 Public Health Act sought to impose certain basic standards upon development but in the twentieth century, and particularly since 1945, statutory land planning has become a major factor in regulating the urban environment. Regulation, or attempts to regulate the sprawl of suburbia associated with continuing physical expansion, has been one significant area of concern, but other planned initiatives such as new towns and green belt planning have also been prominent (Elson, 1986; Munton, 1983; Osborn and Whittick, 1977).

4 Concern for urban enhancement has been a feature of recent urban development. This is reflected in areas of town planning that are

concerned with urban design but was also apparent in proposals for garden cities and model communities at the beginning of the twentieth century, in green belt legislation of the early post-1945 period and in contemporary interests in greening the city (Miller, 1992; Nicholson-Lord, 1987; Relph, 1987; Ward, 1992). Environmental enhancement and the opportunities it affords are particularly relevant to outdoor recreation.

5   Policies for enhancement link closely to a fifth process, urban redevelopment. This has been a recurrent theme but has been especially prominent since 1945. War damage was one catalyst in this but more recently the evident decay and collapse of aged Victorian inner cities has prompted new initiatives at the heart of our cities. Urban development corporations and high profile projects, particularly in former dockland areas, are one conspicuous manifestation of the process (see Imrie and Thomas, 1993), but dereliction of urban land is an on-going process with, in some cases, what were seen as 'solutions' in the 1960s (for example, high rise apartments), providing problems for urban planners in the 1990s.

6   The need for redevelopment arises too because of a sixth process, urban decay. Cities developed in the nineteenth century because they offered work and attracted a youthful population from rural areas. Today, population movements are broadly in the reverse direction, with successive censuses showing population losses from major urban areas, especially the inner cities. High unemployment, poor housing, social stress, crime, traffic congestion and pollution are all symptomatic of a crisis in many contemporary cities that has focused attention on the question of how far modern urban life is actually sustainable. (For a thought-provoking analysis of the problems of London, see Thornley, 1992.) Such debates often tend to adopt a pessimistic or negative perspective, but whilst the problems are not to be belittled, it is also appropriate to emphasise the opportunity for restructuring that such decay actually affords. As we will see, one of the potential beneficiaries of such restructuring is outdoor recreation.

Within the fluid and at times unpredictable process of urban development, the significance of recreational space has fluctuated. In the pre- and early industrial city, recreational space *per se* was limited and was almost always an attribute of social class. For ordinary people, the street (including features such as town squares and markets) was probably the major venue for those few outdoor recreations that existed, supplemented by areas of common land which frequently provided important venues for fairs, meetings and sporting events. Some urban houses in the sevententh century possessed ornamental private gardens, but larger areas of amenity land were rare and, where they did exist, were normally in private ownership. However, as Conway (1991) shows, limited public amenity space did exist in some urban places in the seventeenth century. Although a royal park, Hyde Park in London had been opened to the public as early as the 1630s, and the first municipal park was formed in Exeter in 1612. However, such early initiatives occurred selectively and were atypical.

Of course through time the tendency is for recreational and amenity space to become more widely accessible, in both a physical and social sense. During the eighteenth and early nineteenth centuries, the expansion of good-quality upper- and middle-class housing areas, prominent in cities such as London, Bath and Edinburgh, was also associated with an extension of space for leisure. Private gardens, sometimes attached to individual properties, sometimes as shared (though still private) spaces set within the centres of residential squares, become a noticeable feature. There was also a significant extension in the provision of park-type spaces. Regent's Park (London), for example, was laid out as an integral feature in the prestigious housing development erected in the area by John Nash between 1811 and 1826 and although sections were reserved for property holders, other parts of the new park were freely available for public use. The extent to which such land was effectively available to the labouring masses who were still largely confined to their dense and squalid tenements and back-to-backs is, of course, open to question. Semi-public spaces, for example zoos and botanical gardens, also begin to appear in number at this period, although entry charges would in practice have restricted the clientele, no doubt to those sectors of society for whom such entertainment was initially intended.

Although a Select Committee on Public Walks reported as early as 1833, the real expansion of amenity space that was accessible to ordinary working people resident within towns and cities comes after 1850. In Britain between 1820 and 1849, some 19 urban parks were created, whereas between 1850 and 1880, the figure was 111 (Conway, 1991: 63).

The ornamental Victorian park did not, however, meet the demand for places for urban children to play or for locations for popular sports which developed rapidly after the middle of the nineteenth century. Thus was born the recreation ground, and although few such grounds were completed prior to about 1880, between then and the outbreak of war in 1914 there was a great deal of frequently opportunistic development of small parcels of vacant urban land to provide recreation grounds.

The wider concerns for the quality of urban life which lay behind this expansion of opportunity was further reflected in, first, wider provision of houses with gardens within expanding Victorian middle-class suburbs, and secondly, allotments – a prominent feature of rural life since the Middle Ages – which began to appear in number in an urban context towards the end of the nineteenth century, especially after the 1908 Smallholdings and Allotments Act.

Provision of parks, recreation grounds, public walks and allotments illustrates a paternalistic approach that was epitomised by the efforts of the various open space societies and which was characteristic of this early provision of amenity space. To a degree, this is further evident in important initiatives within the garden city movement and the formative phases of town planning which occurred in Britain in the early twentieth century. New planned model communities, with their parks and open spaces, their tree-lined roads and houses with front gardens and back yards, placed an emphasis on urban amenity and recreational spaces which had been largely absent in the typically uncontrolled expansion of working-class housing in the nineteenth century. Raymond Unwin, one of the founders of modern planning, wrote that 'we have neglected the amenities of life. We have forgotten that endless rows of brick boxes, looking out upon dreary streets and squalid back yards, are not really homes for people' (Unwin, 1909: 4).

The types of city Unwin and his followers wished to plan afforded not just those opportunities for leisure that were already associated with parks and gardens, but extended significantly the scope of the home and the suburban street to support informal recreation and children's play. In time, the utility of the street as a recreational environment would decline in the face of the environmental onslaught of increased road traffic but in, say, the years between 1918 and 1939, the streets of leafy suburbia became an almost unnoticed, but significant, recreational resource.

The style of housing which typified inter-war (and indeed post-1945) suburbia endowed ordinary urban people, for the first time on a widespread basis, with homes that had gardens. Actual use of gardens has, of course, changed, especially in respect of the balance between domestic and household functions that would have dominated a garden in the 1930s, and the leisurely use of the same space in the 1990s. But at this stage, simple recognition of the opportunity is all that is necessary.

Those same suburban areas offered, too, new facilities to support active recreations and sports. The formation of the National Playing Fields Association in 1925 was no accident of history; it reflected a realisation that there was a need for allocations of space within urban areas to support this branch of outdoor recreation. In 1937 the Physical Training and Recreation Act marked the beginning of financial aid from central government to local authorities for the provision of playing fields, gymnasia and swimming baths and these have since come to be basic elements of the recreational infrastructure of most urban places.

The popularisation of leisure and recreation in the years after 1945 is well documented and well understood. Dower's (1965) evocation of the 'fourth wave' to describe the spread of leisure is a familiar but still very apposite metaphor, even though universal access to leisure in the way that Dower envisaged has remained elusive (Dower, 1993). Demand for recreation has prompted response along several lines. At one level, statutory planning procedures now address, as a matter of course, basic provision of recreational space – playing fields, children's playgrounds and open space – within new housing schemes. Secondly, new forms of recreational space have developed, often in association with urban renewal schemes. These include urban greenways, which may make use of disused rail lines or canals; multi-purpose sports complexes in both the public and private sectors which afford a combination of outdoor and indoor facilities; informal sites based upon land clearance or derelict sites; adventure playgrounds; and within some fringe areas, urban forest or country parks. Thirdly, and much more recently, urban enhancement policies have begun to realise the recreational potential of land areas which previously had not developed (or had lost) their recreational utility. The pedestrianisation of town centres, for example, has facilitated a reappraisal of the ways in which we use these districts, and amongst the uses which have gained is outdoor recreation.

These different facets of the urban recreation resource base will be developed and explored later in this book. To summarise, it may be helpful to visualise the development of recreation opportunity within urban areas as having passed through three broad phases.

Phase I – 'Formation'

The nineteenth century may be seen as a formative phase in which the needs for public provision for outdoor recreation in cities became recognised. A foundation of provision, in parks and public walks, recreation grounds and other forms of open space, was laid. Towards the end of this era, the emergence of town planning and influential experiments in urban design led to related improvement in the general quality of streets and housing areas which also had some impact upon local availability of space for recreations. Over this same period the social patterning of urban places became much more clearly established and this, too, had implications for the subsequent development of recreational opportunities.

Phase II – 'Consolidation'

The period from 1918 to 1939 may be viewed as one of consolidation. Trends which had become apparent in the first phase, for example the provision of domestic gardens and allotments, became clearly established whilst newer initiatives, for example the provision of playing fields to support sports, aimed to fill some of the gaps which had thus far been overlooked.

Phase III – 'Expansion'

Post-1945 we have witnessed several key trends. Demand for leisure has grown dramatically and this has been reflected in greater levels and diversity of provision in which traditional resources established in earlier phases have been augmented by new forms of provision designed to reflect the diversity and flexibility of contemporary recreational tastes. The placement of recreation as an item on the statutory planning agenda has given it a prominence which in previous phases it has lacked and the amount of space within cities that supports recreation of one form or another has become truly extensive. Recreation has also been a clear beneficiary of wider urban environmental improvement.

THE SPATIAL PATTERN OF OPPORTUNITY

We have looked at how opportunitities for outdoor recreation have changed through time and how they have reflected some of the ways in which a process of emancipation of leisure (in social terms) has also been manifest over the same period. This leads to a consideration of how such opportunity occurs spatially within the built-up areas of towns and cities.

Urban geographers and land economists have long been concerned with summary models of city form as a convenient approach to the task of imposing an explanatory order upon outwardly confusing patterns of urban form. Classical theories of Burgess, Hoyt and Harris and Ullman still receive attention in contemporary texts on urban geography. (For detailed critiques and explanations of these models see reviews in, amongst many, Johnson, 1972; Carter, 1981; Herbert and Thomas, 1990.)

However, although models of city structure are readily available, the study of outdoor recreation in the urban environment is partially constrained by the fact that the spatial patterns of recreation in urban areas have not been well conceptualised to date. The tendency (which initially is followed here, too) has been to superimpose assumed recreational patterns and gradients over the standard models of city structures, or to draw broad contrasts between recreational opportunities between, typically, city centres, suburbs and urban fringe. In practice, recreation, which is often difficult to conceive in terms of the bid-rent curves (which form a common rationale for classical models of city form) because it lacks a measurable monetary utility, sits very uneasily within those models of cities which owe some of their provenance to assumptions concerning the capacity of different land use to bid for space. Studies of the relationship between processes of urban development and the availability of leisure facilities are therefore rare and often limited in scope. (As an example see Spink, 1989.) In fact, a great deal of recreation provision in urban areas, particularly public open space, reflects historic accident and/or municipal intervention. It survives because it is protected from contemporary development by planning control, reinforced by public desire to see such amenity conserved.

In the absence of theoretical approaches to describing and explaining the pattern of recreation resources in urban areas, the approach to the task must inevitably become empirical. To that end, the spatial occurrence of a range of outdoor recreational spaces within a selection of British urban places was examined, and an example of a typical pattern (in the city of Leicester) is presented in Figure 1.2. Calculation of the mean distance from the city centre of the five types of recreational space used in this analysis (Table 1.5) confirmed a pattern that was broadly to be expected, in which older parks and recreation grounds are concentrated towards the core of the settlement, whilst a scatter of newer parks and grounds associated with inter-war and post-1945 housing produce further significant zones of provision towards the periphery of the city. The outer edges of the built-up area are important for provision of extensive facilities such as sports grounds and golf courses, since these locations are traditionally associated with the types of low-cost land that such provision requires. However, overall, the most striking conclusion from Figure 1.2 is the significance of the suburban environment as a location for recreational provision.

Table 1.5 Mean distance (in km) from the city centre of different types of recreational space (Leicester)

Parks and gardens	Recreation grounds	Playing fields	Sports grounds	Golf courses
2.9	3.6	3.5	3.7	4.6

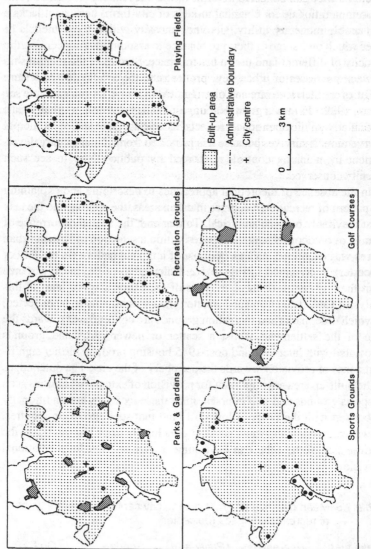

Figure 1.2 Spatial patterns of outdoor recreational facilities in Leicester

Built-up area

Administrative boundary

+ City centre

Playing Fields

Recreation Grounds

Golf Courses

Parks & Gardens

Sports Grounds

0   3 km

Such observations suggest that simple contrasts in the type and level of recreational opportunity will occur in the different zones of an urban area, that they can be identified and, for convenience, summarised. This is attempted in Table 1.6, which also lists opportunities or activities that will not be revealed by a cartographic analysis but which are likely to be present.

Clearly, Table 1.6 presents a generalised pattern and individual places will vary substantially from the profile described, reflecting a diverse range of local circumstances that may deflect or distort any summary arrangement. However, it does suggest that in attempting to define a typical pattern of recreational opportunity within an urban area, it may be helpful to recognise 'gradients' along which the level of opportunity varies as one moves from the urban centre to the periphery. (Sample gradients from the analysis of Leicester are set out in Figure 1.3 to illustrate the idea.) In presenting recreational patterns in this way it should be noted that the notion of a gradient suggests that opportunity is continuous, though variable, whereas in reality it will be discontinuous with tracts of land in which opportunity for any given type of provision or recreational activity simply does not arise. But in so far as these gradients highlight a propensity towards spatial variation in recreational opportunity, they have a value.

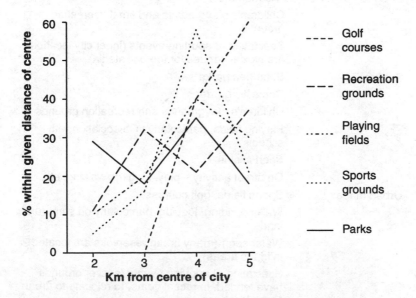

Figure 1.3 Recreational 'gradients' in a typical city (Leicester)

Table 1.6 Possible outdoor recreational opportunities within intra-urban zones

Zone or locality	Likely recreational opportunities
Central area	Small public gardens, sometimes public parks
	Leisure centre recreations (the number of centrally located leisure centres that offer outdoor as well as the usual indoor facilities may be limited)
	Recreational window shopping
	Spectating at major sporting venues (these are not common in central areas but do occur, e.g. Cardiff Arms Park rugby football stadium)
	Street theatre and on-street entertainment
	People-watching
Inner city localities	Park-based recreations, typically in Victorian/Edwardian parks and gardens, some of which may include formal sport (bowls, tennis, soccer, etc.)
	On-street activity, including children's play
	Some garden-based recreation
	Allotments
	Children's playgrounds and small recreation grounds
	Spectating at sporting events (inner city locations are typical venues for football stadia)
Suburbs	Suburban parks
	Domestic gardens
	Children's playgrounds and recreation grounds
	Playing fields, particularly in association with schools
	Sports fields
	On-street activity – play, jogging, walking, etc.
Urban fringe	Sports fields, golf courses
	Walking, riding, jogging, particularly on semi-rural land
	Water sport (many urban reservoirs are located in fringe areas)
	Spectating at sporting events (soccer grounds have tended, in recent years, to relocate to urban fringe locations)

TOWARDS A TYPOLOGY OF RECREATION RESOURCES

Ultimately, we must view the geography of outdoor recreation in an urban area as being a reflection of the local resource base. The concept of a resource in recreational terms, though, is not straightforward. Evaluation, even simple recognition of a recreational resource, is a highly personalised matter, reflecting a complex equation which will include personal interests, awareness and knowledge, and ability to take advantage of such opportunities as are recognised. Recreation resources are not static either, varying in both time and space (Pigram, 1983).

The personalised nature of recreational resource evaluation is not a new idea (see, for example, Clawson and Knetsch, 1966) but it is an important one for two reasons. First, different people will perceive the same recreational facilities in contrasting fashions. For example, Grahn's (1991) study of parks in Sweden demonstrates how groups involving children recognised far more attributes within the recreational space than groups of older people, a reflection not just of different needs but also of the different scale at which the environment was viewed. The small-scale world of the child often magnifies features which adults view as possessing no recreational utility. Secondly, the personal dimension to resource evaluation is significant because it highlights the evident truth that some will find a recreational utility in space or facilities that the majority may see as simply functional and unconnected with leisure. For example a railway station is, for most people, a purely functional facility through which the routine task of travel is conducted. However, for the railway enthusiast it is (potentially) a recreational resource. At a different scale, most adults would view a street primarily as a means of communication and access, yet to the child it may be an important play environment.

The recreational value of a resource may also alter according to the context in which it is being used. Saturday morning shopping for weekly groceries is a routine chore that few would identify as recreational, yet a Saturday afternoon trip to the same shopping centre in search of leisure clothes, books or compact discs might very well be seen as recreational in character. It is, therefore, important to recognise that the resource base for urban recreation is extensive and potentially diverse and that it is not easy to predict how, at an individual level, opportunity may be perceived. Further, to maximise the recreational utility of urban spaces, planning and other regulatory procedures must adopt a flexible and broad perspective and promotion should be educational, widening the scope and appreciation of the resource base and enhancing the ability of urban residents to benefit from its use.

In the light of this complexity, it may be useful to derive a summary typology of recreational resources as both a framework for, and an aid to, further study. Such a task is complicated both by the diversity within outdoor recreation and the problems of resource perception highlighted above, and it is unlikely that a universal summary is attainable. But, nevertheless, a simple typology of resources is here proposed, constructed around seven key variables. These are summarised in Table 1.7.

The variables deployed may be considered as simple descriptive labels reflecting basic resource attributes which, when combined, facilitate some degree of differentiation of resources according to their basic characteristics. It is not desirable to attempt to combine all the variables since this would produce a very large number of typological categories, many of which would be theoretical rather than of practical value. However, by selective combinations, some useful distinctions may be drawn or emphasis placed upon particular types of resource. This is attempted in Table 1.8.

It will be apparent that such schemes can only be indicative of basic contrasts and that certain types of facility can be placed into several categories. An alternative selection of defining variables might also be expected to produce different combinations of resources. Even so, Table 1.8 does point to the significance of two main types of resource area for urban outdoor recreation, the *linear* resources – footpaths, towpaths, streets and thoroughfares – and different types of recreational *areas* – parks, recreation grounds, playgrounds, gardens and allotments, sports fields, water space and urban woodland being examples. This primary division is important because linear and areal types of resource can be expected to display some differences in type of activity as a consequence of their physical forms. From the viewpoint of providers, these spaces pose different management demands.

The activities encouraged by this pattern of resources will tend towards two main types: the range of passive, informal pursuits discussed at the commencement of this chapter; and sports, in particular the common team games. This raises a fundamental question which centres upon whether resource patterns reflect recreational needs, or whether recreational patterns are shaped by resource availability. In order to understand the problem more fully, it is appropriate now to turn attention to the question of how individuals shape their patterns of demand for outdoor recreation (Chapter 2) and how that demand is accommodated (Chapter 3).

Table 1.7 Summary and explanation of key variables deployed within the recreation resource typology

Variable	Sub-categories	Explanation
Design	Purpose-built	Resource is designed for specific recreational uses
	Adapted	Resource has been converted to a recreational use from a previous function
	Annexed	Resource is not designed nor intended for recreational use, but will be used as such by some groups
Organisation	Formal	Resource has a structured design/layout and/or management
	Informal	Resource has no such structure
Function	Single	Resource has one intended recreational function
	Multi	Resource has a diversity of intended recreational functions
	Shared	Resource has a variety of functions, of which recreation is one
Space/use characteristics	Extensive	Individual recreational functions range over large areas with generous use of space
	Intensive	Functions are concentrated with little or no unused/wasted space
Scale	Large	Over 10 acres in extent
	Medium	Between 2 and 10 acres in extent
	Small	Below 2 acres in extent
Catchment	City-wide	Resource draws use from across the urban area
	District	Resource draws use primarily from its district
	Local	Resource draws use primarily from its neighbourhood
Source of provision	Public	Funded/managed by government at either local or national level
	Private	Funded/managed by private individuals/groups for their own use
	Voluntary	Funded/managed by groups acting as co-operatives, clubs or societies, for the use of members

Table 1.8 Basic typology of outdoor recreation facilities in urban areas

	Public facilities		Private/voluntary facilities		Facilities that may be 'annexed' for recreational use by particular groups
	Formal	Informal	Formal	Informal	
Large scale; city-wide catchment	Major parks Major sports fields/stadia Municipal golf courses	Major commons Major urban woodland Major water space Urban country parks	Private golf courses		Major shopping centres Major transport centres, e.g. airports, stations
Medium scale; district catchment	Recreation grounds Small parks	Urban greenways Minor urban woodland Minor water space Cycleways	Sports clubs e.g. bowls or cricket	Natural areas or reserves	Roadways Towpaths
Small scale; local catchment	Children's play areas Allotments	Local footpaths		Domestic gardens	Local streets/pavements Waste ground Grass verges

Chapter 2

Outdoor recreation and leisure lifestyles

In Chapter 1, the resource context in which urban outdoor recreation takes place was outlined and the types of pursuit that are generally characteristic of urban outdoor recreation were identified. This chapter seeks to develop these themes by shifting the emphasis from resources to people through an examination of the patterns of outdoor activity and, particularly, the factors which determine the shape of their recreational lifestyles.

When we examine patterns of activity at the level of the individual (or the local level in spatial terms), we encounter not the generality of an aggregate picture but a complexity and diversity which both reflects and is the product of the very large number of variables which impinge upon and shape personal recreation behaviours. A fuller appreciation of this variation and complexity will be developed later in the book, but it is perhaps helpful to recognise initially that recreational patterns are shaped at a general level by the interaction of 'actors' – particularly the providers of recreational opportunity and the participants – and that patterns of outdoor activity are further influenced by interaction between people and their environment. Then, at the individual or institutional level, the actions of the actors are themselves the product of the interplay of key variables, in particular between desires (or intentions), opportunities and constraints. Figure 2.1 offers a summary of this process and suggests a simple equation in which desires stimulate demand and provision creates opportunity, while the capacity to take advantage of that opportunity is regulated by sets of constraints. These constraints may be personal and specific to the individual but some of the basic variables themselves may also have a limiting effect, especially constraints associated with the character of the environment or with a lack of opportunity resulting from a failure to supply recreational spaces or facilities. The resolution of this equation may produce one of several alternative outcomes.

We will return to consider the forces which act upon providers and the

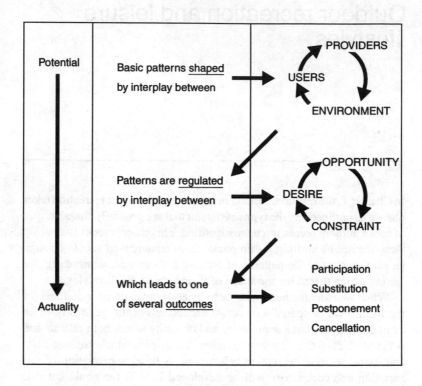

Figure 2.1 Theoretical relationship between principal variables
influencing patterns of outdoor recreation

role of the environment in Chapter 3 but, as a preface to that discussion,
this chapter examines basic activity patterns in urban outdoor recreation
and introduces the important concept of the leisure lifestyle and those
aspects of individual lives that shape demands for outdoor recreation.

ACTIVITY PATTERNS AND THE CONCEPT OF LEISURE LIFESTYLES

An activity pattern may be defined with reference to three basic parame-
ters: time, space and the nature of the event. The element of time defines
both the duration of activity and its placement within a time frame – a day,
week, month, season, etc. Space is primarily concerned with location and
embraces fundamental distinctions between indoor and outdoor activity

and between local and distant venues, whilst the event is the specific recreation or experience in which the participant is engaged.

Although not all the facets of recent developments and change in outdoor recreation are fully detailed within the research literature (especially in areas of casual and informal recreation), we may be confident that within society at large, outdoor recreational activity is increasing. Figure 2.2 charts time series for participation in a range of active pursuits and sports as reflected in membership of accredited organisations, and whilst these activities are not necessarily confined to the urban environment, they are indicative of broad changes. At a detailed level, the trend in all sectors is not always consistently upward since many established activities display a 'plateau' of participation which is characteristic of maturity. Some, for example tennis, even appear to signal decline, although in this instance the use of the number of clubs as a surrogate measure is misleading since actual numbers of players registered with the Lawn Tennis Association have risen over the review period (Centre for Leisure Research, 1991). But overall, participation in recreation out of doors is evidently on the increase.

Excepting the case of outdoor recreation at, or close to, the home, participation requires several primary conditions to be met. These include awareness of potential activities and of where they may be located or pursued; sufficient time to pursue the event and the journey to and from the venue; and an appropriate level of mobility. At least a part of the explanation of the general changes in activity patterns lies within these variables: in changes in the patterns of time availability and use, in extensions to personal space through increased mobility and in changes in recreational tastes and preferences. The general nature and effect of these changes may be briefly summarised.

Time

The important relationship between availability of time and recreational participation has long been understood, and in the post-1945 era the general downward trend in hours spent at work has been of evident benefit to the growth of outdoor recreation. Falls in the length of the working week have been less pronounced over the last twenty years or so, but are still apparent, especially for men (Figure 2.3).

However, the decline in hours worked is only part of the story. In a revealing examination of changing patterns of use of time, Gershuny and Jones (1987) not only confirm that average amounts of time devoted to work have fallen but also show how time has been redistributed. We tend

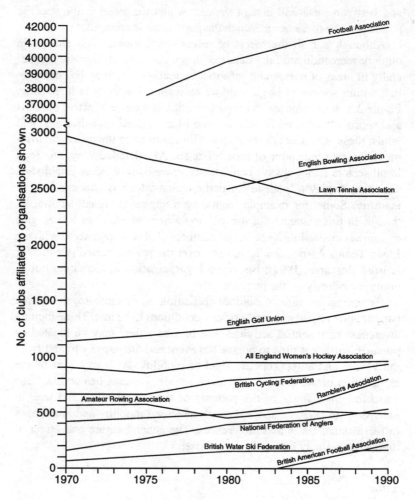

Figure 2.2 Change in numbers of clubs affiliated to accredited
      organisations, 1970–90
Source: Centre for Leisure Research, 1991

now to spend not only less time at work than, say, in 1960, but also less
time on routine personal care and domestic chores. Time liberated from
these duties has been switched, at an aggregate level, into childcare and,
particularly, leisure. Amounts of leisure time vary according to employment status, age and gender (Figure 2.4) but the broad trend remains valid.

Explanations for these changes lie in several areas. The reduction in

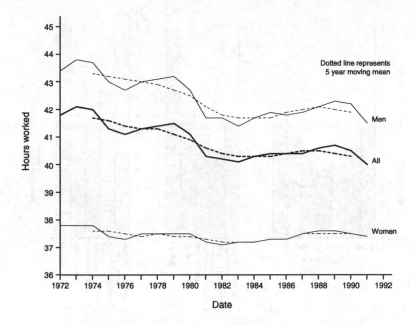

Figure 2.3 Change in average hours worked (including overtime) for full-time employees in all sectors, Great Britain 1972–91
Source: Employment Gazette, various issues

mean hours of work reflects reductions in the working week and, for some, a shift from full-time to part-time employment, whilst the reduction in time spent on domestic chores owes much to the widening use of modern technology in the home: microwaves, home freezers, automatic washing machines, tumble dryers and dishwashers all reduce the time taken to perform routine tasks. Less positively, perhaps, the increase in time allocated to childcare may well indicate a growing reluctance on the part of parents to leave children unattended out of doors for fear of the harm that may befall them. Supervision of young children at play and escorting them to and from school have become commonplace in a way that would have been unusual in the 1950s or 1960s and such duties erode parental free time and limit the activity patterns of children too. We will return to this issue in Chapter 6.

The release of larger amounts of time to leisure has been a significant factor in facilitating development of out-of-home recreation. Gershuny and Jones's (1987) study isolated a mean 43 per cent increase between

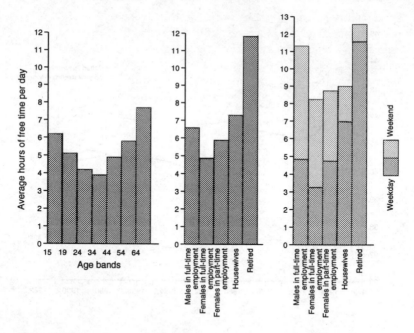

Figure 2.4 Variations in availability of leisure time according to age, gender/employment status, and time of week/age/employment status
Source: Central Statistical Office, 1993

1961 and 1984 in the allocation of leisure time outside the home compared with only an 8 per cent increase in in-home leisure over the same period, while Glyptis *et al.* (1987), in a time-budget study of some 460 adults in Nottingham, clearly demonstrated that recreational activities out-of-home occupied significantly longer periods, an average of 136 minutes for out-of-home events compared to 63 minutes in-home. This is an under-standable pattern given the additional effort and costs involved in many out-of-home recreational trips. (These data relate to out-of-home trips, not necessarily to outdoor recreations.)

Mobility

Alongside changes in the general availability of leisure time, increases in the levels of personal mobility, especially car ownership (Figure 2.5), have also been important in shaping patterns of outdoor activity. For car owners, enhanced mobility extends the geographical extent of activity space and brings more resource areas to their disposal. Further, it may permit different patterns in the use of time by reducing journey times to a recreational venue. Thus smaller time windows within the day become usable for a recreational activity in a way that might not be possible if journeys had to be made by slower modes of travel. The net effect of car ownership is that participation rates in sports and outdoor recreations are significantly higher in households with access to a car (Patmore, 1983).

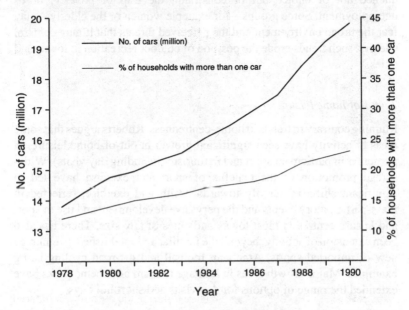

Figure 2.5 Growth in numbers of private motor cars and the percentage of households with more than one car, Great Britain 1978–90
Source: Department of Transport, 1992; Central Statistical Office, 1993

Tastes and preferences

Activity patterns have been influenced, too, by some of the wider changes in recreational tastes and preferences and by the manner in which recreation has been perceived and promoted within the urban community. Roberts (1989) suggests that recent developments may be characterised by four trends.

1. Home-centredness

The role of the home and its facilities has already been noted in Chapter 1 and its convenience, privacy and relative security seem likely to reinforce its central place in the leisure activity patterns of most urban residents. However, whilst noting the evident attraction of the home, it should be appreciated that home-centredness for some can be a consequence not of choice but of constraint, the trap of poverty, or of unemployment. Some groups – for example women or the elderly – may fear the urban environment and the perceived threats that it may contain. Clearly, such trends erode the position of outdoor recreation in towns and cities.

2. Out-of-home leisure

Running contrary to trends in home-centredness, Roberts argues that some areas of activity have seen significant growth in out-of-home leisure, in particular in participant sport and in tourism (including day visits). Widespread promotion of the benefits of sport and exercise have led to significant shifts in activity towards health and exercise, reflected in mass-participatory events and the pervasive development and use of sport and leisure centres in most towns and cities of any size. There has also been extension of activity, beyond the familiar and established, to embrace new or imported sports, American football and off-road cycling being examples. Major growth areas in heritage tourism and theme parks have extended the range of options for day visits and short holidays.

3. 'Connoisseur leisure'

Roberts (1989:55) describes this area of growth as the domain of 'minorities of enthusiasts with finely tuned skills and exceptional knowledge, who commit considerable cash, time and energy to their pastime'. Most recreations have always had their specialists but the growth in this style of activity has been significant, not least for the benefit it may bestow upon the participant. Haworth (1986) illustrates how this form of committed activity can, for the increasing proportion of the population who do not work, perform a range of functions normally afforded by employment, including structuring of time, creation of focal points for interest and facilitating the development and maintenance of social networks with others who share the interest. Connoisseur leisure is not, of course, necessarily directed towards outdoor recreation but where it does occur, the characteristic levels of commitment will encourage the participant into regular and/or lengthy use of outdoor facilities.

4. Programmed leisure

This has been a fourth feature of changing recreation provision in Britain since the late 1970s. Roberts visualises it as a (partial) response to what he terms 'the threat of the mob' – the emergence of a sub-culture of largely urban, unemployed youth. Since the urban riots in Britain in the early 1980s in which this 'threat' became manifest, policy has variously sought to shape a range of recreational programmes, many of them sports-based, with these groups in mind. However, the approach has tended to broaden, and the programming of leisure has been extended to other participants. The Sports Council's 'Sport for All' campaign provides an example at the national level, but locally most authorities have developed programmes aimed at fostering activity amongst a range of low-interest groups, including the elderly, ethnic minorities, the disabled and the unemployed.

Having outlined some basic trends, it is useful to draw a distinction between two broad types of outdoor activity, here labelled as 'routine' and 'special'. At the individual level, activity patterns are built up through a combination of day-to-day recreations (which tend to be commonplace and may even be accorded minimal significance by participants), supplemented by more occasional special events which will be prominent as recreational experiences in the minds of the participant. The routine might include walks within the neighbourhood, exercising dogs, children's play and gardening, where this is enjoyed as a recreation. Special events might include countryside visits, trips to concerts, festivals or major entertainments, and holidays.

The routine and the special may be expected to show marked differences in respect of variables such as location, timing, duration and level of forward planning, as well as some of the less tangible benefits or rewards associated with activity. For convenience, probable patterns are summarised in Table 2.1, the primary distinction being between shorter duration, local, routine activities and longer duration, more distant, special events. There is, of course, nothing to stop a local event commanding special status or vice versa; it is simply here seen as less likely.

So far, the discussion has been couched in general terms and has been concerned mainly with aggregate representations of activity. However, there is ample evidence from the research literature to tell us that at the individual level there is considerable deviation from the norms of behaviour that are suggested in aggregate studies and that descriptions of the

Table 2.1 General characteristics of 'routine' and 'special' recreational events

Status	Location	Timing	Duration	Planning level	Reward
Routine	Local	Regular	Short	Low	Low
I	I	I	I	I	I
Special	Distant	Occasional	Med./Long	High	High

type set out in Table 2.1, for example, whilst encapsulating a pattern of behaviour to which many would conform, will misrepresent patterns of those who view their leisure from different perspectives, or who are guided by specific motivations, or who suffer certain constraints. This has led to a shift in behavioural leisure research, away from *aggregate* studies of populations to observation of how *individuals* shape their activity patterns, the broad term for this approach being the 'leisure lifestyle'. (For a recent review of the lifestyle approach see Veal, 1993a.)

'Lifestyle' has been defined simply by Glyptis (1981:314) as 'the aggregate pattern of day-to-day activities which make up an individual's way of life'; according to Glyptis, 'leisure lifestyle' refers to 'those elements of lifestyle which the individual perceives as leisure'. The benefits of this individualistic approach, which sets recreational patterns clearly in the wider context of personal lifestyles, have been emphasised by a number of authors (for example Glyptis *et al.*, 1987; Gershuny and Jones, 1987; Bernard, 1988; Wynne, 1990). These are primarily that a lifestyle approach affords insights into detailed patterns of activity which are concealed within an aggregated picture but which when exposed advance understanding of the variation that exists within general recreational activity patterns and why such variation might occur. The relevance of this approach will perhaps become clear if we consider how patterns of demand for outdoor recreation are shaped and regulated.

DESIRES AND NEEDS – THE PARTICIPANT

The nature of recreational demand has been explored extensively in the past (see, for example, Clawson and Knetsch, 1966; Mercer, 1980; Miles and Seabrooke, 1977 and Pigram, 1983) and those enquiries have established several aspects of demand patterns that are widely accepted. Principal amongst these conclusions are that (a) levels of demand, or perhaps more critically the ability to translate demands and needs into participation, do not occur uniformly across a population, and (b) there are important differences between various forms of revealed and hidden demands. The revealed demand pattern may be equated with participation levels, but studies have also recognised latent demands, which exist when people who wish to participate are prevented from doing so by some form of impediment; induced demands, whereby people who have no expressed wish to pursue an activity may still be encouraged to do so, especially by provision of facilities; deferred demands, in which participation is postponed until circumstances become more conducive; and substitute demands, in which one activity takes the place of another which is unavailable at the time. These observations are important for two related reasons. First, although recreation participation is often presented as a matter of choice, for many those choices are limited by internal (personal) and external factors. Secondly, this observation readily focuses attention upon the important effects of the constraints that shape recreation behaviours.

Recreational choices and preferences of an individual will normally be governed by a range of variables which may be summarised under four headings.

Physical attributes

These primarily relate to the age and gender of potential participants and may affect several facets of recreational behaviour, including the type of activity chosen and the periodicity and duration of recreational events. Whilst some of the age and gender effects are felt more strongly in combination with others (for example, the impact of gender is commonly amplified by marital status and family responsibilities), there are independent effects too.

Research has suggested several ways in which age may influence participation in outdoor recreation. Interest in outdoor recreation seems most limited at the age extremes. Although many young people, especially males, are active in sports and physical recreations, the consensus is that the recreational lifestyle of youth is centred upon largely indoor pursuits of a relatively passive and/or social nature: watching television, listening to recorded music, reading magazines, visiting or receiving friends, window shopping, or simply hanging around (Hendry, 1981; Willis, 1990; Mintel, 1991a). Elderly people reveal contrasting patterns. It is normal to see some form of decline in participation in physical activities with increasing age, and the geographic range over which old people operate may also be restricted in comparison with, say, a young adult. But there are also differences in the type of recreation pursued. Strenuous and strongly competitive activities tend to wane while so-called 'lifetime' activities (e.g. walking, bowls, golf) figure more prominently. Gardening, too, becomes a significant outdoor recreation for older people, reflecting a home-centredness which is a characteristic of the elderly lifestyle. These trends are reflected in Figure 2.6, where allocations of time to sample activities according to age group are charted. The decline in adherence to sport and exercise and the converse emergence of gardening are well illustrated but it should be noted too how activities which may be construed as 'time-fillers' – window shopping and doing nothing – diminish in significance under the pressures on time that often characterise mid-life (25–54 years), but then recover with the release of time that is a feature of later life, particularly retirement.

Psychological attributes

Age and gender may place some conditions upon demand but more significant is a clutch of psychological factors which relate to personal experience, motivations and interests. Most people have a rather limited range of recreational interests but how these are selected is still, to a degree, unclear. Certainly, early exposure to a pursuit and the experience it brings may foster long-term involvement. Scott and Willets (1989), in a study of adults who were originally surveyed as adolescents in 1947, showed how the experience of high levels of participation in an activity in their youth commonly shaped an interest that was sustained into middle age, especially amongst women. Motivation, the urge to participate, may be nurtured through a variety of channels: experience; perceived rewards which may act as positive stimuli, drawing participants into an activity; or even peer group or familial pressures, which push an individual into participation in a recreational event that they might not otherwise select.

Socio-demographic positioning

This concerns key elements such as marital and family status, the nature and extent of friendship patterns the individual may possess, and perhaps social class. Research has placed great emphasis upon marital and family status and the associated position in the life cycle, since there is ample evidence to illustrate the influence upon recreational demand patterns that events such as marriage, child-rearing and retirement exert (Young and Wilmott, 1973; Rapoport and Rapoport, 1975; Long and Wimbush, 1979;

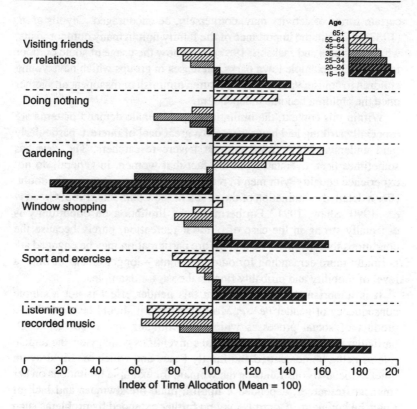

Figure 2.6 Allocation of time to selected recreational activities according to age
Source: Mintel, 1991a

Kelly, 1983). Although certain aspects of these works have been challenged – J. Smith (1987) for example criticises Young and Wilmott and the Rapoports for their failure to take due account of gender – their general conclusions remain valid. Of particular significance are the responsibilities of family care, the common effect being a reduction in the total time devoted to leisure and, normally, a reduction in the range of recreational experiences too. Activity often retreats to a core of sustainable interest such as reading or television viewing, at least until the responsibilities for family care recede (J. Smith, 1987). Since outdoor recreational trips are generally more time-consuming, pressures of family responsibility might well be expected to impact disproportionately upon such events, although certain forms of activity may, conversely, be encouraged. Glyptis *et al.* (1987) highlight the importance of the family unit in many outdoor visits, while Williams and Jackson (1985) show how the usage of some outdoor facilities, for example town parks, increases in groups which have young children to amuse; visits to the park often diminish or disappear altogether once the children become independent.

Within this context, the limitations upon female demand patterns are especially striking and have attracted a great deal of interest, particularly (and understandably) from feminist leisure researchers. The case has sometimes been overstated but the fact that women, in general, do not experience equality with men in recreational opportunity is not in doubt. (For a detailed examination of the problem see Chambers, 1986; Green *et al.*, 1990; Shaw, 1991.) Furthermore, the limitation on opportunity is especially strong in the case of outdoor recreation, purely because the conditions that require to be met before participation may be engaged are normally more demanding for outdoor events – longer blocks of time, a level of mobility and probably financial cost, for example.

It is important to appreciate that this gender effect is not a simple consequence of gender *per se*. More correctly, it should be viewed as a product of social processes which are complex and deep-seated. Of particular importance are those social conventions which view the female role as being home-centred and family-based and which readily draw in other associated constraints on the woman, for example limitations on her financial resources, dependence upon a male breadwinner and lack of financial autonomy. Controls may be further extended by problems such as a reluctance or refusal of male partners to share burdens such as domestic chores, by expectations on the part of the male partner that the woman should be ready to accompany him to recreational events that he wishes to pursue but which she might not, or even by the wider perception of societal norms that some behaviours or forms of activity are unacceptable for females. Fazey and Ballington (1992), for example, note how the masculine image of many sports reduces female participation in physical activity and channels much of what remains to 'feminine' pursuits such as keep-fit programmes and yoga. Women's participation in outdoor urban recreation is, additionally, likely to be limited by the changing image of the city environment. Although young males are far more likely to fall prey to urban street crime, female fear of an environment which is widely seen as becoming more unsafe can only further inhibit female participation in outdoor leisure in both spatial and temporal terms. (For a recent discussion of women's fear of the outdoor urban environment, see Valentine, 1992.)

These effects are not, of course, universal but they are evident, and although there is often a reluctance to attribute too much to social class, a study by Bernard (1988) of a cross-section of adult groups in the Potteries conurbation in England suggests that it is the young, working-class female whose leisure is often most constrained by the lifestyle she leads.

Other socio-demographic variables merit briefer consideration. Social links outside the family are important influences upon demand patterns and, other things being equal, the wider the social network of an individual, the greater will be the opportunity for recreation. For outdoor/out-of-home recreation, social contacts beyond the family are especially important. Glyptis *et al.* (1987) demonstrate that over 90 per cent of in-home leisure is either solitary or family-centred, but out-of-home, friends and more distant relations become a more significant social focus for recreation, although not to the extent that the family influence is supplanted.

The role of social class as a factor regulating or shaping demand is problematic. Traditionally, leisure itself was an attribute of social class, enjoyed by an elite minority and denied to the majority (Seabrook, 1988). But as leisure has taken its place as a universal, albeit variable, component in modern lifestyles, the question has inevitably been asked as to whether recreational patterns can be linked to social class. There are studies to show that certain social groups may be characterised by association with particular activities. The prevalence of particular forms of 'pub culture' amongst working-class men (Franklin, 1985; J. Smith, 1987) or the striking attachment to bingo of women of working-class background (Dixey, 1983) are examples that contrast with, say, the observable middle-class character of most theatre or opera audiences. But whether these reflect real differences that stem from class or a situation that is simply sustained by custom is open to question. Wynne (1990), in a revealing study of contrasting middle-class groups in an urban community in north-west England, shows how each group deployed leisure behaviours to create and then defend a distinctive social position, but the fact that both groups shared common origins in working-class society rather suggests that leisure differences were a construct rather than a direct attribute. Glyptis (1981) has also warned of the risks of taking social class as a causal variable in explaining recreation behaviour, arguing that it is more properly seen as an indicator of a likely pattern, not a predictor.

Socio-economic positioning

One of the factors that appeared significant in Wynne's study was the divergent educational and employment histories of his contrasting middle-class groups, and in practice a great deal of recreational demand patterns reflect factors such as employment status, income level, educational attainment and mobility. These tend to become interrelated and may demonstrate a range of effects. Thus, employment situations may directly foster recreational participation, sometimes through facility provision, but more commonly through social networks that are founded in the workplace and are partly sustained through leisure time activity. Or, educational attainment may influence not only employment status but have a wider impact on participants' awareness of opportunities. Social geographers have demonstrated how urban communities composed of educated, professional households maintain, and have knowledge of, a much wider activity space (which will include recreational facilities) than do communities of skilled and manual workers (see, for example, Herbert and Raine's 1976 study of communities in Cardiff).

At several points in the preceding discussions, reference has been made to the existence of constraints. The variables that have just been outlined may be conceptualised as creating a potential to demand outdoor recreation, but the variation in both the potential and the actuality of recreation participation owes much to the individual's response to the constraints that he or she may face. It is appropriate now to consider briefly the current understanding of recreational constraints and how they may operate.

That recreation participation is subject to the operation of constraints has been acknowledged for some time (see, for example, Kaplan, 1975). However, recent research has gone beyond the simple recognition that constraints exist towards a more detailed articulation of their form and how they function.

Amongst several attempts to conceptualise recreational constraints, Crawford and Godbey (1987) have proposed a model centred upon three categories of constraint. First, they identify *structural barriers*, factors which intervene between leisure preferences and actual participation. People know what they want to do but are prevented by one or more of a range of impediments – family responsibilities, financial resources, scheduling of work time, availability of opportunity or even peer group attitudes to proposed events. Secondly, there are *intrapersonal barriers* which relate to the individual's psychological state and attitude. These include awareness and motivational criteria, levels of depression or stress, perceived skill levels and the extent of previous socialisation into specific recreations. Finally, Crawford and Godbey recognise *interpersonal barriers* which are shaped by the pattern of relationships between different individuals and, particularly, individual compatibilities.

In a subsequent refinement of these ideas, Crawford *et al.* (1991) suggest that in order to participate, people are required to negotiate a sequential series of constraint levels. First, it is argued, the individual must confront the intrapersonal barriers that will be critical in shaping a pattern of recreational preferences – a mental list of activities in which the participant wishes to engage. Next, and depending upon the activity chosen, constraints at the interpersonal level may be encountered. For solitary activity this will not apply but for a group-based event, compatibility with others is fundamental. It is only when this second stage has been negotiated that the structural constraints come into play. If, as the authors propose, these stages are seen as hierarchical – in which the intrapersonal barriers are the most powerful and the structural the least significant – then the process may be conceived as a filter through which the unsuccessful participant will fail to progress.

The relative insignificance of the structural barriers is, to a degree, borne out by results from an interesting empirical study of constraints on an urban population in Stoke-on-Trent conducted by G.A.M. Jackson (Jackson, 1991; Kay and Jackson, 1991; Jackson and Kay, 1992). This study, which focused on the structural barriers, found that recreational constraints were widely perceived (72 per cent of the sample acknowledging the effects of constraints upon their actions), and that a core of common constraints formed the basis to the problem. These included shortage of money to meet participation costs, lack of time, restrictions associated with the family and with work, personal health, lack of mobility and a lack of provision.

Although the results revealed considerable variation in the way in which different constraints were experienced or perceived by various sub-groups within the sample, the researchers were struck by two observations. First, it was noted how many respondents were able to circumvent or reduce the impact of particular structural constraints by adaptations to their behaviour patterns – reductions in the frequency or duration of participation; meeting costs through savings programmes, for example, but rarely cutting out the activity altogether. (This tends to reinforce the proposition of Crawford and Godbey that the structural constraint was the least powerful.) Secondly, it was observed how people who were already frequent participants reported similar or even greater levels of constraint when compared with others who were demonstrably disadvantaged. Bernard (1988), in an investigation of leisure lifestyles in the same urban community, reached a similar conclusion in noting that those whose lives were 'leisure rich' also reported high levels of difficulty in their efforts to manage their commitments in a way that facilitated their recreational preferences. Jackson and Kay (1992) conclude that those who are most active are also likely to be most aware of other activities in which they could engage, and to have frustrated desires as a result.

In summary, this project suggested several broad conclusions. It confirmed the tendency for women to experience constraints associated with family care and domestic responsibilities and, to a lesser degree, problems with access to transport. It did not, however, present a picture in which women felt their leisure to be significantly more constrained than men, nor did it reveal any significant difference between the sexes in the operation of a financial constraint, as has sometimes been suggested. As might be anticipated, shortage of money was experienced particularly by the young whilst, at the other end of the age spectrum, the elderly reported mobility and health constraints as limitations on their recreational activities. In socio-economic terms, what may broadly be termed as 'working-class' respondents tended to report financial constraints whilst middle-class groups were more aware of pressures of time and work, which variously reflected positions of responsibility for many middle-aged people, or the challenges of career-building for the young.

To illustrate how these various constraints conspire with opportunities and desires to produce a pattern of behaviour, we may return briefly to the work of Glyptis *et al.* (1987). The time-budget diaries which this research team gathered in Nottingham permitted reconstruction of individual activity patterns across several days. When charted as time-space diagrams, they provide a revealing insight into where respondents were, how long they had been there, and what they were doing. It thus becomes possible to see how people in different circumstances shape a leisure lifestyle around more routine chores and responsibilities, and how the shape of that lifestyle varies according to circumstance and the sorts of interests and constraints that the individual experiences. (Unfortunately, the timing of this survey in winter limits the extent of recorded outdoor recreation, but as an illustration of basic principles, the case study is still valuable in the present context.)

Figures 2.7 to 2.10 provide contrasting examples of a Saturday in the lives of six respondents (two couples and two single males) which highlight some very different lifestyles. In the case of couple A (Figure 2.7), the impact of responsibility for a young baby with its regular routine is evident for both parents, but especially the mother, whilst for couple B (Figure 2.8) who are middle-aged and whose family is grown-up, a strong hobby interest (in tape recording) produces frequent and occasionally lengthy allocations of time to the activity. But in both cases it is the fragmentation of time into many small blocks that is the most striking

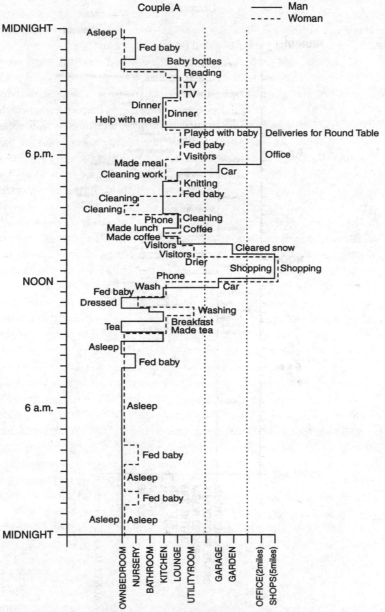

Figure 2.7 Time-space diagram for a young married couple with a child on a sample day
Source: Adapted from Glyptis *et al.*, 1987

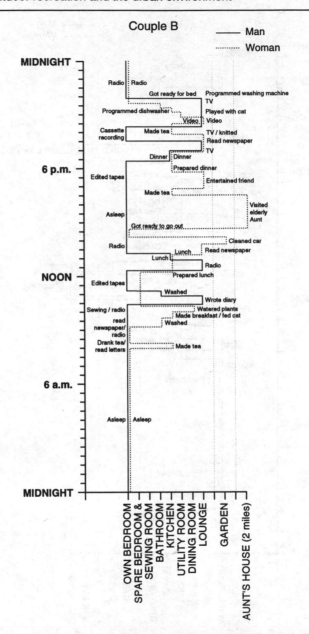

Figure 2.8 Time-space diagram for a middle-aged married couple without children on a sample day
Source: Adapted from Glyptis *et al.*, 1987

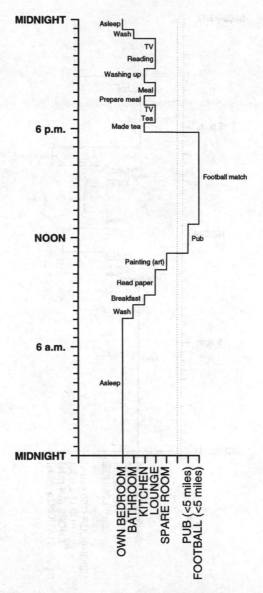

Figure 2.9 Time-space diagram for a middle-aged single man on a
sample day
Source: Adapted from Glyptis *et al.*, 1987

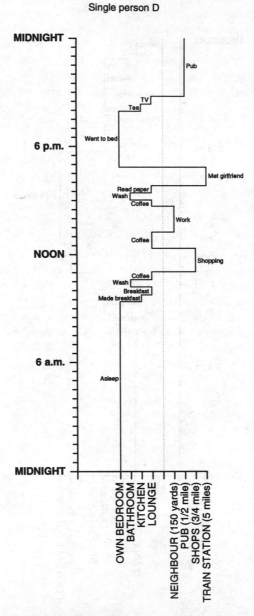

Figure 2.10 Time-space diagram for a young single man on a sample
          day
Source: Adapted from Glyptis *et al.*, 1987

feature of the lifestyles, reflecting not just a diversity of responsibilities but possibly the impact of commitment to the partner, too.

In contrast, the patterns revealed by the single men, one retired (subject C, Figure 2.9) and the other young and in work (subject D, Figure 2.10) are clearly different. Time is blocked into lengthy periods in which the respondent is able to stay in the same place doing the same thing. Here there are fewer responsibilities acting to disrupt the pattern, fewer interruptions of the type that keep, say, the mother with baby busy. There are not necessarily fewer constraints, because the time-space diagrams tell us nothing about the wider conditions under which these behavioural patterns are formed, but nevertheless, there is a vivid illustration of the variety that is to be encountered in personal lives.

Before we bring to a close the consideration of how people express their demands for recreation, it is worth pausing briefly to reflect on the related concept of 'need'. As we will see in Chapter 3, identification of the types of recreational facilities that are needed to meet expressed and hidden demands is a key role for the providers of recreational opportunity and that is one sense in which the idea of 'need' may be considered. However, there is a more subtle question concerning the extent to which recreation itself is a need, in the manner in which other more obvious necessities – such as food, shelter or income – are needs.

For many years, the notion that people might need recreation in a way that other necessities of life are required was not given clear recognition. Roberts (1977), for example, highlights how successive governments have tended to promote certain forms of outdoor recreation, particularly through provision, but suggests that this was not viewing outdoor recreation as an end in itself but as a vehicle to deliver a healthy population of workers and soldiers of upright and dependable character (Roberts, 1977:2.3). He questions (p.2.12) whether people actually possess recreational needs at all, the implication being that although certain physical, psychological and social needs can be met through recreational activity, they could just as readily be addressed via other experiential channels.

But uncertainties over the necessity of recreation have increasingly been challenged by the realisation of the considerable physical and psychological benefits that may be ascribed to recreation participation as well as by the realisation that personal well-being can be reinforced or partially sustained by recreational experience. Wimbush (1986), in a study of relationships between leisure and well-being amongst young mothers with children in Edinburgh, suggests quite clearly that 'regular participation in some form of outside recreation was beneficial to the mother's general health' (Wimbush, 1986:184). The distinction is perhaps a fine one –

people would no doubt survive without the types of recreational opportunity that this book is addressing – but in light of the range of benefits that the outdoor experience potentially brings, particularly where it forms a contrast to the normal environment and routine within which an individual resides, then it seems reasonable to acknowledge that demand for outdoor recreation reflects not just an element of preference, but also an element of real need.

Chapter 3

Creating opportunity – the role of providers in urban outdoor recreation

Accommodating the needs of the urban population for outdoor recreation requires adequate provision of a range of facilities, set within a physical environment that is amenable to the types of pleasurable experience that most people wish to be associated with their recreation. This chapter explores the role of providers in meeting those recreational demands, including the processes and constraints that regulate their actions, and highlights the types of programme that are currently being pursued in an effort to enhance the urban environment and which may be expected to have some beneficial impact on the incidence of recreational opportunity.

THE SECTORS OF PROVISION

The provision of recreational facilities is drawn from three sectors – the public, the private and the voluntary – and while each has its distinctive organisational characteristics and, to an extent, interests too, in the real world of leisure provision there is considerable overlap between their actions and activities.

In meeting the needs for outdoor recreation in urban places, the public sector is the dominant actor. It normally exercises direct controls over key land resources such as town parks and public gardens, recreation grounds and playing fields, children's play areas, allotments, footpaths and cycleways, and may exert indirect controls over at least some of the actions of the other two sectors through local authority regulation of the statutory planning process. Decisions made in the public sector will also influence the nature of development of other elements in the urban fabric which may foster recreational usage, although not specifically intended for that purpose – for example town centre pedestrianisation, traffic calming or land reclamation strategies.

The organisation of and actions taken by local authorities to develop outdoor recreation are very variable and this may be partly attributed to a lack of policy direction from central government. The absence of a clear central policy for leisure has long been noted, most recently by Coppock (1993) and Rodgers (1993), and although general encouragement is given by central government to local authorities to make appropriate provision, for example through planning policy guidance (PPGs) or, occasionally, White Papers such as that issued in 1975 on Sport and Recreation (DoE, 1975), leisure remains a non-mandatory function of local authorities. This leads to considerable variation in the level and character of commitment by local government to leisure provision, reflected both in divergent organisational structures and in actual provision.

The nature of local authority work, with its imposed resource constraints and inevitable tensions between alternative expenditure areas, ensures that public provision for recreation is characteristically the product of compromise. Coalter (1985) draws attention to several areas in which inevitable trade-offs have to be made – between what is equitable and what is economically attainable, between the socially desirable and the cost-effective, and between provision that is universal and that which meets selective demands.

In contrast, the private sector has a much clearer and rational basis for operation since these actors are driven by market forces and investment in facilities needs to be justified by financial returns. In urban recreation in general, the commercial sector of activity is extremely important since it controls many of the facilities around which the leisure lifestyles of probably a majority of people are based, when they are not at home. Public houses, cinemas and entertainment complexes, bingo halls, discothèques, nightclubs and, selectively, provision for sport and physical recreation – for example some leisure pools, bowling centres, snooker halls, squash clubs and fitness centres – are typical of this sector. But, strikingly, there is little provision for outdoor recreation in towns and cities from commercial providers, simply because many of the facilities around which outdoor leisure is focused are those from which it is extremely difficult to raise major revenue. In Britain, as in many countries, there is a culture of non-payment for use of facilities such as town parks, footpaths, playgrounds, shopping centres and perhaps only contributory payments (though seldom at full cost) for use of provision such as sports fields or allotment gardens. There are ways of raising revenue from facilities such as town parks (see Chapter 7), but this is not normally at a scale that would entice a commercial leisure operator into the field.

The voluntary sector falls somewhere between the public and private in its significance as a provider of outdoor recreational opportunities, but because of its internal diversity it is the hardest to characterise. It is normally dominated by community-based clubs, groups and associations which tend to be organised around specific activities. Many will focus upon hobby, exercise or sporting interests (amateur drama groups, gardening clubs, football teams) whilst others may have a wider portfolio that is not activity-specific, for instance rotary clubs or townswomen's guilds. They attract members from across the age and gender spectrum but perhaps feature especially strongly in the activity patterns of children and teenagers, women and the elderly. Access to a voluntary group is usually subject to formal membership and payment of a subscription.

As providers of recreational opportunity, the voluntary organisations occupy a variable position. As organisers and providers of a social context for activity they are very important indeed, but less so as providers of physical facilities. A great deal of voluntary activity is indoors where it is frequently sustained through use of space and equipment which is hired for periodic meetings. Back rooms in public houses, school or church halls or community centres, for example, accommodate the meetings of many voluntary groups. Situations in which the voluntary group actually owns space or premises are rather rarer and that is particularly so in the case of outdoor provision. The majority of urban sports teams play on pitches hired from local authorities or leased from landowners and the ownership of sporting grounds is seldom vested in the club itself. Golf is the clear exception, although the organisational basis of golf clubs, their social profiles and the willingness of members to pay high annual subscriptions perhaps marks this activity as atypical.

In an ideal world, it might be expected that these sectors would arrange themselves in a complementary fashion such that efficiency in the provision of a range of facilities to the urban population was achieved. In practice this does not always happen. There is considerable overlap between some sectors, while other areas are neglected since there is no overall co-ordinating strategy with which to bridge the gaps. Williams (1991) in a study of local practice in an English district authority (District of the Wrekin, Shropshire) discovered only limited evidence of inter-sectoral complementarity and instead, high levels of direct competition, particularly between public and private sectors. The local authority was anxious to develop revenue-earning, commercially- run recreation facilities in order to cross-subsidise loss-making areas of provision, for example parks and gardens. Relationships with the voluntary sector were more cordial and included formal structures through which voluntary groups and the public authority could come together to discuss future developments and strategies.

THE LOCAL AUTHORITY

In view of the significance of local authorities to the provision of outdoor recreation in towns and cities, their structures and working practices merit closer attention. We have seen how individuals have a complex decision to reach in selecting an event in which to participate, where resources, time, opportunities and constraints have to be evaluated and conflicts between these variables resolved. Local authorities have an equally complex task in reaching decisions on investment in recreational provision.

The level and character of provision that originates from a local authority and the manner in which it is delivered will be dependent upon two primary groups of factors: the organisational characteristics of the authority and the political economy in which it functions.

Organisational characteristics

Under this heading will fall the inter- and intra-departmental relationships through which the authority operates, the nature of officer/member relationships, and the character of decision-making procedures. Subsidiary aspects of organisation might also include the extent to which the authority has invested in expertise by appointment of officers with experience and/or training in outdoor recreation provision and management.

Provision of recreation, like several elements within local authority work, requires inter-departmental liaison. One of the notable features of recent change in local government in Britain is the extent to which authorities have designated separate leisure services departments within their structures, rather than perpetuating traditional practice in which such responsibility was seen as a minor concern and subsumed within the work of another area. Such practice still occurs, of course, but it is becoming less common. However, this does place a responsibility upon the authority to create appropriate channels for liaison within its structure; in the case of outdoor recreation, a close working practice with the planning department is important. Linkages need not necessarily be formalised within the authority structure, but they need to be present and their operation understood by those who are required to communicate.

Good working links between the officers of the authority and the elected members of its council are also essential. Normally, detailed policy for an area such as recreation will be made the responsibility of a sub-committee of the full council and interviews conducted by the author with a number of heads of local authority leisure services departments have emphasised the significance of good working relationships between officers and the politicians. The attitude of the chair of the relevant sub-committee can be particularly important to effective delivery of services, a keen, interested and knowledgeable chair being far more likely to win resources and advance provision than someone who lacks those key attributes or who does not work well with the officers. Figure 3.1 illustrates how a typical authority might derive its recreation policy.

Once policy is decided, efficiency in implementation is especially dependent upon effective intra-departmental organisation. Leisure service units in urban authorities can have a surprisingly wide portfolio of responsibilities: parks and open spaces (possibly including cemeteries); recreation grounds; sports and leisure centres; community centres; play-grounds; water space, woodland and general amenity areas being a not untypical range of interests. Optimal management requires clear internal structures in which responsibility is precisely defined. As an example, Figure 3.2 illustrates the internal structure of the Leisure and Community Services department in the Wrekin District authority. It is, not surprisingly, a hierarchical structure in which there is a vertical chain of command that transmits policy from the higher levels to the people who are concerned with implementation and day-to-day management, while co-ordination across sectors is maintained by regular meetings of senior staff from each of the three sub-divisions. Those senior staff are also charged with maintaining inter-departmental links and liaison with external bodies with interests in outdoor recreation provision, for example the relevant regional unit of the Sports Council (Williams, 1991).

Political economy

The manner in which a local authority addresses the question of recreational provision also reflects the prevailing political economy. This will embrace basic elements such as budgetary allocations (and the potential constraint of budgetary shortages surely needs no emphasis), but less tangible factors such as the degree of political inclination to support recreation in the public sector and the general nature of central government guidance are also important.

Outdoor recreation provision is expensive, current local authority expenditure on parks and urban open space, for example, running at more than £500 million (CIPFA, 1992). It follows, therefore, that public supply of recreation opportunity is likely to be constrained by budget shortages, particularly since this area of expenditure is discretionary. It is not surprising that the flood of new urban sports and leisure centres, which typified much of the urban development of leisure in Britain in the 1970s,

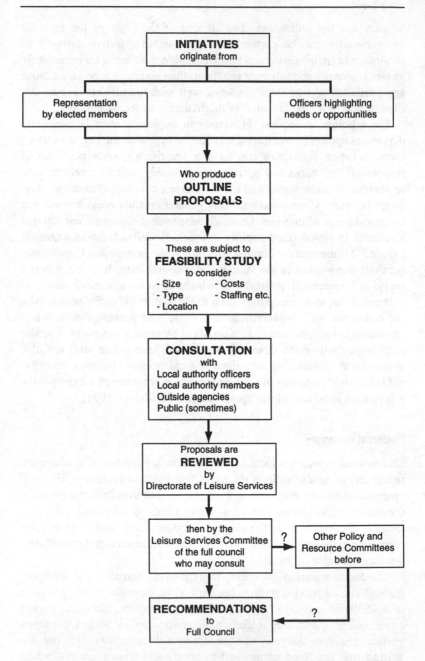

Figure 3.1 Derivation of recreation policy within a typical local authority

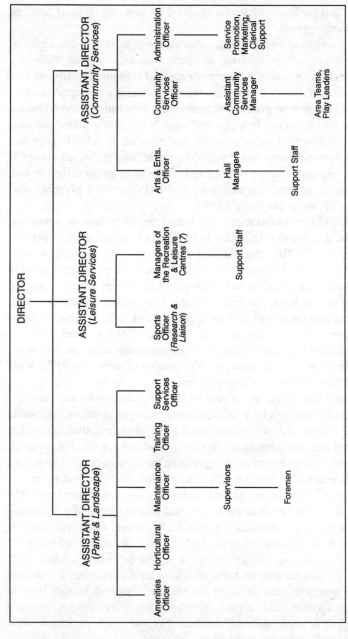

Figure 3.2 Internal structure of a typical local authority leisure services department

Source: Williams, 1991

DIRECTOR

ASSISTANT DIRECTOR (*Parks & Landscape*)
- Amenities Officer
- Horticultural Officer
- Maintenance Officer
  - Supervisors
    - Foremen
- Training Officer
- Support Services Officer

ASSISTANT DIRECTOR (*Leisure Services*)
- Sports Officer (*Research & Liaison*)
- Managers of the Recreation & Leisure Centres (7)
  - Support Staff

ASSISTANT DIRECTOR (*Community Services*)
- Arts & Ents. Officer
  - Hall Managers
    - Support Staff
- Community Services Officer
  - Assistant Community Services Manager
    - Area Teams, Play Leaders
- Administration Officer
  - Service Promotion, Marketing, Clerical Support

slowed to a trickle after 1979 and the election of a central government with firm and persistent views on the need for controls on local taxation and local expenditure.

This observation underlines the importance of political philosophy in decision-making. Although local leisure service units may be staffed by professional practitioners with experience and training, the structure of democratic government ensures that their decisions and recommendations are always subject to political approval, so the ultimate constraint on provision for recreation is a political one. None of the major political parties in Britain is outwardly hostile to the notion of publicly provided recreational opportunity, but it would be remarkable if they all accorded it the same significance and priority and of course, in practice, they do not. (For a useful general discussion on the links between planning and political philosophy see Rose, 1984.)

The 1988 Local Government Act introduced an additional complication for local authorities in Britain in the form of compulsory competitive tendering (CCT). This requires that the management of most services provided by local authorities, including leisure, be put to competitive tender. Authorities are required to compete with private enterprise for the contracts to run their services, and this has caused additional work, complexity and uncertainty for local government. CCT is aimed at management not at provision of facilities, but Veal (1993b) argues that CCT has encouraged local authorities to think through the aims and objectives of their services in more detail, and this may have ramifications for what is provided as well as how it may be run.

Although only sketched in outline here, the organisational basis for provision of recreation by local authorities emerges as structurally quite complex. Proposed developments need to be identified, their feasibility established and then prioritised; resources need to be secured in competition with other departments making calls on the local authority budget and proposals eventually must be subject to scrutiny and approval by appropriate council sub-committes and, normally, the full council too. The process inevitably becomes protracted and in some areas of recreational provision that is a limitation. Recreation, like many social activities, is prone to fashions – short-term, high-interest activities, which grow quickly in popularity, sustain a short peak, but decay with almost equal rapidity. The organisational basis on which local authorities are obliged to work makes it very difficult for them to respond to this type of recreational pattern, and the time-lag often means that provision coincides with decline in participation. Skateboarding and BMX cycling are two recent examples of these problematic activities.

LOCAL AUTHORITY PLANNING FOR RECREATION

The basic objective in local authority planning for outdoor recreation is to establish the physical requirements necessary to support the urban population's recreations and to facilitate those activities through structured patterns of provision. This objective is easier to elucidate than it is to deliver, principally because of the subtlety of the demand side of the equation, especially the fact that levels of participation may be equated only with what is termed 'expressed demand' and that there will be additional demands that lie hidden within the population. User surveys, for example, will always be underestimates of the true demand level since they only tap that element of demand that is revealed through participation. The problem, and it is one to which there is no clear solution, is how to measure hidden demand in such a way that it may be taken into account in forward planning. People are unreliable when asked directly about facilities they may wish to see – they may subscribe to views which they actually do not hold, express interests which cannot be effectively fulfilled because of other constraints, or simply overlook things they actually would like to do. It is also understood that usage can be created through provision, even when there is no expressed wish amongst the population to engage in the activity in question.

Thus, planning for leisure tends to become an exercise in estimation, with reliance upon a professional instinct for what is needed supplemented by fairly simple standards or spatial deficiency approaches to provide a form of factual basis to support proposed provision and make whatever case may be necessary to secure financial and political support.

Veal (1993b) suggests that the development of recreational planning in Britain has passed through three distinct phases. The first he styles the *demand phase*. He locates this between about 1960 and 1972 and characterises its aims as being 'to measure and forecast the totality of leisure demand and then put in place policies to provide for that demand' (Veal, 1993b:85). This was a period of a wide-ranging, almost undiscerning, response to the growth in leisure, in which the answer to the challenge of Dower's 'Fourth Wave' was seen as provision on a wide scale. Local government, for the first time, began planning for leisure in earnest, reinforced by new quasi-governmental agencies, the Sports Council, the Countryside Commission and the tourist boards being the most prominent.

Between 1973 and 1983, Veal argues, recreational planning entered a *needs phase*. This reflected a significant shift in thinking, a growing realisation that leisure had a role to play in the improvement of life quality for urban residents and the view that a policy with a sharper focus on the needs of particular groups was appropriate. This shift was mirrored in overt targeting of sub-groups perceived to be disadvantaged in their access to facilities; ethnic groups, the elderly, the disabled and women were variously highlighted as potential beneficiaries of such policy. (The Sports Council, for example, has actively campaigned to broaden the base of participation in sport; see for example, Sports Council, 1982, 1988, 1992a, 1992b, 1993). Veal also hints at an element of political pragmatism in this approach. If local government were to operate in a financially constrained environment, then public leisure services would be better placed to defend their budgets if they were seen to be meeting a social and worthy objective.

Eventually, the political philosophy of the Thatcher governments caught up with local leisure provision and planning for leisure entered what Veal calls the *enterprise phase*, broadly from about 1983 to the present. Here the emphasis has fallen upon the ability of the market to discover people's real recreational needs and on the potential for the leisure industry to create wealth and employment. The introduction of CCT is seen by Veal as the culmination of the enterprise approach to provision (Veal, 1993b:89).

The changes encapsulated in Veal's 'enterprise phase' highlight the plain fact that planning for leisure within local government structures is not a straightforward task, since it takes place at varying levels and with differing degrees of enforcement. At one level, the pattern of provision of outdoor recreation will be shaped and guided by the statutory planning process while, in many authorities, a second level of service planning guides the work of the leisure service departments.

Statutory planning

This refers to the legal control of physical development as regulated by local authority planning departments. Policy is cast within the structure plan/local plan system whereby the structure plan sets a broad agenda for physical development, usually at a county level, and the local plan interprets and implements policy at the district level. Excepting a small number of 'permitted developments', any physical development of land or change of use requires formal consent (planning permission) which is granted through the development control process. (For fuller detail on the structure and workings of the structure plan system see Cullingworth and Nadin, 1994.)

Although there is a policy vacuum in urban leisure at the national level, central government (through the Department of the Environment – DoE) does seek to guide policy directions for all areas of planning concern, including recreation. This is now exercised through the issue of planning policy guidances (PPGs), PPG No. 17 (DoE, 1991) being the guidance for sport and recreation currently in force. Table 3.1 distils the key advice as it relates to urban recreation and it may be seen that beyond the general encouragement to authorities to make appropriate provision, the guidance highlights several areas of specific concern. These include open space strategies (with emphasis upon playing fields, urban fringe areas and afforestation projects), provision for sports (including spectating) and issues of access, via orthodox rights of way and also through reclamation of features such as disused railway lines which have clear potential for redevelopment as recreational routeways in both urban and rural locations.

Policy guidance (and the official circulars which preceded them) have certainly promoted recreation policy into a more prominent position in most local plans, as the place of recreation as a bona fide urban land use has been recognised. A review of some 50 local plans from urban authorities in England conducted as background research for this book established that just over two-thirds of authorities saw recreation as being of sufficient importance to warrant its own discrete section within the local plan and all articulated a recreation strategy to varying degrees, normally within a wider discussion of environmental policy.

Statutory planning is, however, constrained by the fact that it is essentially a means of indirect control. Land may be zoned for designated uses within a local plan and permissions for development may be granted in accordance with normal criteria, but the planning process *in itself* is restricted in the extent to which it can ensure that approved developments actually take place. Developers are not required to take up planning permissions which have been granted. The general exceptions to these observations relate to the areas of 'planning agreements' (or 'obligations' as they are now termed) and the associated 'planning gain', and these have become an especially important means through which planning authorities have been able to extend the provision of recreational facilities.

Planning obligations are agreements between a developer and an authority whereby the developer undertakes to provide (or contribute to the provision of) public facilities as part of a larger commercial development. The facilities which result are referred to as the 'planning gain'. Originally, planning agreements were made under the terms of Section 52 of the 1971 Town and Country Planning Act and tended to relate to housing areas where roads, public space and landscaping formed common subjects for an agreement. More recently the scope has been extended to embrace major commercial and retail projects, and sport and recreation has edged itself into a position of sufficient prominence to warrant

Table 3.1 Principal statements in Planning Policy Guidance 17 in respect of urban recreation

Government policy is to promote the development of sport and recreation in the widest sense; to enable participation and to encourage provision of a wide range of opportunities (para. 2).

Planning authorities have a responsibility to take full account in their development control decisions of the community's need for recreational space (para. 3).

Local plans should generally cover:– the specific needs of mainstream and specialist sports facilities, the particular recreation needs of the elderly and disabled people, the protection of public and private open space and the availability of public rights of way (para. 15). Local plans should also include a statement of the extent of the community's requirements for sports pitches and policies for the protection of playing fields (para. 44).

Local authorities are encouraged to draw up their own standards of provision based upon local need (para. 16).

Local plans should contain policies on the potential for reuse of disused railway tracks which have an important part to play in offering recreational opportunities (para. 19).

Local authorities are encouraged to consider entering into planning obligations to secure provision of recreational facilities as part of larger mixed development (para. 20).

Where the urban land supply is limited, priority will often need to be given to intensive forms of provision, for example multi-purpose indoor/outdoor sports centres (para. 29).

Authorities should consider the scope for encouraging recreational facilities and increased public access to open land on the urban fringe (para. 32).

Authorities are asked to give sympathetic consideration to afforestation initiatives in urban fringe areas and, where possible, to enhance the rights of way network (para. 33).

Playing fields are of special significance for their recreational value and their contribution to the green space of the urban environment and, with certain exceptions, should normally be protected (paras 41/42).

Local planning authorities are asked to give sympathetic consideration to development proposals designed to achieve the aim of all-seated accommodation at Football League grounds, although major football stadia cannot be regarded as appropriate development within an approved Green Belt (paras 47/50).

Source: Department of the Environment, *Planning Policy Guidance* 17, September 1991.

guidance from the Sports Council on ways in which obligations for sport and recreation might be approached (Elson and Payne, 1993). PPG 17 directs attention to several circumstances under which such obligations may be pursued and Elson (1993) has charted a variety of local planning situations in which obligations for sport or recreation have been sought. These are summarised in Table 3.2.

Table 3.2 Examples of local plan situations in which planning obligations for recreation have been sought

1. On-site provision in major housing schemes where the need has arisen through the new development
2. Contributions to off-site provision, in lieu of on-site provision, where housing schemes are small
3. Replacement facilities where existing provision is lost through development
4. Contributions to off-site provision when larger developments create an impact, e.g. through extra use of existing facilities
5. In conjunction with major office or retailing schemes
6. To secure after-use of mineral or waste disposal sites
7. To secure new patterns of access

Source: Elson (1993)

Service planning

As the pressures on local government to make effective provision for recreation have grown, so has the incidence of strategic forward planning within leisure services departments. These plans afford an opportunity for the authority to review progress to date and set out a preferred agenda for development over the period ahead – normally three to four years. A service plan will thus need to take account of the requirements for facility development, identify potential sources of funding, indicate the capital and revenue implications and perhaps address alternative management strategies for specific facilities or types of resource (Mann, 1990).

As non-statutory devices, strategic service plans are primarily management tools which stand alongside the local plan, normally reflect its policies but are otherwise independent of it. But they do have a direct relevance to the forward planning of facilities where they are used for the identification of deficiencies and, at a more detailed level, they are relevant to how facilities are made available to the using public, times of opening, incidence and timing of concessionary periods, organised programmes, club usage and so on, all of which affect 'opportunity' in the widest sense.

COMMON PLANNING APPROACHES

Identification of deficiency in provision, whether through the medium of a service plan or within the formal context of a statutory local plan, is a key element in planning for outdoor recreation. In the light of the practical difficulties in estimating true demand outlined earlier, we should expect to see some divergence in the manner in which the task is addressed. Veal (1982) has proposed eight contrasting approaches to facility planning, although in practice most authorities subscribe to a smaller number of preferred methods. Three are worthy of emphasis as being particularly popular with planning/leisure services departments, whilst a further two may be noted as possessing more limited application.

Standards approach

This is the most firmly established method for setting levels of provision, the standard for open space, for example, dating back to recommended levels first voiced by the National Playing Fields Association (NPFA) in 1925. The basis of all standards planning is that a fixed level of provision is associated with a given population base – the NPFA standard, for example, recommends 6 acres of open space per 1,000 population. Over the years, quite a number of different agencies have suggested standards for specific areas of provision; allotments, children's play space, sports centres, golf courses are all examples of facilities that have been subject to recommended standards at one time or another. Although standards-based provision has been criticised for its uniformity in approach and its limited capacity to take into account local demographic, economic, social or physical conditions, it is still being urged upon local authotities as an appropriate approach to facility planning (DoE, 1991), albeit through locally derived standards rather than the application of national norms.

The advantages of a standards-based approach to provision rest largely in its simplicity and its perceived equity, although equity is not a particular advantage when specific groups are being targeted and, by implication, others being ignored. There is also some benefit for planners where there are difficulties in forecasting demand, since a standards system provides some measure of release from the uncertainties of identifying hidden demand, by simply assuming a fixed level. If population levels are known or can be forecast with some accuracy, then it is a straightforward task to deploy a standard to calculate any shortfall in provision levels.

Spatial approach

A standard may well define a level of deficit in an urban area but, in itself, it provides less guidance as to where new facilities should be located. For such decisions, planners may well turn to a spatial approach. Specific facilities will have a catchment area that may be marked on a map and from beyond which little or no use will originate. The extent of the catchment will vary in relation to the existing distribution of provision, the degree of specialisation of the facility and the characteristic patterns of use – for example a children's playground will normally have a very small catchment whereas a golf course will draw users from a much larger area. By plotting the catchment areas of existing facilities on a map of the urban area, places that are deficient because they lie beyond the normal range of travel for the services provided will be highlighted. This then permits planners to target new provision into these geographical gaps, assuming that the population within those zones is of a character that is likely to demand the specific facility under consideration. Figure 3.3 provides an actual example of such an exercise conducted by the City of Plymouth to identify zones of deficit in respect of children's play space.

Organic approach

This is Veal's (1982) term to describe a situation which is very common in facility planning. Essentially it reflects an incremental approach in which authorities take regular (or even irregular) stock of their existing provision, assess its patterns of use and highlight any deficiencies that analysis suggests. Deficiency is then addressed according to the con-straints of resources and the prioritisation of development that may be resolved within the appropriate departments or may be a political decision imposed from above. There is a convincing reality surrounding this type of approach. Local authorities do not have the resources to provide for all types of recreation in all parts of their domain. The pattern of provision does tend to grow in an incremental fashion, sometimes in an *ad hoc* manner, reflecting the fairly lengthy history of resource development to which reference has already been made.

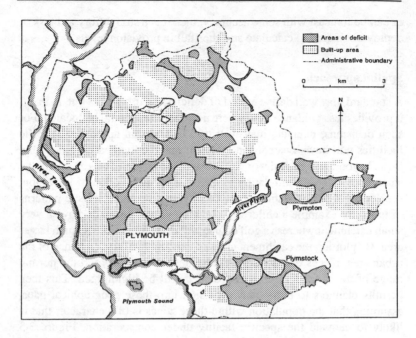

Figure 3.3 Example of the use of catchment analysis to highlight
deficiency in provision for children's play in the City of
Plymouth
Source: Data provided by City of Plymouth Planning Department

Other approaches

Organic approaches are common because in British recreational planning
the local conditions rarely permit a large-scale strategic approach to
provision. There is too much existing development which will disrupt any
broad and ambitious agenda. The one exception to this is the case of new
towns and it is interesting to note that in these special circumstances, other
planning techniques become prominent. One, in particular, is worth
mentioning – the hierarchical approach.

This is founded in conventional central place theory as expounded by
Christaller, which recognises a hierachy wherein a small number of large
and/or specialised facilities (which attract users from a large catchment)
occupy the upper echelons of the hierarchy; at the base we encounter a
larger number of small non-specialist forms of provision with a much
more localised appeal. This can provide a rationale for planned provision

of recreational facilities, especially where there is no existing provision that might disrupt the model pattern. (Figure 3.4 displays a theoretical example of a hierarchical approach to open space provision. An example of an attempt to implement such an approach in Leicester is illustrated in Figure 7.3 in Chapter 7).

Figure 3.4 Theoretical open space hierarchy

One final, and contrasting, approach is the community development approach (Veal, 1982, 1993b). This is very much a product of the democratisation of planning in the 1970s (when public participation became a feature of the new planning process) and of the 'needs phase' in recreational planning described above. The community development approach is centred upon public consultation as a way of informing planning of the requirements for recreation that local people feel are current. As noted earlier, consultation is an important mechanism through which public authorities can keep in touch with the work of the voluntary sector, and the extension of the principle to embrace interest groups within the community who are not necessarily providers but who reflect local opinion allows the needs of the community to be identified and addressed.

PLANNING AND THE URBAN ENVIRONMENT

In many of these planned approaches, whether as part of the statutory local plan or as developments steered by a strategic service plan, manipulation and enhancement of the urban environment is part of the process of creating opportunity for outdoor recreation. The character of the environment can be crucial in determining the levels and types of leisurely use that urban space may attract and sustain. If a townscape presents a pleasing prospect, is interesting and safe it will draw recreational use. If it is ugly, monotonous or dangerous, it will not.

Urban planning has become very much more attuned to the value of the built environment (as part of a wider awareness of environmentalism in planning that has developed since the 1970s: Cherry, 1984a) and a number of policies have been initiated within urban areas in general which attempt to enhance the character of cities and towns and which create significant new opportunities for outdoor recreation. For example, in many industrial urban centres a substantial problem of land dereliction has been created, not only by the final expiry of nineteenth-century industries and their associated infrastructure, but also by the premature decline of certain forms of twentieth-century development. Kivell (1993), whilst enumerating a number of problems in accurate measurement of derelict (and vacant) land in Britain, nevertheless suggests that in 1988 as much as 40,500 hectares lay in this state, about half of which were in urban zones and with most concentrated in major metropolitan areas and regions of traditional heavy industry. Kivell also shows how the problem of dereliction has a capacity for self-renewal as new dereliction erodes the apparent gain derived from clearance of older sites. The incidence of derelict factory sites, for example, actually increased during the 1980s.

Across urban areas in general, land reclaimed from former use has been put to a variety of new purposes, housing, industry and commercial development (including retail and business parks) being typical. One of the primary beneficiaries of reclamation policies has been recreational space, and at a local level the focus on recreation has occasionally been pronounced. The City of Stoke-on-Trent, for example, reclaimed more than 570 hectares of derelict land between 1970 and 1980 of which approximately 87 per cent went to public open space, 12 per cent to industry and just 1 per cent to housing (Bush *et al.*, 1981a). Reclaimed land devoted to recreation has normally been set out as open space of varying character. Parkland, playing fields, simple open land and water space are common forms of after-use, but occasionally more ambitious schemes for mixed development have been planned. The Festival Park redevelopment is one example: here the redundant Shelton steelworks site was redeveloped first as the location of the 1986 Stoke National Garden Festival and subsequently as an area of mixed housing, open space and business, with a prominent emphasis upon leisure. Figure 3.5 illustrates the site whilst still an industrial zone and as redeveloped for amenity usage.

Within the broad area of land reclamation, dockland redevelopment has provided a conspicuous example of planned urban renewal and one in which recreational space has often been integral to the development concept. From a position perhaps 20 years ago in which old dockland areas

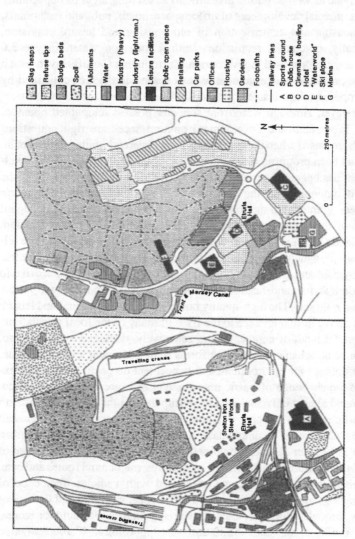

Figure 3.5 The Garden Festival site, Stoke-on-Trent, before (left) and after (right) redevelopment

Source: Data provided by Stoke-on-Trent City Planning Department

were viewed with despair by local authorities, these zones have emerged (often under the guidance of urban development corporations and deploying private as well as public investment) as exciting areas of opportunity for commercial development of office space, hotels, pubs and restaurants, new housing and gentrification of old housing and leisure provision, especially, of course, recreations with a focus on water. Figure 3.6 illustrates the proposed redevelopment surrounding Cardiff Bay in which leisure provision is a prominent user of space and the area contained by the proposed tidal barrage a potentially valuable zone for water sports.

However, although waterfront schemes possess undoubted potential when investment and development circumstances are right, questions have been raised when these schemes have apparently failed to deliver all that had been promised or was expected. The London dockland redevelopment has begun to attract extensive criticism, not least because of the level of autonomy that the London Dockland Development Corporation has been granted and the manner in which it has been able to disregard many of the preferred policies of local government in East London. Coupland (1992) itemises a failure to provide a balanced form of development in which opportunities for local people to achieve suitable employment and affordable housing have been neglected in the drive to provide a stylish and fashionable zone of development that will attract affluent migrants. The high-quality hotels, restaurants, marinas and leisure centres have little relevance to the lives of many of the local population.

Derelict land, of course, occurs selectively, dockland even more so, and in some urban contexts such forms of development are not an issue. Other policies for environmental enhancement do occur widely: for example the challenge of traffic management and 'greening the city' now command almost universal attention from local authorities. The problem of traffic in towns which was signalled over 30 years ago by Buchanan (1963) has become an unavoidable issue. The increase in car ownership noted in Chapter 2, when combined with the growth in road haulage of freight, has ensured that town and city centres, major axial routes and even suburban streets have become congested with vehicles. Incidence of atmospheric and noise pollution, air turbulence, vibration and the risk of injury through vehicle accidents have risen sharply. For outdoor recreation, traffic is a major limitation on opportunity. If routeways to recreational areas are congested or made dangerous by traffic, if the environmental quality of localities is diminished by vehicle noise and pollution from adjacent roads, then the utility of those areas is significantly reduced.

Policy which seeks to minimise such impact is to be welcomed and the

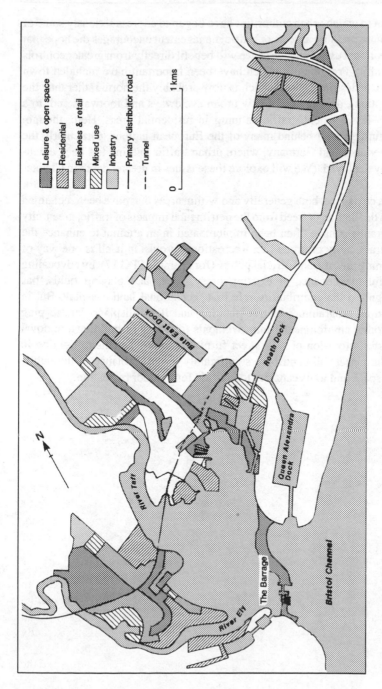

Figure 3.6 Proposed land use zones within the Cardiff Bay Development Corporation area

Source: Data provided by Cardiff Bay Development Corporation

extent to which urban authorities have begun to address seriously some of the more pressing aspects of traffic management encourages the hope that recreational use of outside space will benefit directly from greater controls on traffic. Programmes which have been important have included town centre pedestrianisation (which is now probably the norm rather than the exception), designation of new urban cycleways and footways and, to a much lesser extent, traffic calming in residential areas. Here, though, Britain lags well behind many of the European nations, particularly the Netherlands and Germany, where urban traffic calming has been extensively deployed. (We will explore these issues in greater depth in Chapter 5.)

In city space, both generally and within areas that have been reclaimed from dereliction or freed from the detrimental impacts of traffic, green-city programmes have often been implemented in an attempt to enhance the general quality of urban life. Recreational provision itself is one way of greening the city, and official policy (for example PPG 17), by advocating careful maintenance of existing open spaces and playing fields, has recognised the contributory role that recreational land can play. But in addition, programmes of tree-planting and floral displays, landscaping and other environmental improvements (cleaning of buildings, removal of litter, provision of new street furniture, improvements to lighting in public places) all contribute significantly to the ambiance of the public city space and to its capacity to provide for outdoor recreation.

Chapter 4

No place like home – the role of domestic gardens as recreational spaces

THE SIGNIFICANCE OF THE PRIVATE GARDEN

'Gardens are mirrors of ourselves . . . by making gardens, using or admiring them, and dreaming of them, we create our own idealized order of nature and culture.' So wrote Francis and Hester (1990:2) in a timely reminder that gardens, in all forms and scales, have a significance that extends beyond simple formal qualities and associated patterns of use to a position of some importance in contemporary conceptions of, and life within, towns and cities. Although this chapter is primarily concerned with the manner in which domestic private gardens (and similar garden-type spaces) are used for outdoor recreation, the wider significance of gardens should be acknowledged since so much of what we do in the management and usage of private space reflects wider perceptions and values that society at large places upon these areas. Gardens possess a meaning and a value more than is manifest in usage patterns alone and it is not an exaggeration to suggest that the evolution through time of urban culture and society has been sharply reflected in, amongst many things, the provision, style and use of gardens, both public and private.

In developing this theme, Francis and Hester (1990) suggest a number of perspectives from which gardens may be viewed, several of which have a bearing upon recreational use of domestic gardens. First, they commend the notion of gardens as a medium for the expression of ideas. Gardens illustrate, for instance, a particular view of human relationships with nature, especially a version of nature in a regular and domesticated form. This applies most clearly to large-scale public parks and gardens, but even on the domestic plot the opportunity to control natural systems is present and for some people is a motive for the way they choose to develop and manage their garden. Gardens have also been used as a means of expressing religious belief (whether as metaphors, settings or symbolic designs) and as expressions of political or monarchical powers, for example in the ostentatious creation of ornamental gardens attached to buildings of importance.

Secondly, gardens may be viewed as places and, by extension, as resources – to be used for productive purposes, as aesthetic zones which enhance the environment of the home and street, as venues for a range of activities and recreations, as extensions of the indoor living space, as a refuge to which people may resort for enjoyment, repose, restoration or personal re-creation. Within these forms of use, the activity of gardening itself has a special significance, affording a number of direct and indirect benefits: relaxation, education, exercise and interpersonal contact with family, neighbours and friends who share the interest. Gardening is a creative art that brings rewards (and failures); a sense of achievement and enhancement to self-esteem that comes with successful management of a garden is prominent, as are the simpler pleasures that come with enjoyment of the visual quality of plants and flowers, and perhaps the wildlife that the garden will attract.

Thirdly, gardens are an expression of cultural values and beliefs. The garden is but one manifestation of the human tendency to make sense of the world around us by imposing an order – on nature, on people, on events and on environments – and this becomes a surrogate expression of common cultural values. For example, the exclusivity of gardens in the towns and cities of Georgian England reflected a prevailing culture in which the social order was clearly etched and actively maintained, whereas the ubiquity of the contemporary suburban garden (and perhaps too its uniformity of character) reflects a different culture in which the social order has been eroded in the attempt to create a more equitable society based upon (theoretical) equality of opportunity. Within such egalitarian societies, gardens provide a comparatively rare opportunity not just for projection of shared cultural beliefs but, perhaps more significantly, for expressions of individual personality. In the bland and uniform suburban environment, the garden (and especially the public front garden) provides an arena in which the individuality and creativity of the occupants may be exhibited to a wider public gaze.

Whilst these less apparent attributes of urban gardens may for convenience be identified separately, Francis and Hester (1990) argue that the real significance of gardens is only revealed when they are viewed holistically. The garden is one of several forms of space that we are considering in this text for which the recreational utility has tended to be overlooked and it is perhaps the failure to take an holistic perspective that has led to the consistency with which gardens have been neglected as recreational spaces. Simple usage, alone, belittles and belies a wider philosophical and cultural value which, when taken into account alongside the more practical considerations of how extensive tracts of land are absorbed by urban domestic gardens and the diversity of uses to which they may be put, should place gardens much more highly upon any agenda that is concerned with the manner in which people in urban places live.

The significance of gardens as recreational spaces should not be in doubt even though only a handful of empirical studies have considered the recreational roles of domestic gardens. Theoretical and conceptual appraisals are even rarer. Studies of recreation in the home (e.g. Cherry, 1982, 1984b; Glyptis and Chambers, 1982; Glyptis et al., 1987) confirm that the domestic environment dominates contemporary leisure lifestyles for all but a tiny minority of people, although none of these studies looked systematically and in depth at the role of the garden in home-based leisure. The assertion that gardens occupy a primary position in the outdoor recreation resource base may be supported through, for example, the apparent attractions of gardening as an activity. Forty-eight per cent of respondents in the 1990 General Household Survey (GHS) had gardened in the four weeks prior to survey (OPCS, 1992), the highest level of participation in any physical activity. Scott (1990) shows how the value of business in the gardening sector has grown from £126 million in 1971 to over £2 billion in 1990, based upon healthy sales levels in plants and seeds, tools and equipment, patio furniture, home barbecues and other garden-related leisure goods. The value of sales in garden buildings and leisure equipment increased by 51 per cent between 1986 and 1990 (Euromonitor, 1991), which suggests that the convenience and appeal of private outdoor space is real enough. Halkett (1978:14) summarises the recreational value of the garden as a resource 'that can be used spontaneously and without incurring travel costs . . . without competition with users other than the members of the household', a space that is 'more flexible than other outdoor facilities', one that 'can be modified to meet the household's requirements' and 'used simultaneously or sequentially for a variety of leisure activities'.

THE PROVISION AND EXTENT OF PRIVATE GARDENS

Kellett (1982) argues that the private garden is a distinctly English feature, noting that in Europe, and indeed even in Scotland, a different tradition in apartment- or tenement-style living has tended to make the garden plot attached to single dwellings less commonplace. This is not to assert any measure of uniqueness in the British experience for, after all, suburban forms of housing across the developed world tend to be associated with private gardens, notably in North America and Australasia, but the high level of incidence of British gardens is genuinely remarkable, with some estimates suggesting that over 80 per cent of British households have access to a garden or garden-type space (Euromonitor, 1993).

In Britain, although some medieval town plans show the presence of burgage plots (long, narrow parcels of land with cultivated spaces to the rear of the dwelling), urban domestic gardens seem to have emerged in number in the Georgian period. A common form of initial development, and one that is well demonstrated in Georgian London, was for communal gardens to be set within squares, around which the more exclusive terraced town houses were arranged. These spaces were fenced and locked to keep out non-residents but inasmuch as they were visible from the street, they could have been enjoyed indirectly by a wider group who benefited from their amenity value. However, developers soon appreciated the potential of reversing the pattern and placing the communal gardens at the rear of the houses, thereby creating private gardens that were largely freed from the curious gaze of the ordinary classes.

The fashion for private gardens was quickly adopted and their communality declined so that by the time that John Nash was setting out the Regent's Park area of London (c.1811–26), most of the new villas that formed the basis for the high-class housing in this area had enclosed and private gardens. The properties were also, by now, most often detached rather than terraced. This established a common pattern of building for subsequent construction of Victorian villa developments which, in the nature of fashions of the time, spread rapidly. Figure 4.1 shows such an area of high-quality Victorian housing, developed in the spa town of Great Malvern during the middle decades of the nineteenth century. The low density of housing and the ample provision of private gardens are striking features of this illustration, especially when compared with Figure 4.2, which is drawn at the same scale.

The first development of semi-detached housing is thought to have been the Eyre Estate at St. John's Wood, London (c.1830–40). Edwards (1981) has suggested that patterns of terraced housing limited the role of the garden as a usable space, since the property severed the main access at the front from the garden at the rear. But the innovation of semi-detached housing now provided the opportunity to integrate more fully the house with its garden and in so doing, enhanced the ability of the garden to fulfil a wider range of functions, some still domestic but others pleasurable.

Working-class housing of the mid-nineteenth century was not generally favoured with gardens. The characteristic dense pattern of terraced or back-to-back houses realised little space between properties in which to develop anything other than small service yards. Even the so-called 'by-law housing' that was developed over extensive tracts of land following the 1875 Public Health Act and which was guided in its layout by more generous minimum standards for spacing of properties, still created plots that normally were insufficient to set out gardens (Figure 4.2).

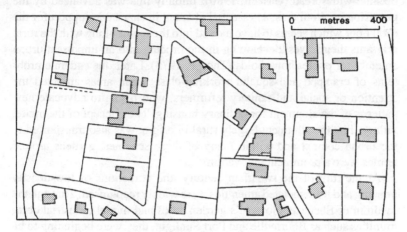

Figure 4.1 Layout of mid-Victorian villas with private gardens, Great Malvern
Source: Traced, with simplifications, from 1:2500 Ordnance Survey extract

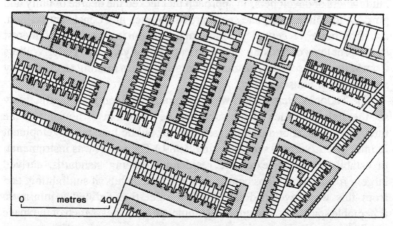

Figure 4.2 Layout of late nineteenth-century industrial housing with yards, Stoke-on-Trent
Source: Traced, with simplifications, from 1:2500 Ordnance Survey extract

However, gardening was considered to be one of the 'rational recreations' that Victorian paternalists tried to encourage amongst the working population. As an activity, it reflected and embraced key Victorian virtues – hard work, thrift in the management of resources, self-reliance and self-improvement – and it is no surprise that as the nineteenth century advanced, attempts at imposing sobriety and a measure of social order upon industrial communities through productive activity of this type became widespread (Gaskell, 1980). Initially this was advanced by the provision of allotments, an essential element in charitable support for the rural poor which seems to have moved into the towns along with the rural migrants themselves, developing in the process into an important urban amenity for poorer households (Thorpe, 1975). Later, the endemic problems of cramped and squalid working-class urban areas attracted the attention of social and sanitary reformers, who began to advocate new patterns of development for ordinary housing. The concept of the model village, like the allotment largely rural in origin, was also transported to the urban context and within many of these schemes, gardens around homes were a prominent innovation.

At the turn of the twentieth century, the attractions of low-density housing and its associated amenities were widely recognised. Through the medium of Ebenezer Howard's garden cities and model industrial communities such as Bournville and Port Sunlight, they were beginning to be realised. Whitehand (1991) notes that before 1914 control over house-building was exercised through by-laws and restrictive covenants of landowners or developers, an approach that lacked the degree of unity and purpose to deliver adequate space around homes in a consistent fashion. By 1918, however, central government had begun to take a keener interest in the problems of housing development. In that year, the Tudor Walters Committee was set up to examine a range of issues relating to the density and design of housing.

The Tudor Walters Report was enormously influential and effectively set the style for much of the suburban development of housing of the inter-war years. (For a useful case study of public housing development in inter-war Liverpool see McKenna, 1989.) The report was instrumental in establishing more extensive residential spacing standards, derived largely from assumptions concerning adequate levels of sunlighting, and from this was developed the '70-foot rule' that defined a minimum acceptable space between opposing domestic frontages. Much of the space would be absorbed by roadways, pavements and verges, but there was still a significant residual space from which to fashion the suburban front garden. The 70-foot rule has had its detractors. Edwards (1981:106) notes that it became 'an unwritten, unexplained but universally accepted code of practice, and extended throughout Britain the unhappy proportion of building height to intervening space'. There is no doubt that the visual tedium of inter-war suburbia owes much to the uncritical application of simple building regulations of this type but they also ensured that most forms of public and private housing built in Britain after 1920 (excepting flats) possessed private garden space. During the inter-war period in particular the combination of high demand for owner-occupied housing, its wider affordability through the mortgage system and the relative cheapness of former agricultural land led to vigorous development of low-density housing with extensive garden plots (Figure 4.3) (Whitehand, 1991).

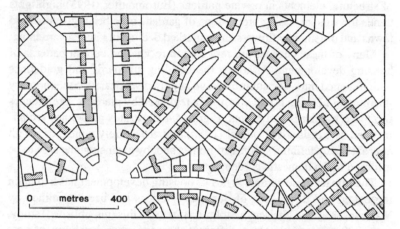

Figure 4.3 Layout of 1930s suburban housing with private gardens, Newcastle-under-Lyme
Source: Traced, with simplifications, from 1:2500 Ordnance Survey extract

Following the Second World War, the pattern of housing and garden provision altered, especially in response to constraints upon urban development that followed the introduction of statutory land planning procedures in 1947. Densities of housing increased as designation of green belts (which were intended to halt urban sprawl) created shortages of land within built-up areas, as land prices rose and as land redevelopment established tower blocks of flats in place of older industrial housing, especially in the inner cities. Gardens became smaller but, as the Parker Morris Report noted (Ministry of Housing and Local Government, 1961), the uses to which people put their gardens were changing too. Up to perhaps the mid-1950s, gardens had primarily been used for domestic storage and as productive spaces for cultivation of fruit and vegetables. This reflected not just vestigial links with a rural tradition (Gaskell, 1980) but the more practical reality of the needs of ordinary families. Improvements in post-war standards of living changed the ways in which gardens were used. The garden became an extension of the home, used for outdoor living – reading, sunbathing, sleeping, sitting out, active games and sports and social activities such as entertaining (Halkett, 1978) – while the gradual invasion of the domestic environment by central heating, automatic washing machines, tumble dryers and deep-freezes, diminished or eradicated the need to allocate garden space for such routine functions as fuel storage, drying of laundry, and vegetable production. Recent analysis of structural elements in private gardens (Euromonitor, 1993) highlights trends towards increasing proportions of garden space being given over to lawns and ornamental flowers and a marked decline in kitchen gardening.

Many of these changes are reflected in recent and current patterns of housing development. Although the building standards and guidelines which shaped inter-war suburbia have largely disappeared, contemporary planning of housing is still effectively regulated by planners' preferences for space standards and norms. Figure 4.4 illustrates guidelines recommended by Leeds City Council (1980) that are entirely typical of recent approaches to defining spacing of homes and, by extension, the area to be afforded to the domestic garden.

The impact these various styles of housing development has had upon the extent and disposition of domestic gardens has been examined by Williams, Kay and Nielsen in Stoke-on-Trent. In this (unpublished) study, some 900 domestic plots from different phases of urban development were measured for their overall size and disposition of land around the house. Several aspects of garden development were illustrated.

First, with reference to the areal extent of domestic plots, Table 4.1 reinforces the general observations made above on the changing pattern of plot size through time. Only a small number of houses survived from the period before 1875 and, as properties of substance, these were associated with large plots. They contrasted sharply with the largely industrial, terraced housing of the period between 1875 and 1914, where the mean area of the plot available as garden space was less than 60 square metres. These would, of course, have been mostly service yards. The new perspectives on housing density signalled by the Tudor Walters Report and the generous opportunities afforded by patterns of inter-war housing development are revealed in a significant increase in the mean sizes of both

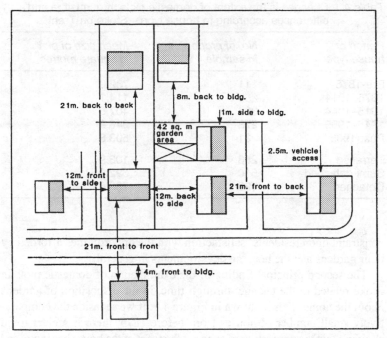

Figure 4.4 Example of guidelines on minimum spacings between
residential properties
Source: Leeds City Council, 1980

plots and gardens between 1915 and 1944. However, after 1945, increasing land prices and the application of tighter planning controls caused a significant reduction in plot and garden sizes as housing densities increased, although for the most recent period, the survey of properties in Stoke suggests that garden sizes have started to increase once again. This is a result of the high number of detached properties that happened to fall within the sample of recently constructed homes and may, as a result, mislead. Whilst modern detached properties do indeed tend to possess larger gardens than semi-detached homes of the same period, and the demand for detached homes has probably increased in recent years, there has also been a parallel but contrasting growth in small starter homes and mews-type housing, where garden allocations are typically very modest. This trend was amongst several noted by Winter *et al.* (1993) in a comparative study of new residential areas in Cardiff and Hampshire where the small size of many modern gardens was observed as a potential

Table 4.1 Changes in the extent of domestic plots through time and
differences according to house type – Stoke-on-Trent

Period or house type	No. of properties in sample	Mean size of plot in square metres
Pre-1875	11	732.0
1875–1914	259	114.1
1915–1944	306	407.6
1945–1965	278	346.9
Post-1965	31	503.8
Terraced	263	103.9
Semi-detached	510	322.8
Detached	120	738.6

constraint upon residents' satisfaction with the opportunities afforded by
their gardens and the housing developments in general.

The second principal finding of the examination of domestic plots in
Stoke related to the change, through time, in the disposition of gardens
about the home. This is shown in Figure 4.5. If we set aside the comparatively small number of houses from before 1875, there is a clear trend
showing that the proportion of space at the front of the house has increased
through time, while that to the rear has contracted. This may be indicative
of two processes, the first being a tendency to locate the home further back
on the plot, to gain a degree of privacy and separation from the activity of
the road. This is important on modern open-plan developments where
fences and walls at the front are not usually permitted. Less positively, the
increase in the proportion of the land at the front can be interpreted as a
consequence of reductions in the overall size of each plot. Planning space
standards such as the 70-foot rule tend to fix the position of the house
relative to other elements in the development, so where plots are smaller,
proportionately more space will occur at the front, by default. The implications for the recreational use of gardens of this shift in land disposition
are significant since they signal a relative movement of space out of the
recreationally more valuable private area at the rear of properties, into the
more constrained public domain of the front garden.

THE RECREATIONAL USE OF GARDENS – THEORY AND PRACTICE

Having outlined the manner in which the provision of domestic gardens

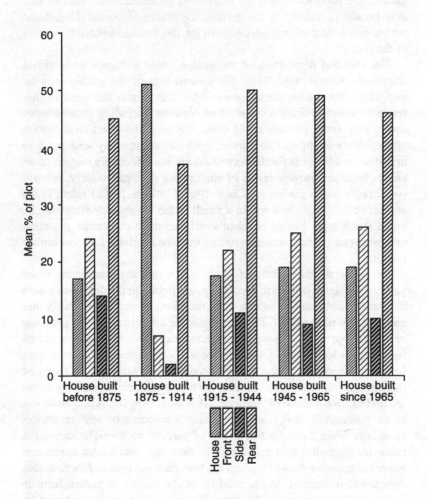

Figure 4.5 Trends in the disposition of land within domestic plots in Stoke-on-Trent

has developed, we may turn now to a consideration of how garden spaces might be used for recreational events. Theoretically, we may expect the pattern of recreational use to be dictated by several factors, including the composition of the household, the value its members place upon the garden, the presence within the household of recreational interests that may be accommodated in the garden, the nature of the neighbourhood within which the garden is set, and perhaps, too, the size and configuration of the plot.

The size and disposition of the garden could influence recreational activity in several ways. First, the overall size of the garden may be important. The greater the space available, the greater the scope of that space to absorb a diverse range of recreations (including simultaneous uses); very small gardens could constrain or prohibit activities which householders might wish to pursue. Such constraints may arise because minimum space needs for the recreation are not effectively met or, more likely, because adequate levels of sunlighting and, particularly, privacy (which encourages garden use, Cook, 1968; Coulson, 1980; Kellett, 1982) are not so easily attained within a small space. (It should, of course, be noted that a large garden could in itself become a constraint, the more extensive tasks of maintenance eroding the time available for other leisure pursuits.)

Secondly, the disposition of space is theoretically significant. Front gardens, although private in ownership, are public in the degree to which they are visible and to which they therefore contribute to the wider environment of the street. Privacy levels are often low and the presence of unseen, but usually powerful communal expectations regarding norms for front garden use and levels of care will often impose a pattern upon front garden spaces. They tend to become neat, tidy and, in terms of recreational use, limited to activities such as car maintenance and gardening and the passive role of 'scenery'. This latter function is not, however, to be diminished as it readily provides a resource of real substance, especially when the collective effect of gardens on a neighbourhood is taken into account. It is interesting to note too, that where communal expectations and values of gardens are low, care and usage of these spaces diminishes in parallel. In the conduct of the survey of garden form in Stoke-on-Trent, several local authority housing areas with a reputation for roughness were visited. In these areas, almost without exception, front garden spaces were poorly maintained and clearly not used for any practical or effective aesthetic purpose.

The extent to which the size and disposition of garden space actually influences recreational behaviours is one of the themes in an empirical study of recreation in gardens being conducted by Nielsen. This work (which is yet to be formally reported) is centred on a household study in Stoke-on-Trent employing both conventional questionnaire and time-budget diary analysis of how people use gardens and the factors that shape those patterns of activity. Nielsen's preliminary findings suggest that there is some evidence to show that recreational activity is partly related to the size of available spaces, households with large gardens (>625 square metres) reporting a higher mean number of different activities than properties with small gardens (<200 square metres). However, the differences are not great and the evidence points to a core of common garden activities which recur almost regardless of garden size. Cook (1968) reached a similar conclusion in his study of the links between the size of gardens, their usage and the levels of satisfaction with garden spaces. The identification of size thresholds around which significant changes in attitude to the garden would occur proved elusive, variations in activity pattern seemingly owing more to the composition of the household and to levels of privacy. Coulson (1980) agrees, and suggests that in most situations householders are content to adapt their activity patterns to fit the size of the gardens they possess.

However, an unpublished analysis by Kay of a survey of garden activity conducted by a major garden equipment manufacturer did highlight a pattern in the relationship between the size of the garden and its usage. Respondents were asked to estimate average time spent in a typical week on a range of garden-based activities. The conclusion (see Figure 4.6) showed that the larger gardens required, as would be expected, significantly greater amounts of time on maintenance, leaving lesser amounts of time for what Kay defined as leisurely activity. In contrast, for medium and small-sized gardens, the average expenditure of time on leisurely pursuits exceeded that required for routine maintenance. This distinction ignores, of course, the fact that the activity of gardening might very well be part of the recreational use of the garden, but it does afford an alternative perspective from which the links between the availability of space and its manner of use may be viewed.

If the association between garden size and recreational utility is obscure or inconsistent, the influence of disposition of space is more evident. In Nielsen's study, the arrangement of space to the front or rear of the house emerged as a significant factor in regulating layout and usage. Owners showed themselves to be particularly attuned to the question of privacy. Where front gardens were generally shielded from public gaze, for example by perimeter fences and/or mature vegetation, usage of front spaces was more extensive and diverse. But when housing layouts created largely open front areas, respondents adopted a more circumspect view of how the areas should be used and revealed quite high awareness of the need to make a contribution to the character and standard of the neighbourhood through regular garden maintenance. Halkett (1978:19) agrees, noting that

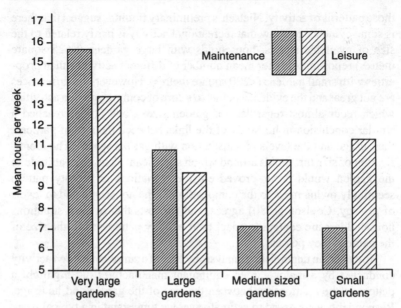

Figure 4.6 The relationship between garden size and time allocations to
maintenance and leisurely garden use
Source: Kay (unpublished)

amongst his sample of Australian homes, 'the back garden was used for
recreation' whilst 'front gardens tended to be used for display'. These
patterns were particularly characteristic of areas of better-quality housing.

The core of garden-based activities which Nielsen identified is set out
in Table 4.2 alongside comparative findings (Table 4.3) from the only
other empirical study that is directly comparable, Halkett's (1978) examination of garden use in Adelaide. (Hall's 1987 survey of garden use in
Chelmsford identified an abbreviated list of garden uses centred on
gardening, clothes drying, children's play, sitting out and care of pets, but
did not place these in an overall ranking according to popularity.)

Both Nielsen and Halkett have developed their data by subdividing
activity into functions which are domestic or recreational in character, but
the pattern proposed by Nielsen is arguably the more discerning since it
recognises an intermediate category in which the named activities could
be recreational events or domestic chores, depending upon the inclination
of the participant and the specific circumstances of engagement. The
classification derived from Nielsen's work also benefits from a further
subdivision into primary, secondary and tertiary activities, according to

Table 4.2 Classification of garden functions and activities

Domestic	Intermediate	Leisurely
Primary activities (all over 75%)		
Drying clothes	Gardening	Reading
Storing refuse		Relaxing
		Sunbathing
		Entertaining
		Talking to neighbours
		Feeding birds
Secondary activities (between 10 and 75%)		
Fuel storage	Car maintenance	Children's play
Vehicle storage	Care of pets	Play with pets
		Games and sport
Minor activities (less than 10%)		
Laundry (other than	Knitting/sewing	Listening to music
drying)	Business work	Woodwork
		Painting
		Watching wildlife

Source: Nielsen (unpublished)

Table 4.3 Garden activities in Adelaide, Australia

Activity	% of households using garden
Recreation	82
Passive – reading, sunbathing, sleeping	70
Active – playing games or sport	49
Social – eating, entertaining	59
Gardening	95
Household	99
Drying laundry	99
Vehicle maintenance	71
Keeping animals	66
Storage of large items	35

Source: Halkett (1978)

their levels of popularity. Halkett reports a more consistent pattern of involvement in garden activity that is less amenable to such a subdivision and which probably reflects the fact that the warmer, drier climate of Adelaide will be less of a constraint on garden activity than the seasonality of weather in England.

The two studies reinforce the notion of the garden as an outside room with largely passive and sociable recreational forms dominating in both listings. Gardening, not surprisingly, is the most widely encountered activity, followed by reading, relaxation, sunbathing, entertaining and socialising with neighbours, especially through the habit of conversing over the garden fence or across front lawns. Children's play, games and sport occur more selectively, as do activities such as vehicle maintenance and the tending of animals. Australians appear to be more involved in car maintenance and care of animals than the residents of Stoke-on-Trent, but in both cases the lower levels of participation are a reflection of the fact that these are interests that we would expect to be taken up by only a portion of the urban population, whereas the primary activities are not interest-related events *per se* and will have a much broader appeal as a result.

Aggregate descriptions of this type, of course, tell only part of the story. Nielsen develops her data by looking next at the periodicity of garden use according to activity. Her findings are summarised in Table 4.4. These reveal the patterns for summer usage of gardens (the winter being a period of negligible garden activity in Britain) and permit further refinement of Table 4.2. It becomes possible to distinguish between activities that are widely encountered and the subject of frequent engagement (e.g. gardening, feeding birds, children's play, relaxation and socialising with neighbours) and activities which, although defined as 'primary' events in Table 4.2, are enjoyed on a more occasional basis (e.g. entertaining). Vehicle maintenance emerges in an intermediate position, between the frequent patterns of daily routines and the occasional entertainment of friends.

Part of the variation in incidence of different garden activities will be explained by the composition of the household and especially the incidence of children. Hall's (1987) study revealed that the presence of a garden was an important factor in selecting a home amongst those families with children, and Cook (1968) has shown how the relative significance of activities fluctuates according to the numbers of children in the household. Figure 4.7 illustrates that as the number of children increases, the activities of gardening and, to a lesser degree, sitting out, decline in popularity. Presumably, the clamour of children at play is a minor disin-

Table 4.4 Frequency of garden use (during summer) for different activities – Stoke-on-Trent (%)

Frequency	Entertaining	Reading	Relaxing	Talking to neighbour	Children's play	Games and sport	Work on garden	Work on car	Attend to pets	Feed birds
Daily	2.1	15.3	22.5	16.6	19.9	11.0	22.9	—	22.9	48.3
2–3 times a week	8.5	25.0	24.5	30.9	8.9	5.9	44.1	0.8	4.2	19.9
Weekly	11.9	23.7	15.7	19.5	5.5	5.5	19.5	19.9	3.0	7.3
Fortnightly	12.2	9.7	10.6	5.1	0.4	1.3	5.9	8.1	0.8	0.8
Monthly	24.2	3.0	2.5	2.5	3.9	1.3	1.7	3.8	1.7	0.8
Less	20.3	4.2	3.4	3.8	7.2	1.7	—	3.4	—	0.8
Never	20.8	19.1	20.8	20.8	54.2	73.3	5.5	62.7	67.4	22.0

Source: Nielsen (unpublished)

Table 4.5 Variation in the most important garden use (%) according to household size – Chelmsford

Persons per household	Gardening	Laundry	Children's play	Sitting out	Pets	Other
1	25	17	—	42	12	4
2	32	22	—	41	2	3
3	22	31	11	31	5	—
4	21	15	35	23	2	4

Source: Hall (1987)

centive to sitting out in proximity to their activity, while gardening is a likely casualty of incidence of physical damage to the fabric of the garden resulting from play, especially ball games. In households without children (or where the children have grown up) the fortunes of gardening as a pastime are notably higher and, as Figure 2.6 (p.41) shows, the attraction of gardening becomes progressively more important as people grow older. Data presented by Hall (1987) and reproduced in Table 4.5 tend to confirm that gardens belonging to larger households possess a reduced utility as places in which to garden, to sit out or care for pets, but become important venues for children's play and (less consistently) drying of laundry.

ALTERNATIVES TO THE PRIVATE GARDEN

From certain perspectives, the characteristic uses of domestic gardens may appear mundane and trivial, and some proponents of higher-density urban housing have questioned the wisdom of allocating generous amounts of land to private outdoor space. But such a view surely undervalues the types of casual interaction that gardens facilitate and which for many urban people form the central core of their recreational lifestyles. Kellett (1982) argues further that people value gardens for reasons beyond the merely functional, as status symbols, as a medium for personal expression and as defensible spaces. Privacy and security are primary attributes of domestic

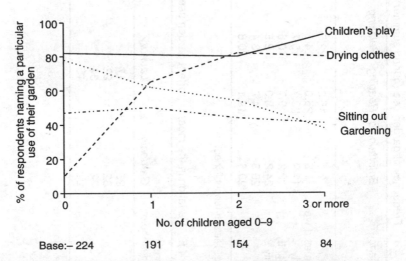

Figure 4.7 The effect of children within a household upon garden use
Source: Cook (1968)

garden spaces and whilst Newman's (1972) theory of defensible space has yet to be adequately validated in the specific context of domestic gardens, there can be little doubt that many garden owners perceive the relative safety of their gardens as a positive advantage. The reduction in the levels of perceived safety of public urban places can reinforce the value of private space for outdoor recreation, particularly for women, young children and the elderly.

But how may the advantages that a garden bestows upon its users be extended to those members of the urban community who do not enjoy personal use of garden space: those who reside in flats, older forms of industrial housing, or even modern small homes developments which provide little more than a paved court outside the rear service door? Although the urban garden in Britain is widespread, it is not ubiquitous. Data from the Central Statistical Office (1993) show that in Britain as a whole, over 21 per cent of dwellings are flats, many of which will lack private garden space, as will a proportion of the 29 per cent of homes that are terraced. These contrasts are also mirrored in socio-economic data, research by Euromonitor (1993) suggesting that whilst most households in the professional groups (AB) have access to a private garden, such access is much more selective amongst manual and unskilled households.

In areas of continental Europe (including Austria, and especially the Netherlands) where large urban populations reside in high-density apartment complexes, a tradition in the provision and use of 'leisure gardens' has been developed. These are plots of land that are leased or purchased by householders to provide opportunities to garden and to recreate within garden-type environments. Typically, leisure gardens are grouped together on sites which, being often peripheral in location, are physically removed from the home and the immediate neighbourhood of the household concerned. Space within the leisure garden may be devoted to productive forms of fruit and vegetable growing, but many holders take the opportunity to lay out areas of lawn, paving, ornamental flowers and trees and construct summerhouses which may be sufficiently well served to provide an effective weekend retreat. Individual sites are often maintained to a high standard and the composite effect of groups of leisure gardens is an enhancement of the urban environment which, in the best cases, extends beyond the immediate boundaries of the site itself.

Continental leisure gardens developed significantly after 1945 but to date have made little impact upon British traditions in provision for garden spaces away from homes. The most concerted attempt to import the idea followed the publication in 1969 of the Report of the Committee of Inquiry into Allotments (generally known as the Thorpe Report, after its chairman). Thorpe's enthusiastic advocacy of the concept of the leisure garden (which he also reinforced through a number of demonstration schemes: Figure 4.8) did produce a modest response amongst several urban authorities, including Birmingham, Bristol and Cardiff (Crouch and Ward, 1988). However, the failure of government to act upon any of the substantive recommendations of the Thorpe Report, either through legislative change or through new resource allocations, has tended (for the present) to consign the leisure garden concept to little more than a footnote in the story of British urban gardening and horticulture.

The focus of the Thorpe Report was the urban allotment and the proposals for a new form of leisure garden arose directly from what was perceived to be something of a crisis in the provision and use of these spaces. Thorpe saw the leisure garden as a way of invigorating and providing a new direction to a form of land use bounded by traditional practice and in the latter stages of a terminal decline. In fact, the allotments have survived rather better than Thorpe envisaged and to that extent, they still provide the only widely available alternative to the private garden in urban Britain today.

The significance of the allotment as a form of urban land use has fluctuated markedly through time. They were introduced into the Victorian city as a form of relief for poorer people and to provide meaningful recreations to counteract the socially pernicious influence of public houses. Their practical utility was of suffecent importance to warrant official recognition and promotion through the Smallholdings and Allotments Act of 1908. This placed an obligation upon local authorities to make allotments available and there was, consequently, a marked increase in the number of holdings (Figure 4.9). The two world wars created short-term and significant fluctuations in the provision of holdings and Kay (1988) has noted that as a result it has proven difficult to establish the true level of demand for allotments. However, the consensus is that levels have not fallen below the figure of around half a million allotments that was recorded in 1973, even though precise calculations are now rendered impossible through a removal of requirements for local authorities to keep records of plots in their areas (Crouch, 1991). So despite the view of allotments as untidy anachronisms that is prevalent in some authorities, it would seem that there is a strong residual interest in urban allotment gardening and, perhaps surprisingly, current numbers of allotments are unlikely to be significantly below the level that existed immediately before the First World War.

Empirical studies of allotment use are rare. The Thorpe Report provided a full analysis of patterns in the 1960s, a useful résumé of which

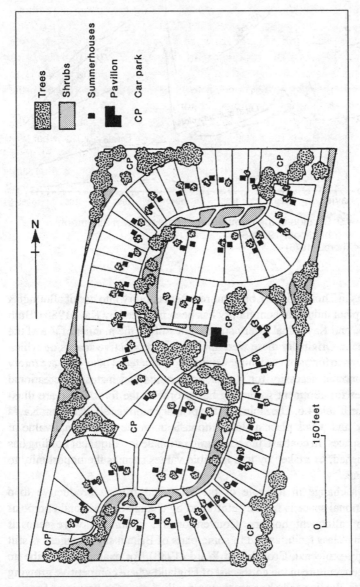

Figure 4.8 Westwood Heath leisure garden, Coventry
Source: Thorpe, 1975

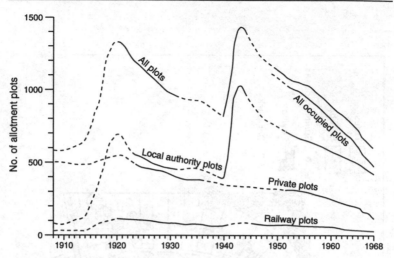

Figure 4.9 Change in the numbers and categories of allotment
holdings, 1908–68
Source: Thorpe (1975)

appears in Thorpe (1975), but a more recent enquiry into use of allotments
in a typical industrial community has been provided by Kay (1988). Both
Thorpe and Kay signal a very significant shift in the manner of use of the
allotment. Originally these were intended as productive spaces on which
subsistence forms of gardening would be conducted. Today they are rarely
an economic necessity for poorer households and instead, recreational
motives for allotment gardening have come to the fore. These are illustrated in Table 4.6. The table lists the primary motives elicited from Kay's
sample and which place a clear emphasis upon the recreational value of
these spaces. In contrast, the economic rationale for allotment holding has
diminished, overtaken by less tangible values such as the opportunity to
be alone.

   This change in the role of the allotment from a productive to a
recreational space is further reinforced by change in the social composition of allotment holders. Conventionally, allotments were seen as
working-class facilities and in some parts of Britain such imagery is still
strongly projected. Crouch and Ward (1988), for example, describe an
allotment culture in the north-east of England where competitive growing
of leeks, dahlias and chrysanthemums, allied with the keeping of racing
pigeons provides a powerful focus of popular attention amongst the urban
industrial communities and their working men in particular. But processes

Table 4.6 Motives for allotment holding – Stoke-on-Trent (%)

Motive	Very important	Important	Little importance	No importance
Hobby/recreation	70.6	26.7	2.1	0.5
Source of fresh produce	60.4	33.2	5.9	0.5
Opportunity to work/ be alone	50.5	31.9	12.6	4.9
Saving on household expenditure	32.4	29.1	29.7	8.8
Supplementary source of income	8.7	7.1	14.7	69.6

Source: Kay (1988)

of urban gentrification allied with changing perspectives on environmentalism, the attraction of organic foods and moves towards new lifestyles that emphasise the value of exercise and health-related fitness, have induced a movement into allotment holding by professional and middle-class groups too (Crouch, 1989a). Crouch and Ward (1988:80) assert that 'the most remarkable result of the cultural changes of the post-war years is the sheer diversity of today's allotment holders', and although there is a natural tendency to high turnover rates amongst newcomers to allotment holding, those that have stayed with the hobby have helped to diversify the socio-cultural profile of allotment gardening.

The degree of gentrification of allotments probably varies spatially. In the predominantly working-class community of Stoke-on-Trent, Kay (1988) identified the allotment clientele as being largely of a traditional social character (in terms of allotment use), drawing upon housing areas that were concentrated in the older inner city zones of the conurbation. The conventional profile of Stoke's allotment holders was further conveyed by the fact that holders were overwhelmingly male and middle-aged or elderly, 40 per cent actually being retired (Table 4.7). In contrast, Crouch and Ward (1988:232) observed that in Haringay (north London), there was significant demand for allotment gardens from 'new arrivals, often young professionals seeking places of character and influenced by ecological ideas, disenchanted with commercially produced food and the prevalent attitudes to the environment'.

Such divergent experience emphasises the importance of locality in shaping patterns of allotment use. This may be seen, superficially, in the

Table 4.7 Profile of allotment holders – Stoke-on-Trent (%)

Age	
Under 25	1.1
25–40	10.6
40–60	45.2
Over 60	43.1
Gender	
Male	92.0
Female	8.0
Employment status	
In full-time employment	45.0
Self-employed (full-time)	4.8
In part-time employment	1.6
Unemployed	7.4
Retired	38.6
Other (housewife, student, etc.)	2.6

Source: Kay (1988)

spatial relationship between homes and allotments. Kay's (1988) study showed, for example, that walking to the allotment was the preferred mode of travel, that journey times were short (Table 4.8) and that catchments seldom extended beyond a radius of 1 kilometre (Figure 4.10). Like many urban recreation facilities, allotments are primarily local in their appeal.

But Crouch (1989a, 1991) argues for a deeper significance too. Explicitly he rejects perspectives that suggest that people do not want the kind

Table 4.8 Travel patterns to allotments – Stoke-on-Trent (%)

Journey times	
Under 10 minutes	79.3
10–20 minutes	16.5
21–30 minutes	4.2
Over 30 minutes	—
Travel mode	
Walk	77.7
Bicycle	2.1
Car	19.7
Motorcycle	0.5
Bus	—

Source: Kay (1988)

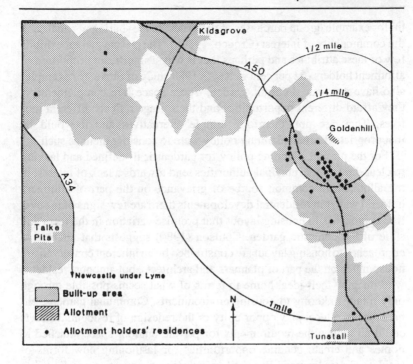

Figure 4.10 Catchment area of allotments at Goldenhill, Stoke-on-Trent
Source: Kay, 1988

of local control and links with tradition implicit in local production of landscape (such as is evident in the creation of allotments) and argues instead that 'people are in fact becoming more rather than less concerned about local identity' (Crouch, 1991:327). Allotments represent an increasingly rare opportunity to resist the commodification of leisure (Crouch, 1989b) and 'a chance for creation of a landscape by ordinary people, in contrast to the predominant landscapes around us that are the product of the business sector or the state' (Crouch, 1989a:261). Such a thesis reinforces the deeper cultural significance of garden spaces that goes beyond their evident recreational utilities.

The heading of this section suggests that spaces such as allotments might be considered as an alternative to the private domestic plot, but in truth they are not analogous. The success of an allotment typically depends upon its co-operative nature: in its organisation, control and, sometimes, ownership; in the presence of reciprocal arrangements amongst holders in, for example, group purchases of materials; in the sharing of rituals and the commonality of interest (Crouch, 1989b). The private garden exhibits few of these attributes and perhaps that is why a significant proportion of allotment holders (62 per cent in Kay's 1988 study of Stoke, for example) also have a private domestic garden. These spaces are complementary, they afford different opportunities and their usage reflects different motives. They are not, therefore, simple alternatives and it would be inappropriate if urban planning policy were to consider them as such.

For the present, planning policy for gardens is ill-defined and lacking in clear direction. Municipal authorities tend towards a lack of interest in the allotment (a common source of grievance on the part of allotment holders) whilst in residential developments there are few signs of innovative approaches to housing layout that promise variation in the form and style of the domestic garden. Coulson (1980) suggests that alternative approaches to housing layout are constrained by an inherent conservatism, not so much on the part of planners and architects, but amongst residents who imagine their ideal home in terms of what seems possible through only minor tinkering to housing environments. Communal gardens, enhancement to local play opportunity or the redesign of residential streets could all reduce the requirements for private outdoor space attached to homes and create genuine opportunities for fashioning new forms of residential development. But until such time as the question of who *needs* garden space and what form such space might take has been adequately addressed, the presumption in favour of provision of gardens is likely to remain. From a recreational perspective, given the undoubted utility of a private garden as an informal leisure space and the trend towards a greater emphasis on home-centred leisure lifestyles that was noted in Chapter 1, this is perhaps as it should be.

Chapter 5

On the street – urban thoroughfares as recreational spaces

'Streets are an important part of the landscape of everyday life. People rely on them for such activities as travel, shopping and interaction with friends and relatives' (Francis, 1987a:23). Streets are also a key element in urban outdoor recreations, although within the extensive literature on streets that significance is not always afforded the attention it merits. Moughtin (1991a:57), however, is one who does emphasise this wider diversity of roles in noting that the street, as well as providing a link to permit movement of people and goods, has 'the less tangible function in facilitating communication and interaction between groups', and 'its expressive function also includes its use as a site for casual interaction, including recreation'. This range of roles applies also to other public thoroughfares within urban places; footpaths that are not associated with roadways, cycleways and canal towpaths, for example, which although intended as means of circulation within the urban environment, attract other uses not directly concerned with the particular function of movement. Jacobs (1961), in her memorable diatribe on modern planning, argues persuasively that these wider functions of streets and public places are every bit as important to the proper functioning of cities as is the movement that thoroughfares facilitate.

People at leisure may use streets and paths in a number of ways. They are, of course, a means of access to other recreational resources in the built-up area but they are also recreational resources in themselves. Some people take advantage of the linear quality of the resource and use it as intended – as a means to get from one place to another, either for a particular purpose or perhaps for the intrinsic value of a recreational journey, whether on foot, on a bicycle or in a vehicle. Others use just part of a route as a venue for activity – a child playing on the street outside the home, for instance – and here the fact that the street forms part of a wider route network is irrelevant. It is simply a convenient space.

Historically, streets and other urban rights of way formed an important location for recreation or quasi-recreational activity; they were venues for entertainments such as street fairs, for political, religious or cultural meetings, for markets, for children's play, for socialising, for some forms of sporting activity, and for walks and promenading. The chronology of decline in these functions is not easy to locate since it varies according to activity and in both space and time, but it is generally true to say that the advance of urbanism in the twentieth century has been associated with a significant and widespread reduction in the utility of streets and thoroughfares as recreational spaces.

Any review of recreational opportunities afforded by contemporary streets and pathways would probably conclude that the recreational utility of these areas varies inversely with the significance of the route and the incidence of road traffic. Modern transport networks provide a hierarchy of routes, at the head of which we encounter urban motorways from which all but wheeled, powered vehicles are prohibited by law. Such roads have limited recreational utility and even the potential for pleasurable recreational driving is minimised by the technical challenge that is posed by urban motorway conditions, by the frequency with which traffic is brought to a standstill by congestion and road repairs, or by the dull prospect that the view from the car window on motorways so often manages to afford.

Next we encounter major arterial roads and dual carriageways and whilst these are theoretically available to pedestrians and cyclists at leisure, the weight of traffic that typically uses major roads is a powerful discouragement to such use. It is only when we enter the lower levels of the road hierarchy – the local distributor roads and particularly the residential streets and culs-de-sac – that the recreational utility and potential of street areas becomes truly apparent. This is partly a consequence of the reduction in traffic volumes associated with these minor routes, which allows people rather than vehicles to become more prominent, but is also an indication of the character of the built environment that such routes habitually service. People live alongside these streets in large number in a way that is untrue of motorways and less characteristic of major roads (although obviously it occurs). This immediate proximity of people and streets leads to a spillover of activity such as socialising and children's play, alongside the bona fide recreational use of streets such as walking and cycling.

These ideas are summarised in Figure 5.1, which also shows that where surfaced roads stop, the networks of footpaths and other routeways take over. As traffic-free routes these perhaps possess the greatest potential to support outdoor recreation, especially where they diverge from areas of congestion and take users into quieter and perhaps environmentally contrasting areas of the town or city, or to the fringes of the countryside. Indeed, many urban areas reveal networks of unofficial paths that have been forged simply by people creating their own routes, as short-cuts perhaps, or as a means of access to areas of interest that cannot be reached by road. Children, in particular, are skilled at such route creation.

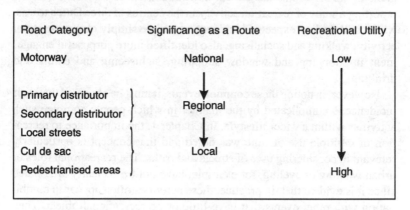

Road Category	Significance as a Route	Recreational Utility
Motorway	National	Low
Primary distributor		
Secondary distributor	Regional	
Local streets		
Cul de sac	Local	
Pedestrianised areas		High

Figure 5.1 Theoretical relationship between road capacity and recreational utility

The other traffic-free areas that are significant recreationally are those town and city centre areas that have been pedestrianised as a part of environmental enhancement policy. Scrutiny of current local plans for urban centres in Britain shows that adoption of pedestrianisation is becoming almost universal within selected zones of town and city centres and whilst the scale and character of pedestrian schemes is variable, the potential value of such spaces for recreation activity is to be noted.

RECREATIONAL USAGE OF STREETS AND THOROUGHFARES

Streets, pedestrian zones and pathways habitually support a range of recreations that may be considered characteristic. These include traditional street activities such as walking, cycling, shopping, children's play and socialising, together with more recently popular recreations such as road running or jogging. Incidence and character of street activity varies within different urban zones, a central pedestrian precinct, for example, revealing a different blend of activity to that afforded by a quiet residential street. Gehl (1980), in a study of residential street activity in Canada and Australia, identified six primary activities: people sitting or standing about; people engaged upon domestic chores – car maintenance, repairs to property, etc.; walking; social interaction; children's play and movement of traffic along the street. In contrast, Jansen-Verbeke (1988), reporting a study of recreation activity in the centres of three Dutch towns, whilst still finding expected incidence of people simply observing street activity, walking and socialising, also identified more purposeful engagement in shopping and window shopping, sightseeing and eating and drinking.

However, in noting these common events, it must be observed that their incidence is complicated by the manner in which people combine such activities within a wider lifestyle. In Chapter 1, the importance to recreation of multiple use of time was noted and that concept is particularly relevant in considering uses of streets and paths. The recreational roles of urban walking or cycling, for example, have not been clearly articulated since it is evident that, in practice, these activities often appear in combination with other events that have little or no recreational object. They tend, therefore, to become obscured or overlooked and it becomes difficult to disentangle recreational motives from purely functional objectives when, say, a parent, in escorting a child to school, chooses to walk rather than drive the car because of the pleasurable benefits that might be associated with the exercise, or when a journey to work is undertaken by cycling, perhaps to conserve financial resources, perhaps to gain physical exercise and, maybe simultaneously, for the recreational experience of the event. Dividing lines between recreational and non-recreational elements in street activity are blurred and inconsistent and this problem must be noted as a caveat to ensuing discussion.

Walking and cycling

Walking is the natural means of locomotion for people so it is unsurprising that it should emerge at the head of lists of common outdoor activities. Eighty per cent of journeys of less than a mile are conducted on foot (Department of Transport, 1992) and most of us walk somewhere every day. Figure 5.2 illustrates average weekly walking distances divided according to age and shows that for groups such as children and teenagers, walking is a primary mode of travel. Regular recourse to walking is probably a consequence of the types of short journey pattern which characterise the lifestyles of children and young people, their often limited

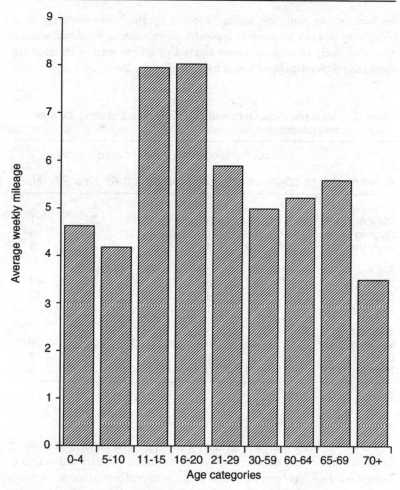

Figure 5.2 Average weekly walking distances according to age
Source: Department of Transport, 1992

financial resources with which to purchase public transport services, and prohibition on driving or inability to drive a motor vehicle. But even in households where a car is available, not all members will have equal access to the vehicle and this ensures that many journeys in apparently mobile households will, of necessity, be made on foot. Data reveal that men are more likely to walk than women, when it is a chosen activity, and with the exception of elderly people over 70 years, such walking is fairly uniform across adult age bands (Table 5.1). But when walking is an obligatory activity attached to typically short, routine journeys, women are more likely to walk than men and old people as well as children are especially dependent upon travel by foot (Tolley, 1990).

Table 5.1 Adult participation in walking, cycling and running, by age and gender

	% participating in the 4 weeks before survey							
Activity	16–19	20–24	25–29	30–44	45–59	60–69	Over 70	Mean
All groups								
Walking	45	42	45	43	44	42	25	41
Cycling	24	11	11	11	8	6	3	9
Running	15	10	9	7	2	—	—	5
Men								
Walking	48	44	47	46	45	46	33	44
Cycling	33	14	16	14	8	7	5	12
Running	22	16	16	11	3	1	—	8
Women								
Walking	43	41	42	40	42	39	20	38
Cycling	15	8	7	9	7	5	1	7
Running	10	6	4	3	1	—	—	2

Source: OPCS (1992)

However, while quite a lot is known about general patterns of walking in towns and cities, a lot less is known of urban recreational walking, except where it has been examined as a common form of usage of parks and open spaces. A great deal of attention has been focused upon countryside walking and a range of policies developed to address the supposed needs of countryside walkers (Countryside Commission, 1986, 1988, 1993), but although surveys such as the General Household Survey (OPCS, 1992) tell us that 41 per cent of the population took a walk of over 2 miles in the four weeks preceding the survey, they don't tell us where that walk took place and what the motivations behind the walk might have been.

But despite the absence of sound empirical observation, we may be confident that walking in cities occurs in a range of circumstances. Some walking will be of a purely functional nature, selected as the fastest or most convenient way to travel between two locations as part of a task that is necessary to employment, domestic duties or some other routine. Secondly, and at the opposite end of the spectrum, some walking will be entirely recreational. In most residential neighbourhoods, at varying times of the day, people will come on to the street, perhaps to walk dogs (which may, of course, be a chore) or to stroll around the block, observing gardens and street activity, socialising with other residents, or merely taking the air. Between these poles will be a range of contexts in which walking may take place, all of which will be characterised by a duality of recreational and non-recreational uses of time: a walk to post a letter, to collect children from school, to visit the shops or to journey to work. Aggregate data suggest that in Britain, about 45 per cent of walking trips are associated with personal business and shopping, 25 per cent with journeys to schools and colleges and the remainder, some 30 per cent, are recreational or leisure-related (Department of Transport, 1992). Such simple descriptions should, however, be accorded some caution due to the plurality of motives that may be combined in such trips.

Rapoport (1990) argues that the degree to which different urban societies engage in walking is primarily a reflection of two factors. The first relates to perceptions of the environment and the extent to which it supports walking in public places. Physical comfort, levels of safety, the attraction and diversity of the townscape, all can exert a strong influence on the propensity to walk. But perhaps of greater significance is the cultural affinity with walking within the urban community. Here Rapoport is struck by contrasts between Britain where, he observes, streets in town centres are not much used in evenings, and countries such as Spain or Italy where, in the evenings, the streets come alive with people at leisure. In part this reflects certain climatic differences, the incidence of afternoon siestas in many Mediterranean countries and the habit of reopening shops in the evenings but, climate apart, these are divergences in custom that appear deeply ingrained in contrasting cultures.

The risk in non-use of street areas, especially after dark, is that these spaces become the domain of particular sub-culture or lifestyle groups whose presence then becomes a deterrent to other users. Most cities and large towns have their 'rough' areas in which crime, drug-related activity and prostitution are prevalent and in which people from outside will not normally walk. Jansen (1993) notes this problem in the context of contemporary Amsterdam but the risks of surrendering the street through non-use were voiced more than three decades ago by Jacobs (1961), so it is scarcely a novel perspective even if municipal authority has been slow to heed the advice.

The fortunes of cycling as a recreational activity have fluctuated noticeably. In Britain, the 1960s and early 1970s were a period in which cycling provided a rare example of an outdoor recreation in relative decline (Patmore, 1970). Since then, a combination of factors which include wider awareness of the benefits from health-related fitness, increasing costs of motoring, media coverage of major cycling events and the popularity of new forms of cycling, especially mountain-bike riding, have assisted in restoring interest in the activity. The number of bicycles in the UK increased by almost 80 per cent during the 1980s (McClintock, 1992) and the GHS shows that 9 per cent of the adult population engaged in cycling during the period preceding survey. However, Britain lags significantly behind many of its continental neighbours in bicycle use: in the Netherlands, for example, 29 per cent of all trips are made by bicycle, in Denmark 18 per cent, in West Germany 11 per cent, but a mere 4 per cent in Great Britain (McClintock, 1992). In Britain, cycle use is sharply skewed towards the young and towards men rather than women (see Table 5.1) but the overall low levels of bicycle usage probably reflect, once again, cultural perspectives in the population at large, as well as a failure to plan transport systems in which bicycles may safely be used.

Whilst it is possible to chart the incidence of cycling at an aggregate level, cycling shares with walking the practical difficulty of isolating both the occurrence of purely recreational cycling and the locations where people actually ride. Given the poor traffic conditions on urban roads in Britain, it is probable that where the object is recreational, although most cycle journeys will originate in towns and cities, destinations may well be rural or semi-rural. But as with walking, there will also be extensive mixed-motive journeys made by bicycle and in countries such as Denmark or the Netherlands, where there is a much stronger tradition in urban cycling, the full scope for such journeys is very apparent and is well supported through planned provision of appropriate cycleways and associated facilities (Michels, 1992).

Shopping

As an activity, shopping is not, of course, necessarily a recreational event, nor is it conducted entirely out of doors. Indeed, trends towards movement of stores to indoor environments are tending to erode the position still further. However, in most cities there remains a significant outdoor element in shopping; in the use of street markets, in the incidence of window shopping or in patronage of stores that display goods on pavement areas and, in most central areas, shopping remains a prominent activity that brings people on to the streets.

Recreational shopping has been accorded rather more attention than urban recreational walking although understanding of the activity is far from complete. Bussey (1987) suggests that leisure and shopping combine in three distinct ways: as direct retailing of leisure goods; by the provision of leisure facilities as part of the retail environment, for example restaurants, pavement cafés and amusements; and through the incidence of shopping as a recreational activity. To this we may also add the observation that in Britain, increasingly, recreational facilities have been provided as a result of planning obligations placed on retail development, the leisure facilities forming part of the planning gain (see Chapter 3).

Of these, it is recreational shopping that is most directly relevant to the present discussion, and recent work conducted in the Netherlands has illuminated a number of aspects of this activity as a behavioural area. First, recreational shopping is particularly attractive to younger people. For example, Jansen (1989) shows how extensive parts of inner Amsterdam have enjoyed a commercial revival centred on 'fun-shopping'; its streets draw large numbers of young people who enjoy the crowds, the loud music that accompanies modern retailing of clothing, shoes, fashion accessories, videos and compact discs, the relative cheapness of goods in 'popular' areas and the availability of fast food. The custom of 'free entrance' shopping in which stores display goods on the street and where premises usually open directly on to pavement areas encourages forms of window shopping that are probably attractive to younger people who value the social context of such activity without necessarily possessing the resources to make extensive purchases. Older people, in contrast, tended to reflect unfavourably on the way in which the shopping environment had changed, perceiving a movement down-market. They might still use such areas for specific purchases but were less likely to dwell in these popular retail locations, absorbing and enjoying the activity on the street.

A second aspect of recreational shopping noted in Amsterdam was that the social context of the shopping trip was a significant factor. Jansen concludes that, in general, visits that were made alone tended to be of the functional type, with a specific purpose and destination in mind, whereas when shopping took place in a group, there would at least be an element of recreational activity. Respondents suggested quite strongly that trips to central shopping areas were viewed as an 'outing' that would combine a range of activities including shopping, window shopping, eating and drinking, socialising and observation of activity on the street.

Thirdly, there are differences according to gender in the manner in which shopping is perceived and conducted. Jansen-Verbeke (1988) established that women go more frequently to towns for shopping, window shopping or visits to street markets and that while engaged upon the activity, expend more time and money than is characteristic of men. The recreational element in this is not easy to determine, although patterns of expenditure amongst Jansen-Verbeke's sample showed that purchases other than routine daily needs were the most important element. The author does not make the point, but it nevertheless seems likely that although men tend to spend less time on shopping than women (reflecting conventional gender roles as much as anything), when they do shop, a greater proportion of their time will be spent on leisure shopping as distinct from convenience shopping for routine domestic goods.

Fourthly, recreational shopping is a prominent activity amongst urban tourists. Bussey (1987) shows that shopping accounts for around a quarter of tourist expenditures (second only to the purchase of accommodation) and that where cities attract significant numbers of visitors, their recreational shopping will be a valued contribution to local economies. Urban developers have learned the value of tourist shops, as redevelopments in areas such as London's Covent Garden or Liverpool's Albert Dock testify.

Children's play

Children are the biggest recreational users of streets and thoroughfares and play is their primary activity. This is especially so in the residential zones of the city where the high levels of use reflect the accessibility of the street (through proximity to the home), the suitability of its hard surface for many forms of play and its convenience as a meeting ground for other children. Moore (1987) observes that even where children are faced with attractive alternative locations, a substantial amount of play will still occur on the street. Policy which seeks to limit or prohibit such activity is unrealistic and in all probability doomed to failure, for whilst some children are pushed towards streets and associated spaces because of a lack of alternative play opportunities, others are drawn by the special attraction of these areas simply because they are not duplicated elsewhere (Moore, 1987:52). (For a fuller discussion of children's play, see Chapter 6.)

Socialising

Streets, historically, were social spaces and although some of the more overtly anti-social trends that have emerged in post-1945 urban life have suppressed some of the manifestations of this role, it remains close to the surface and readily reappears when conditions are adjusted to suit gregarious forms of activity.

Such activity occurs in various guises. People-watching is a popular recreation in many public places and the activity of the street, whether observed from a stoop on an apartment block in New York, from a bench in a London park or a pavement café in Paris, Rome or Amsterdam, is a major focal point of interest. Oosterman (1992), charting the dramatic rise of sidewalk cafés in Holland, perceptively observes how the seats typically face outwards 'as chairs in a theatre are placed towards the stage' (p.161) and comments (p.162) that in street areas 'it is not the meeting of strangers that is important but the spectacle provided by them'. For people on the street, it is an opportunity to parade and to be seen by the watchers, a desire that reaches its most ostentatious in chic urban resorts, especially along the French and Italian Rivieras.

A much more routine and widespread social use of streets is the simple maintenance of contacts with friends and acquaintances. A striking feature of many British town centres is the manner in which groups of teenagers congregate in shopping malls and other public places on Saturday afternoons during the school year, to converse, perhaps to eat and drink or window shop, but primarily to socialise in a recreational manner. Elsewhere, observers have noted how suburban streets also facilitate incidental social contacts. Gehl (1980), writing of Canadian and Australian streets, and Eubank-Ahrens (1987) reporting behaviour patterns in two German *woonerfen* (see p.117), both note how routine chores conducted at the front of the house (and hence in the public gaze from the street) often took exaggerated periods to complete because the people undertaking the work were regularly and willingly called into conversation with passers-by and children at play close at hand. Both concluded that this interaction was consciously sought and the activity therefore had a mixture of recreational and non-recreational motives. The task at hand, to a degree, became an excuse for being on the street.

Road running and jogging

One further area of activity merits brief attention – road running and jogging. This, like several of the areas that have already been considered, is a clearly observable recreational use of streets and pathways, but one which has escaped systematic documentation. The following observations on the British experience are perhaps relevant.

In the 1960s, road running in Britain was a serious sport, pursued by comparatively low numbers of participants in a highly competitive context. Much of the participation was focused upon clubs where men were in an overwhelming majority and club matches were a prominent feature of the sport although sometimes, it should be noted, such matches took place as part of wider community-based festivals. By the start of the 1980s, the situation had changed. Promoted partly by growing public awareness of issues of health-related fitness, jogging had become a popular recreation and participation in road running and jogging had broadened to include women and older people, many of the latter returning to the activity as 'veterans'. The first televised London Marathon in 1981 prompted a surge in interest, and for a while 'marathon mania' spawned new events and attracted large numbers of participants. This has not been sustained and the number of full marathons run each year has tended to decline in total, with runners focusing upon a smaller number of high-profile events. However, in their place has developed a significant number of half-marathons, 10-kilometre races and 'fun-runs' which draw not just the committed athlete, but fitness enthusiasts and casual participants too, many of whom will have used streets and pathways extensively in their preparation for events. As Table 5.1 illustrates, participants are most likely to be young males, but the fact that both men and women up to the age of 60 appear to participate regularly reflects the manner in which road running and jogging has diffused through the adult population.

STREETS AND THOROUGHFARES AS RECREATIONAL RESOURCES

The ability of streets and routeways to support recreational activity is being affected fundamentally by three sets of problems. The first group are physical difficulties that stem largely from the presence of road traffic but should also include the quality of design of streets and public spaces. Secondly, certain trends in the economic organisation of cities have not assisted in maintaining public interest in streets, whilst thirdly, recreational use has been influenced by societal problems, especially those associated with crime and the fear of crime.

Road traffic is arguably the biggest single obstacle to pleasurable use of streets for recreation, creating a number of difficulties. Of these, the threat of injury and death in road accidents is the most serious. In Britain in 1991, 14,822 pedestrians and 4,145 cyclists were killed or seriously injured (Department of Transport, 1992), statistics which, if they occurred in any other arenas of activity apart from transport and warfare, would be socially and politically quite unacceptable. Between 1967 and 1987, more than 135,000 people (in all road use categories) were killed on the roads in Britain, and in some European countries the figure was even higher. West Germany, for example, suffered more than a quarter of a million road deaths over the same period (Whitelegg, 1990). Yet in Britain, North America and Western Europe there is still a prevailing culture that puts the motor car first, a preoccupation that in Britain even leads to a failure of official statistics to document walking and cycling journeys of less than a mile and which encourages a misrepresentation of the role these modes of travel actually play in urban areas (Hillman, 1990).

Alongside risks of injury, air pollution from traffic is a second problem. Spirn (1987) shows how pollutants from vehicle emissions concentrate in the vicinity of roadways, and where physical design of streets reduces air circulation (for example by juxtaposition of tall buildings) bad air becomes trapped at street level. For the motorist cocooned in the vehicle that may not be a particular source of discomfort, but for the pedestrian, the cyclist, the window shopper or the patron of the pavement café, vehicle fumes are a noxious health hazard that quickly devalues other pleasures that may be associated with being on the street.

Road vehicles are, furthermore, a source of noise and of air turbulence. For cyclists, the close passage of a large vehicle at speed creates momentary and unpredictable air turbulence which can unbalance a rider and lead to an accident. For the pedestrian, air waves are unlikely to affect balance but vehicles commonly whip up dust or create spray in wet conditions, which directly assaults people walking on adjacent pavements. None of this does anything to enhance the capacity of the street as a place of leisure; indeed the effect is quite the opposite.

Poor urban design will also limit the recreational utility of streets and public places. In city centres, much of the leisurely use of streets is in casual, observational forms of activity, so streets need to be physically comfortable and, especially, interesting places in which people will choose to recreate. Natural light at street level, for example, is an essential requirement (Bryan and Stuebling, 1987). The types of street that will encourage walking, window shopping, sightseeing or people-watching will be safe and will engage an observer – through diversity, even complexity, in form, style and layout, in textures, colours and materials embodied in the townscape (Rapoport, 1990). There must be adequate provision of public seating, lighting, street signage and, ideally, trees and vegetation too, the latter often having a significant positive influence on people's perceptions of public space (Sheets and Manzer, 1991). In residential areas, design requirements are rather different in detail but still stress safety and creating interest in street environments through good design and equipment of public space.

Frequently, of course, design characteristics of central urban areas are influenced by the economic requirements of commercial and retail businesses. Since the 1960s, however, there have emerged several trends in spatial location of such activity and the way it is organised and patronised, and these have undermined the traditional role of shopping streets. Most significant has been the move towards relocation of retailing to peripheral sites dominated by a small number of multi-purpose stores and hypermarkets or, less commonly, new regional mega-centres such as Merry Hill (Dudley) and the Metrocentre (Gateshead). The impact of such development upon conventional town centres has sometimes been catastrophic. Vidal (1994) reports that the town centre shops in Dudley have recorded a reduction of 70 per cent in retail turnover since the opening of Merry Hill and many have closed, while lesser impacts have been felt in Stourbridge and West Bromwich which lie a little further away from the shopping complex. Unless alternative forms of retailing develop, as reported by Jansen (1989) in Amsterdam, then many older retail centres may eventually lose a primary function and the recreational activity that goes with it. In March 1994, the government announced new planning guidelines aimed at restricting further the development of out-of-town service zones and re-emphasising the need to develop vacant sites in urban centres (DoE, 1994), but whether such policy reversal will be sufficiently effective to arrest a process that has now generated considerable natural momentum, and is backed by powerful commercial interests, remains to be seen.

Alongside these spatial shifts has been a more insidious change through the so-called privatisation of shopping by its relocation from outdoor streets to indoor malls. This was a conspicuous trend in retail reorganisation in Britain in the 1980s and has been widely encountered in cities in developed nations (Reynolds, 1992). Whilst at one level such development affords a more comfortable and convenient environment for shoppers to make their purchases, the management of such malls often prohibits many of the street activities that add colour to central urban areas (street theatre, buskers, pavement artists, etc.) and, come close of trading, the malls are locked and barred so that night-time window shopping and enjoyment by passers-by of illuminated window displays becomes impossible. Such change undermines the vitality of streets by taking away points of interest that might attract users or cause them to pause *en route* to another destination.

The vitality of the street and the activity it fosters is essential to the maintenance of personal safety in public places (Jacobs, 1961; Moughtin, 1991a). The problems of urban society – homelessness, poverty, drink and drug-related deviancy, crime against property and person, prostitution – manifest themselves most conspicuously on public streets. It is a simple fact, but perhaps needs emphasis nevertheless, that people enjoying recreation will not place themselves in situations in which they are likely to be confronted by such problems. It has even been shown that pedestrians in large cities walk more quickly than those in small towns (Walmsley and Lewis, 1989) although how much of this is attributable to a desire to avoid the less palatable situations which streets in major centres seem to give rise to is unclear.

What is clear is that people feel safe when they are in a crowd and when they are confident that public places are under surveillance, whether by officialdom in the form of police or by the informal surveillance of a community that is attentive to its street areas (Oc, 1991; Valentine, 1990). The deserted street which no one oversees is a dangerous street and it is widely perceived as such, especially by groups such as women and elderly people who are particularly prone to limiting their activities due to fear of crime (S.J. Smith, 1987; Valentine, 1990). As a discretionary area of behaviour, outdoor recreation will be more prone than most to the constraints of fear of the street.

RE-CREATING THE STREET

What can be done to redress the balance and ensure that the utility and potential of streets and throughfares, both as functional and as recreational places, is maximised? Urban policy must address a wide range of issues if this objective is to be realised, but for convenience they may be grouped under four broad headings.

Taming the car

The environmental impacts and the threats to personal safety that emanate from motor traffic require that in any programme to enhance the recreational value of streets, road traffic needs to be brought under a measure of control. This is a fundamental requirement and in its absence there can be no meaningful advance in the recreational roles of streets and other public spaces to which vehicles have access. Two general types of strategy are currently available through which the deleterious effects of traffic may be regulated: traffic exclusion and traffic restraint (or calming).

Traffic exclusion and the associated pedestrianisation of streets has a lengthy and honourable history, being encountered in, for example, ancient Rome, medieval Venice, Georgian London and Paris and the garden cities of the early twentieth century (Hass-Klau, 1990). Historically the incidence of traffic-free areas was, of course, spatially limited and mainly confined to areas of civic importance or social exclusivity, but nevertheless, the principle is an established one.

The widespread use of traffic exclusion in western cities is largely a product of the post-1945 era; in the 1970s countries such as Britain and West Germany applied the idea widely (Hass-Klau, 1990). However, although many urban authorities have embraced the concept of traffic exclusion, either on a total basis or with traffic excluded according to vehicle type or within designated 'core' hours, the locations affected are primarily central shopping areas. In residential areas, the use of exclusion is harder to execute simply because residents tend to object if they cannot obtain vehicular access to their properties, for themselves and for service vehicles such as those of refuse collectors or emergency services. But the experience in British new towns shows that, on a limited scale, traffic-free zones can be created in predominantly residential areas, while in areas of redevelopment or expansion in established settlements, localised traffic-free spaces have also been established.

Where such traffic-free spaces are created, the potential for development of street-based recreation is considerable. Not only do conventional street recreations such as window shopping, people-watching, play and socialisation become immediately more pleasurable, but other activities which enhance the appeal of public places become possible. Furthermore, in many town centres the removal of most of the traffic and its associated pollution has made cleaning of civic buildings and tree and flower planting programmes viable.

If traffic exclusion is limited in its spatial application, traffic restraint can be applied much more widely, especially in residential streets. The principal thrust of traffic restraint/calming is to reduce the impact of road vehicles by a combination of reduction in their number and limitations on the speed at which they are permitted to move. As Tolley (1989:19) notes, the intention in traffic-calmed areas is not that cars be banned but that they be 'admitted on the residents' terms – that is slowly and without superior rights' and traffic calming is intended 'to achieve calm, safe and environmentally improved conditions on streets' (Russell, 1990: iii).

Traffic calming policy achieves its desired effect primarily through road engineering, supported by certain legal limitations on use of calmed areas by through traffic and on maximum permitted speeds. The observable tendency for motorists to disregard speed limits, however, places the emphasis in calming policies on physical restructuring of the road to enforce such speed reductions – by realignments of carriageways, insertion of pinch-points and speed ramps (sleeping policemen), deployment of elevated surfaces, cobbling or rumble strips and placement of bollards or other obstructions to slow the traffic.

The benefit of traffic calming for street users – the pedestrian, the cyclist, the child at play or people chatting on their doorsteps – is that the road vehicle which is restrained generally emits less pollution, makes less noise and, in the unfortunate circumstance of an accident involving a pedestrian or cyclist, is much less likely to inflict serious injury or death. Research in Switzerland reported by Tolley (1990) suggests that in collisions at less than 25 kilometres per hour, only 3 per cent of pedestrians sustain serious injury while in impacts at over 50 kilometres per hour, fewer than 10 per cent survive. These advantages make the calmed street significantly more amenable to use in play, in walking and cycling and in socialising.

The outstanding example of the calmed street is probably the Dutch *woonerf*. This novel concept, first discussed in the Netherlands in the early 1960s and widely applied in that country and West Germany during the 1970s (Hass-Klau, 1990), affords an unusual combination of outdoor living space and vehicle access. Seats, planters, parking space, even children's play space may be sited within the centre of the street itself, while the carriageway navigates between the obstacles and over the speed ramps and raised sections. Studies confirm the positive benefits of the idea. Eubank-Ahrens (1987) in a survey of two quite unprepossessing *woonerfen* in Hannover, West Germany, found significant increases in social interaction between residents, people spending longer periods of time in the street and children, especially, spending much longer at outdoor play in which new street 'furniture' often formed 'play props'. Spatial patterns changed too, with activities spread conspicuously over the full extent of the *woonerf* (Figure 5.3).

The task of calming streets is, however, not to be underestimated. As Russell (1990) comments, the ubiquitous nature of pedestrians, cyclists and children at play permits most streets to make a *prima facie* case for calming. In Britain, the resources to support widespread retrospective treatment of residential streets simply do not exist and in the Netherlands too, since the early 1980s, the expense of creating *woonerfen* has seen a simplified form of the idea (at lower cost) replacing the more elaborate versions of the 1970s. But much more could be done through the planning process to ensure that new housing development espoused these laudable design principles from inception instead of expensive retrospection. There

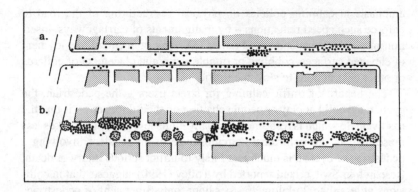

Figure 5.3 Change in the incidence of use of a street area (a) prior to
and (b) after traffic calming, Hannover, Germany
Source: Eubank-Ahrens, 1987

is, though, little sign that this is being done and Britain lags many years behind its European neighbours in its support for these improvements (for a full discussion of traffic exclusion and calming policy, together with further examples, see Tolley, 1989, 1990; Hass-Klau, 1990; Kroon, 1990; Monheim, 1990; Ullrich, 1990; McClintock, 1992).

New provision for walking and cycling

Traffic exclusion and calming policies essentially create space, some of which may be used for recreational activity, but policy needs also to recognise the significance of recreational walking and cycling and provide appropriate routes to support these activities. The requirements for good walking and cycling in towns are not obscure. Table 5.2 sets out recommendations advocated by Hudson (1982) specifically for cycling; Ramsay (1990) has articulated a similar set of requirements for walking (Table 5.3). Actual provision of routes may pursue a number of contrasting though complementary approaches.

For personal safety and physical comfort, it is preferable that paths and cycleways be physically separated from roads or at least segregated from other road users. This is an important requirement when recreational motives are prominent, since the enjoyment that people will normally wish to be associated with their walk or ride is all too easily destroyed by close proximity to traffic. What is required is dedicated, discrete space for these uses.

Table 5.2 Requirements for effective provision of urban cycle routes

— Routes should be as direct as possible.
— Routes should avoid heavily trafficked areas.
— Routes should have convenient access points and be signed, including destinations.
— Routes should not end at hazardous locations.
— Routes should have a smooth surface and be regularly maintained.
— Routes should be well lit and have clear lines of sight.
— Routes should be as continuous as possible, taking in attractive zones (e.g. parks and open spaces) wherever possible and avoiding areas of climatic extreme (e.g. exposed sites with strong winds).

Source: Hudson (1982)

Table 5.3 Requirements for effective provision of pedestrian routes

— Availability: the routes must be accessible by right to all users.
— Negotiability: the routes and their surfaces should not present significant barriers to normal user groups.
— Safety: the routes must be reasonably free of danger from traffic or threats to personal security.
— Economy: users should not be subject to congestion or undue delay when using the routes.
— Convenience: detours to the route should be avoided wherever possible.
— Comfort: users should not have to suffer adverse conditions, whether climatic or social.
— Amenity: routes should be planned to provide as pleasant an environmental experience as possible.

Source: Ramsay (1990)

In urban Britain there have been relatively few attempts at developing discrete pedestrian or cycleways, primarily because of resource constraints, official attitudes and the limitations posed by existing patterns of urban development. Several of the new towns, including Stevenage, Telford and Milton Keynes, have taken advantage of their development on 'green-field' sites and planned separate road and pathway systems as an integral design feature. In Telford, reclaimed land, existing woodland and disused mineral rail lines are being forged to create a 'green network' of spaces and paths for walkers, cyclists, horse-riders and so on (Figure 5.4), most of which is quite separate from the road system and forms a key

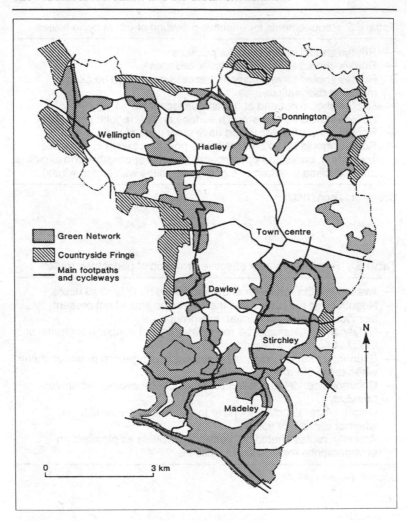

Figure 5.4 The Green Network and associated facilities, Telford
Source: District of the Wrekin, 1990

element in the town's recreational amenity (District of the Wrekin, 1991). This approach is not, however, typical of older settlements, although there is considerable scope for development of path networks by the selective use of reclaimed sites such as disused railway lines and canal towpaths, together with parkland, open space and existing footpaths. Such opportunities are becoming more widely recognised. For example, in Bristol, Cheltenham, Macclesfield and Edinburgh, disused railway lines have been converted to pedestrian or bicycle use (McClintock, 1987), while in Birmingham restorative work on some of the extensive network of urban canals has created new paths that penetrate right to the heart of the city.

These cases are perhaps exceptional and a more common solution is the designation of cycleways as part of main carriageways or the development of cycleways and footpaths paralleling roads. The technical challenges of integrating walkers and cyclists with road traffic are substantial, though not insoluble (see Hudson, 1982; Untermann, 1984) and although the continuing proximity of walkers and cyclists to motor traffic is a far from ideal arrangement, such initiatives are welcome if only as a move towards a more balanced urban transport strategy.

An example of this approach, with a specific focus on provision for cycling, is afforded by the city of Nottingham. In the 1980s the Department of Transport sponsored several schemes to develop urban cycle networks and the experience in Nottingham has been fully documented (McClintock, 1987, 1990; McClintock and Cleary, 1993). The Nottingham cycle network had to confront the common practical problem of adding cycleways in an area that was already heavily developed, and this is perhaps reflected in the variable impact of the experiment so far. McClintock's analyses showed some evidence of an increase in cycle usage in areas served by the network and a reduction in the levels of accidents. But the scheme is clearly limited by a number of factors: by its low total route length at just 37 kilometres and its restricted spatial coverage, by the fact that much of the network runs alongside existing roads without the screening from traffic or soft landscaping that would enhance the physical attraction, and by the fact that with a clear focus on routes linking suburbs to the centre, recreational cycling, involving rides around neighbourhoods or to the urban fringe, is not facilitated.

A more impressive example which combines provision for walking alongside carriageways with routes that depart from trafficked roads is currently being developed by the City of York. Figure 5.5 provides an illustration of this scheme, which is attempting to set out a network of footpaths (with some provision for cyclists too) based upon a system of designated routes defined according to type. The positive aspects of this scheme are that it is spatially comprehensive, that it recognises and provides for the different motives for pedestrian journeys (including recreation) and that in developing the network, the planners are incorporating footpaths along roadways with paths that cross open space, follow existing short-cuts or passages and, where they occur, previously desig-

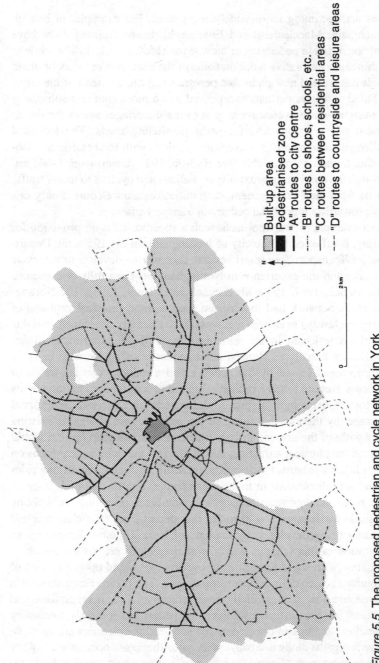

Legend:

- Built-up area
- Pedestrianised zone
- "A" routes to city centre
- "B" routes to shops, schools, etc.
- "C" routes between residential areas
- "D" routes to countryside and leisure areas

0   2 km

N

Figure 5.5 The proposed pedestrian and cycle network in York
Source: York City Council, 1993

nated heritage trails and leisure walks. A technical standard has been adopted to ensure minimum specifications in width of paths, proper surfacing, engineering and lighting, together with provision of signposting, seating and litter bins along the routes.

The footpath network in York perhaps indicates that British planners are at last beginning to learn from the more extensive experience of some European countries that have been quicker to respond to the challenges of urban walking and cycling. There are clear parallels between the approach now being deployed in York and the development of the cycle network in the Dutch city of Delft. Here, by integrating cycle lanes into existing streets and supplementing these with new cycle paths, including several new bridges and tunnels, planners created a hierarchical network of routes (Figure 5.6). Major corridors were designed to connect districts to primary service areas, central shops, places of work and major recreational facilities, while local routes performed secondary and tertiary functions, such as linking neighbourhoods to local schools and shops. Evaluative studies of the Delft experiment (Hartman, 1990) showed higher levels of bicycle usage with associated reductions in car mileages and some evidence of a reduction in cycle accidents too, demonstrating clearly the potential benefits from transport strategies of this type.

Rethinking urban design

The alacrity with which people will use traffic-free spaces and routes for recreational walking, cycling and other leisurely activity will depend to a considerable extent on the quality of urban design. Critics of British planning have argued that design considerations are too often relegated below primary concerns for regulation of land use, and that the naturally fragmented manner in which development control is applied (taking each case on merit and often in isolation) makes it harder to evolve coherent design characteristics over wider areas of urban land (Hall, 1990). Punter (1990:13) attacks what he terms 'mindless plagiarism' in which urban designs are replicated from place to place, producing a predictability and uniformity that disregard the local context and do little to engender safety, comfort, diversity and richness in our streets or create quality in the public realm.

Precisely how these attributes may be incorporated into urban development is a moot point. One of the most interesting and original thinkers in this field is Rapoport. In a detailed and extensive cross-cultural study of street form and visual quality, Rapoport (1990) derives a detailed list of attributes that, he argues, will be encountered in streets that are truly

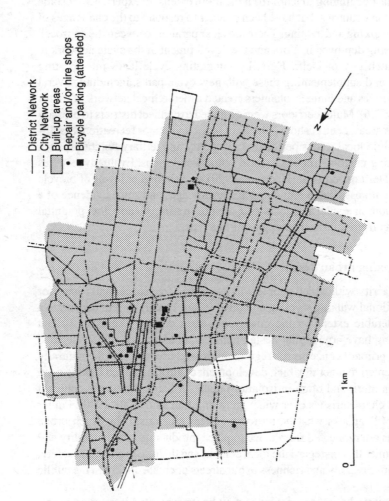

Figure 5.6 The bicycle network in Delft, The Netherlands
Source: Data provided by Delft City Council

Legend:

— District Network
—·— City Network
▨ Built-up areas
• Repair and/or hire shops
■ Bicycle parking (attended)

N

1 km

0

supportive of pedestrian activity. These are summarised in a condensed form in Figure 5.7. In part they reflect the prevailing thesis of Rapoport's study, which is that historic precedent has much to contribute to contemporary design principles and it will be apparent how far many modern developments (for example post-1945 shopping precincts) depart from the guidance Rapoport's analysis provides. But it is also striking how some

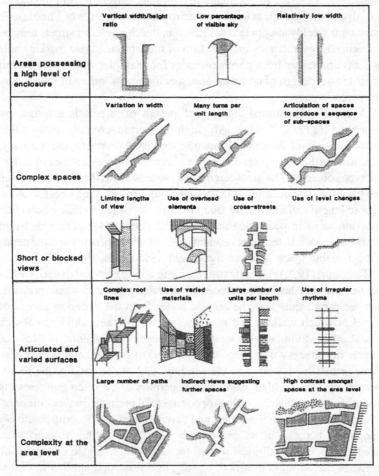

Figure 5.7 Attributes of streets designed to be supportive of pedestrian activity
Source: Adapted from Rapoport, 1990

of the most successful street areas, particularly in historic places, combine at least some of the elements he advocates.

Rapoport is at pains to stress that these design ideas, with their focus upon intimacy, structural diversity and variation in visual form, should not be prescriptive but should provide principles for better design of public space, as opposed to models to be copied. He also acknowledges that the utility of streets varies according to the societal values that are placed on these areas and the situational contexts of their use, the explorative walking of a tourist, for example, being rather different from the casual socialisation of groups at leisure or the routine movements of a housewife busy with weekly shopping. Furthermore, the character of streets may be influenced by temporary implantation of movable features: market stalls or seats and tables from pavement cafés for example, which may permit short-term redesign of space to meet specific needs, many of which may be recreational.

A more conventional analysis of design of streets is afforded by Moughtin (1991a, 1991b). Although Moughtin concurs with some, though not all, of Rapoport's thoughts on visual diversity and intimacy, he draws further important distinctions between design qualities of different types of street. The great ceremonial routes such as the Mall in London are ideal for state occasions but are poor routes for walking because of the visible length and uniformity along their route, whilst 'public streets that function as main pedestrian and vehicular networks require a different design approach to the quiet residential street where privacy and the needs for defensible space are more significant' (Moughtin, 1991a:58).

Rapoport (1990) elaborates this theme in noting that design needs differ between streets that are dominated by vehicles and those where pedestrians are prominent. This, he argues, arises from the different speeds of travel at which walkers and motorists move and their ability to absorb visual information. The slow rate of progress of the walker dictates that interesting streets will possess a higher level of intrinsic complexity than those primarily viewed from the windows of a motor car. For the pedestrian or cyclist, the tiled walls of an underpass or the often uninteresting street windows of banks, offices or commercial premises are monotonous, while for the motorist a complex and diverse street can become positively dangerous because of its capacity to distract. If further support were needed, this is an additional reason for favouring a degree of separation between the different modes of travel, since it is apparent that in design terms, streets that suit the motorist will not engage the pedestrian.

Sustaining living streets

Design considerations link, quite naturally, into the final policy area that urban authorities which are trying to enhance the recreational value of their streets and public areas must consider. Sustaining living streets is concerned with a medley of actions and provisions that make streets effective as areas in which people will wish to recreate, as well as pursue the routine functions of these areas. The reciprocal benefits of policy that addresses recreational provision and concerns for the wider quality of urban life should not be overlooked or underestimated. Five basic strategies are here advocated and together these form a convenient summary for much of the argument that has been advanced in this chapter.

First, make streets and public thoroughfares comfortable. People will enjoy the experience of the street more if natural light penetrates to street level and they are afforded opportunities to sit or walk in sunlight or, conversely, gain a measure of protection from the elements, whether it be shade from hot sun or cover from wind and rain. Comfort will also be a function of the availability of food and drink, toilets and rest areas and places to sit that are neither obstructed nor obstructing.

Secondly, make streets congenial and attractive. Good civic design can do much to make public spaces attractive; street cleanliness, particularly freedom from litter and dog-fouling, is important too. If a street or public square is attractive and well maintained, people will be more readily encouraged into such spaces and their presence, provided it is not malevolent or anti-social, makes the street congenial.

Thirdly, make streets safe. This means that traffic should be removed or calmed, that public places should be adequately lit and subject to appropriate surveillance. Taken in isolation, some of the design principles advanced by Rapoport outwardly offer the types of confined and unobserved spaces that some critics argue are a source of perceived danger and fear of crime (Valentine, 1990). Those concerns can be countered, to a degree at least, by arguing that if street design is such that it entices people to use these spaces, the presence of other users is a better deterrent to street crime than are design adaptations.

Fourthly, make streets green. Outdoor recreation benefits from the interplay of activity and environment and, in general, a green environment is more amenable than one in which greening is absent. Tree planting, creation of open grassed spaces or water features and floral displays can all enhance the ambiance of public streets and squares; in residential areas, private front gardens too make a vital contribution to the character and quality of the public street and support activities such as walking. Indeed, greening philosophy may also extend to positive planning for the so-called green modes of travel – walking and cycling.

Finally, make streets interesting. Although interest is a personalised response, we know enough of the psychology of the street to realise that interest is fostered by the presence of other people and of activity, as well as the attributes of physical design that were outlined above. To this end, there is a case for resisting tendencies towards decentralisation of functions such as shopping to peripheral sites and for supporting the planned maintenance of traditional shopping and service centres. There is a case for relaxation or greater flexibility in the application of by-laws and regulations which, in Britain at least, limit the extent to which private activity can spill over into public streets – in pavement cafés, in street vending or in entertainment. If we pedestrianise our city centres but then don't permit those spaces to be used in new ways, much of the opportunity of the exercise is lost. So there is a case, too, for fostering activity through planned events: festivals, street carnivals, town centre fun-runs or cycle races, exhibitions, displays and entertainments, all of which can contribute significantly to a revival in the role of public streets as recreational spaces.

Chapter 6

Swings and roundabouts – patterns of use and provision of children's play space

'Children,' writes Ward (1978:86) 'will play everywhere and with anything', yet all too often provision for their needs operates on one plane, whilst children operate on another. Herein lies the essential dilemma that confronts the providers of play opportunity. Play is complex – a complexity derived from the different ways in which children play and utilise resources as they develop, the variable benefits that are derived from such activity and, fundamentally, the internal diversity of the group which, perhaps too readily, we label simply as 'children'. This chapter explores these themes by looking first at the significance of play, secondly at patterns of play amongst children in the urban environment, and finally at the role of providers in meeting the challenges raised by the need to accommodate play.

THE SIGNIFICANCE OF PLAY

Virtually all forms of recreation have a significance that goes beyond the activity itself and forms part of a wider experience from which a range of potential benefits to the participant may be derived. This is especially so in the case of children's play since it is not just an activity through which entertainment and pleasures may be gained but also, and much more significantly, a medium for the development of a child as an individual and a means of assimilation into an adult world. The particular significance of play therefore demands some further elaboration, not least since any critique of policy requires that the full importance of play be understood. The word 'play' can very easily become a pejorative, it can imply (quite wrongly) that there is no serious intent on the part of participants and if activity is not perceived to have a significance, there is a risk that policy will accord it none.

The universal incidence of play amongst children has attracted attention from the very earliest times in which people began to observe the societies within which they lived (see Heseltine and Holborn, 1987). The literature concerned with the developmental role of play in the lives of children is voluminous in extent and often specialised in content. As Child (1985) illustrates, play has been conceptualised in terms of physiological, biological, psychological and socio-cultural approaches, but these contrasting, although often complementary, perspectives generally concur about the significance of play in the formation of the individual. Barnett (1990), in a valuable summary of theoretical perspectives, shows how play experience has been seen as central to cognitive, social and emotional development in children, while Moore (1986:12) puts the case quite simply in stating that 'playing is learning' and that 'the child's playful interaction with the environment and his or her absorption of worldly experience produces a feeling of competence, a sense of mastery and control over the environment'. It follows, too, that if opportunities to play are restricted (by whatever means), then the child's competence (or at least those competencies derived through play) may be eroded, which may lead to a sense of inferiority, inadequacy, low self-esteem and lack of motivation.

The German educator Scherler (quoted in Moore, 1986) has suggested six broad areas in which children develop personal competence through engagement in play and these cast a more detailed light on the general benefits that may be gained. Play may be conceived as possessing:

1   an *adaptive function* in which physiological skills and abilities are fostered, the development of strength, stamina, speed and agility being especially pronounced. Structured activities, such as sport, provide an obvious medium through which such functions are advanced, but direct observation of forms of unstructured play (which occupy a great deal of children's play time) shows that balancing, running, jumping, skipping and throwing are often integral to activity.

2   an *expressive function* in which children learn to experience and cope with basic emotions: excitement, fear, tension, curiosity, pleasure and annoyance, for example. Play is not necessarily an exercise in harmony; there is potential for rivalry, conflict and anxiety and a number of developmental psychologists have signalled the significance of play as a medium through which children learn to manage stress-related events (see Barnett, 1990).

3   an *explorative function*. Play at all ages has an explorative dimension to it, and a child's awareness of different physical, environmental and social conditions is commonly enhanced by exposure to variations in these through play. Exploration is also linked to the development of

imaginative faculties, perhaps as an aid to interpretation of that which is discovered but not necessarily understood, or as a constructed context or scenario within which a game is placed. Sebba (1991) suggests that independent exploration is especially important and shows how environments recalled by adults when asked to reflect upon their childhood tended to have a greater significance when they were experienced personally and without adult mediation.

4   a *productive function*. Children learn how to make and alter things as part of routine play. This may occur within the confines of an organised activity in which there is a planned focus upon (literally) constructive use of time, but will also be a prominent feature of unstructured play generated by the child. Productive play of this character may advance the development of manipulative skills or the ability to co-operate with others. Collection of objects, including flora and fauna, a widespread element in play patterns of most children, may similarly be construed as a facet of the productive function of play.

5   a *communicative function*. Children acquire, through play, experience in how to relate to others; to co-operate, to accept rules and to maintain networks of social contacts. They learn with whom they may associate and those who are best avoided; they learn who to trust, who to fear, those with whom they empathise and those with whom there is little opportunity for shared experience.

6   a *comparative function*. Play affords one of the media through which children learn to compare themselves with others. Where playground pecking orders are defined by strength, size and ability, a child will quickly learn his or her place within that order and the concept of winning and losing is central to a large number of children's games.

For many children, the outdoor environment is especially important as a location for play, and research shows a marked preference amongst most children for outdoor play, wherever possible. Parkinson (1987) argues that the outdoors offers a counterbalance to the parent-dominated indoors and affords a domain which is explorable, provides engagement with living systems and the prevailing culture. It is a continuing source of novelty, there is space, the potential of more children with whom to interact and a variety of terrains. The outdoors is a dynamic environment, in a word, 'interesting'. Sebba (1991) shows too how it is memorable, in so far as adults tend strongly to identify the most significant places in their child-hood as being out of doors.

The outdoor environment is, additionally, more amenable to manipulation by the child as a part of their play. Children reconstruct environments in both a physical and, less obviously though no less importantly, a perceptual sense. Objects or places in the environment take on a different meaning for a child compared to those espoused by an adult, partly because of the different scale at which they are viewed, but partly because they derive a significance through use in play. For example, adults typically view urban trees and vegetation as part of landscaping and visual amenity but as having little direct utility. The child at play, however, may view a tree as a resource – something that is to be climbed, or employed as a surrogate set of cricket stumps, or as a reference point, while vegetation is a means of cover in games of hide and seek, or a refuge from which to watch the activities of others, or a hunting ground in which to find insects or small animals. Sometimes the most nondescript of objects in the adult world – a tree, a street corner, a wall, a lamppost, a patch of wasteland – become empowered with a significance as landmarks in the child's environment – as meeting places or even as quite contrary places of solitude – the special place to which the child retreats in order to be alone and which they may recall with fondness throughout their adult lives. Sebba (1991) argues that children experience the environment in a deep and direct manner, not as a background for events but as a factor and stimulator, and Hart (1979) signals the significance of the physical environment to the child by noting the relative ease with which the child may alter it, compared with their limited capacity to influence the social environment. This is reflected in the child's endowment of their playscape with toponyms that only they, their friends and perhaps their parents, might recognise. Personalisation of space in this manner is a further indication of the singular way in which children view their environment and its importance to them.

THE PATTERNS OF PLAY

Children are particularly prone to constraints upon their recreational patterns. In general, they have more time at their disposal than, say, their parents, although they will spend more time asleep, may have some responsibility for lesser domestic chores and errands, and could have their time taken up by the requirement that they accompany parents on routine tasks, for example shopping, because they cannot be left unsupervised. But the net effect is not normally such that constraint on time becomes significant in regulating levels of activity, although if time blocks are fragmented, it may influence where activity takes place. There may be a seasonal effect upon play, the colder, wetter weather and shorter days of winter causing some measure of withdrawal from outdoor play, but it is often only a partial withdrawal and children's play is probably the form of outdoor activity that is influenced least by seasonal contrasts.

Of more importance, perhaps, are limitations on the child's personal mobility and the fact that most children have very modest financial resources, expenditure of which may be subject to parental approval. Here, ultimately, is the biggest single constraint upon the pattern of play of a child – the limitation imposed by parents (or supervising adults) which will usually influence when and where children may play and, in certain circumstances, will also regulate what they do and with whom they associate. Children are unique in the way in which they normally have to seek permission as part of their decision to engage in recreation.

Parental protection of offspring is, of course, a quite normal part of life, and is intended to shield the inexperienced child from potential hazard. In the urban environment, several such hazards are widely encountered, road traffic being the most significant. Crude accident statistics from the Department of Transport (1992), the reliability of which must be accorded some caution, show that as pedestrians, children up to the age of 14 are twice as likely to be killed or seriously injured as people over 14 (children: 494 per million; teenagers/adults: 252 per million) and whilst at an aggregate level accident rates for cyclists are lower (children: 124 per million killed or seriously injured whilst cycling; adults: 74 per million), the figure is likely to be higher were it to be expressed as a proportion of those who actually cycle, as opposed to the population in total. Accidents while at play must be a significant part of those incidents. 'Dangerous places', such as areas of water, building sites and disused premises, rubbish dumps and railway lines, occur more selectively and are a lesser hazard in reality, although they may not be perceived as such by parents. Deaths from drowning by children aged five to fourteen, for example, are half the average rate for the population as a whole, while children aged between one and fourteen are actually the least likely to suffer death from falling (OPCS, 1993). The data do show that boys are at a significantly greater risk than girls from such hazards although, overall, that risk is still slight.

However, in many homes, parents are increasingly concerned about the harm which might befall children at the hands of other people. The fear of crime is a factor upon which we have already touched but it should be reiterated in the discussion of children in the urban environment. Although it has not been charted in detail, it is very apparent that over the course of the post-1945 period, behaviour patterns of parents with children have altered significantly in response to growing fears over the safety of their children in towns and cities. Whilst statistics reveal that serious assaults (including murder) and abductions involving children are extremely rare (and children are actually under a greater risk of coming to harm in the home, from other children and from people they actually know as opposed to strangers) the inevitable high publicity which the small number of criminal cases involving children attracts, serves to reinforce latent parental anxieties. These worries, in turn, translate into restrictions upon the play patterns of their children or in high levels of direct parental supervision which, in itself, becomes a limitation on the child, since the parent has to be available to take the child to the swings or the swimming pool and when he or she is not, the child may not play. Fears of potential misfortune tend to diminish as the child matures, although parental concerns may then shift to other perceived risks, for example drug-taking, substance abuse and under-age sexual relations, which may perpetuate parental attempts to ensure that their children come to no harm and which influence patterns of recreation as a consequence.

It does appear that children growing up in the 1990s have a different experience of play and outdoor recreations to that of their parents and although those parents will often reminisce fondly on the way in which they roamed freely as children, many feel unable to accord the same freedoms to their own offspring (Moore, 1986). A study of changing patterns of children's play in New York City over a 60-year period (Gaster, 1991) concluded that the age at which children were allowed unsupervised into the neighbourhood had risen, whilst the number and quality of the settings they visited had been reduced. Furthermore, obstacles and barriers to activity (including social obstacles in the form of areas dominated by street gangs) had become more widespread and this was reflected in a wider incidence of supervised and programmed play. The general conclusion was that the neighbourhood's capacity to support children's outdoor activity had declined substantially.

The observed effect of parental restrictions and the other constraints, particularly mobility, is to produce an interesting territoriality to children's play. The territory, or the range over which the child operates, will be determined by several factors, including the outcome of negotiation with parents as to where and how far the child may go, what physical barriers to their exploration may be encountered (especially major transport routes that cannot be crossed, or river or canal courses) and the child's mental map of their territory (the places they know and habitually prefer to occupy). Moore (1986) suggests that this produces a pattern in which three types of space may be recognised (Figure 6.1 presents a visual adaptation of the idea). First, the contiguous space immediately around the home forms an *habitual range*, the accessibility to which ensures

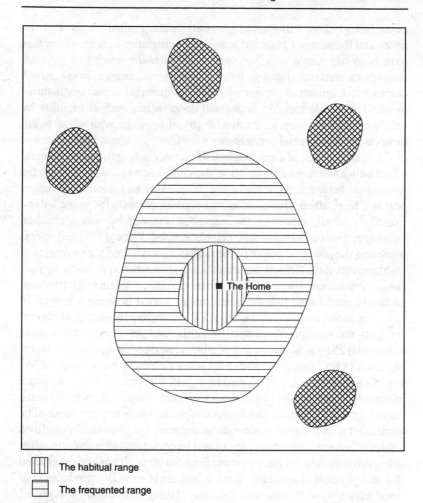

▤	The habitual range
▤	The frequented range
▨	The occasional range

Figure 6.1 The play ranges of children
Source: Adapted from Moore, 1986

regular daily use, especially when time is a constraint. Thus the street or
the garden becomes a play space for fragmented or short time-periods, for
example between the time that children return from school and the evening
meal, or between that meal and bedtime. Secondly, the habitual range will
be extended to produce a wider *frequented range* which defines the area
within which the child normally plays when not constrained by time or

other factors. This will typically be outside the immediate sight of the home and the parental gaze, but within the boundaries to the territory that have been negotiated with the parents or which are defined by physical barriers or hazards. Thirdly, there exists an *occasional range* which embraces a fragmented and spatially discontinuous set of play destinations to which access is variable, dependent upon factors such as mobility by public transport or bicycle, the availability of someone with whom to go, or upon special parental permission.

The physical size of these ranges will vary according to age, the general effect being an increase in extent as the child becomes older, though the distinction between, particularly, the frequented and occasional ranges will still be retained. However, in many urban contexts the range will be extremely small, reflecting the imprecise manner by which children develop spatial cognition of their neighbourhood (Piche, 1981) and re-emphasising the powerful nature of the factors which bound the territories of children and the localised nature of their interactions. A study of play ranges in inner city Birmingham, for example (Richardson and Parkinson, undated), established that the mean ranges varied between a low of 58 yards for nine-year-olds, to a high of 280 yards for children aged eleven; for girls the average figure was 81 yards, and for boys a rather more substantial 251 yards. Ownership of a bicycle extended the normal ranges, particularly for boys. Boys with a bicycle exhibited a mean range of 345 yards, compared with just 90 yards for girls who owned a bicycle, and a miserable 77 yards for boys without a bicycle. These values represented ranges agreed by parents and do not reflect the likely higher values to be associated with journeys made without consent, but even so, the confined nature of areas within which play would be concentrated is striking, often being no more than the spaces visible from the home. It has been suggested that the physical character of inner urban areas naturally produces confined play ranges (Coffin and Williams, 1989), but an earlier study by Holme and Massie (1970) of the wider urban context, although identifying a slightly more generous mean range of around 200 metres for an unaccompanied child, was still describing clearly limited horizons for children at play.

These data have clear implications for planners and policymakers since they reinforce the fact that play is normally a neighbourhood-based activity and thus the character of the neighbourhood, its style of housing and associated development, will be crucial in determining the richness (or otherwise) of the local play opportunities. Moore's (1986) study of children in the Holland Park area of London found compact and well-defined play territories, bounded by major roads and focused upon a small number of parks and playgrounds, reinforced by unofficial spaces which were illegally colonised by children in search of play areas. In contrast, the children Moore studied in Tunstall (Stoke-on-Trent) enjoyed more extensive and diverse opportunities as a direct product of the much looser physical structure of this declining industrial region, with its networks of official and unofficial paths, its derelict and reclaimed land, and its formal and informal parks and playgrounds. Kerten (1988) examined evidence of links between the character of urban development and patterns of play, concluding that incidence of home-based play (especially in gardens) is prominent in areas of good housing, whilst streets and associated 'greens' – grass verges and so on – become significant in areas of council flats and poorer housing where provision for play is often extremely limited (CPAC, 1988). In zones of old terraced housing where there are few gardens and greens and the street is less than alluring, Kerten suggests, playgrounds become significant, almost by default.

Part of the problem in making provision for children's play is that children do not constitute a homogeneous group. In fact, quite the contrary: for a demographic group which covers such a comparatively short age span (perhaps 5–14 years) children are remarkably diverse in character and interests, and that diversity translates immediately into patterns of play. Coffin and Williams (1989) summarise the evolutionary development of play with age by suggesting a fivefold division:

(a) Toddlers (aged 1–3), who tend to play alongside rather than with other children and whose activity focuses upon experimentation with new-found abilities and role play.
(b) Pre-school children, who show higher levels of inquisitiveness, practise new physical skills, enjoy constructional play and materials such as sand and water and begin to acquire skills in social play. Fantasy and role play, which is continued from the earlier age group, may be supplemented by mimicry.
(c) Primary school children (aged 5–10) commonly develop interests in the environment (animals and plants in particular) and explore their environments more widely. They continue to enjoy constructional play and materials, play involving movement (running, jumping, climbing, etc.), ball play and wheeled objects. This age group is also highly sociable.
(d) Older children (aged 10–13) are more competitive, show wider incidence of sexes playing apart and roam further from home. Playing games and organised activities is important for this group and more

time may be spent in conversational and social activity. Constructional and movement play continues to be important.

(e) Adolescents (aged 14–16) display more focused patterns of activity, including interests in hobbies, music and dance; greater independence, which may be reflected in informal street-based groups, and some return to mixed group activity. It is debatable whether this group actually recognise their actions as 'play'.

This provides a useful outline of development trends, but to establish where children actually play and the types of resource that attract their interest, we need to consider some empirical evidence.

Parkinson (1987) reports on the findings of a pilot study of some 1,680 children aged between 5 and 14 years and their spatial and temporal patterns of play. In terms of locations for play, the study highlighted the significance of streets, conventional playgrounds and gardens as primary locations with, of secondary significance, friends' houses, organised play schemes and wild areas (which included non-urban space). The study also touched upon places about which children were not specific but, rather frustratingly, chose not to pursue what is probably a revealing line of enquiry. Streets are particularly important play areas which afford several advantages: proximity to home and its attendant convenience and security; ease and freedom of access; opportunity for spontaneous and temporary grouping; interest and variation in street activity; and the suitability of the paved or tarmac surface for several popular types of play or games (Play Board, 1985).

The significance of the different locations varied both with age and gender. Figure 6.2 depicts the pattern according to age and reveals several trends. First, the need (perceived or real) to supervise the youngest age category in the study (those aged between five and six years) is reflected in high levels of usage of domestic gardens, the homes of friends and playgrounds (to which, presumably, most small children were accompanied). Outings with parents were also widely reported by this group but young children were comparatively modest users of street areas, special play schemes and wild areas.

In contrast, the emerging independence of older children is illustrated in the fact that for, say, the 13- and 14-year old, the street becomes the primary play venue with, in comparison to the younger groups, limited interest in the rather more controlled environments of the garden and playground. Older children were also the most numerous on organised play schemes and special activities, were prominent as users of wild places and, although not shown in the figure, were also the more likely to make

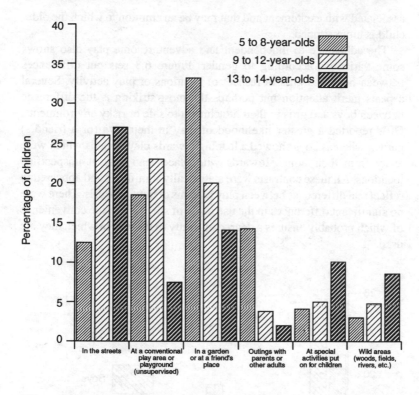

Figure 6.2 Locations of children's play according to age
Source: Parkinson, 1987

reference to unspecified play locations. Playgrounds were most popular with the 9–12-year-old group, which perhaps reflects a form of transitional status in these middle-age children. They are old enough to be allowed out of sight of the home but not sufficiently independent to roam further, or at least, admit to it! Part of the explanation for the manner in which play-site selection changes may be attached to the role of risk. The Play Board (1985) suggest that the seeking of adventure and risky situations becomes prominent as children develop play skills. This has been variously interpreted as an intrinsic response to the need to keep the central nervous system primed and to avoid boredom, and as a means to demonstrate bravery and skills to impress and gain the respect of peer groups. More simply, perhaps, we should recognise that risk-taking in play is associated with excitement and that may be an emotion to which the older child is more attuned.

The adherence to independent and adventuresome play also shows some variations according to gender. Figure 6.3 sets out differences between boys and girls in respect of locations of play activity. Several aspects merit attention but perhaps the most striking is the difference between boys and girls in their attachment to safe or risky environments. Girls reported a greater likelihood of play in their own (or a friend's) garden whereas boys showed a leaning towards playgrounds which were away from their home, towards wild places and play at unspecified locations. All these contrasts were statistically significant and appeared to reflect real differences between play patterns of boys and girls. There were no significant differences in the use made of street areas, the convenience of which probably ensures a degree of equity in the way in which they are used.

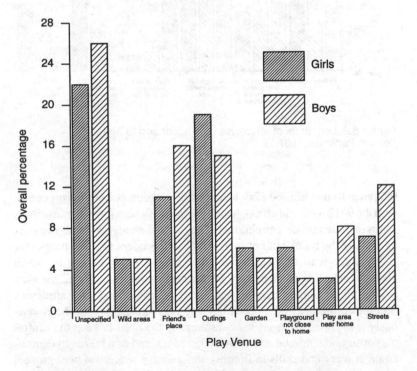

Figure 6.3 Locations of children's play according to gender
Source: Parkinson, 1987

When age is reintroduced as a variable, further aspects of these patterns are highlighted (Figure 6.4). Play in the street establishes a 'plateau' of popularity by around the age of 8. For boys, this is maintained until about the age of 12, at which point the venue becomes more popular with girls. This latter trend is not articulated in the report, nor is it really explained, but is probably a case of male substitution of street areas with another type of environment which holds greater appeal, the likely places according to the data being wild and/or unspecified locations.

Play in conventional playgrounds becomes popular by the age of 10 years and appears to hold its attraction, for boys in particular. This should not, however, necessarily be assumed to indicate interest in, or attachment to, playground facilities *per se*. Observation of these areas suggests that for many older children they act as a convenient meeting point at which children may assemble, either by appointment or simply in an opportune fashion, and that once a group has assembled, it moves off to another, preferred location. As suggested above, for boys in particular, those locations are likely to be the wilder or unspecified parts of the local environment which emerge strongly as areas for play amongst boys of 11 and above. The play area which declines most consistently and sharply with increase in the age of the child is the domestic garden, and the data suggest that boys lose interest in the garden especially quickly.

Explanation for the divergent patterns of play amongst boys and girls probably requires that some emphasis be placed upon processes of social conditioning. The influence of parental controls on patterns of play has already been aired: perception of urban environments as potentially hazardous is undoubtedly a factor that encourages many parents to restrict the activities of their children, girls in particular. The problem is that such processes may readily become self-reinforcing and assist in establishing and maintaining societal norms of behaviour which perpetuate an unnecessarily protective approach to girls, encouraging or even constraining them into preferred and relatively secure patterns of activity while allowing boys a more extensive range of environments and pursuits with which to engage. This pattern is indicated in Figure 6.5, which shows consistently higher levels of unsupervised play amongst boys, right across the age range. Furthermore, cultural pressures may influence differences between the sexes not just in where play takes place, but also in what form it takes. Carvalho *et al.* (1990) explored one facet of this process – the perceptions of children themselves as to what were appropriate forms of play for boys and girls – and whilst there was evidence that gender-stereotyping declined with age, of the activities studied only one (playchasing) was perceived to be generally a game for both boys and girls.

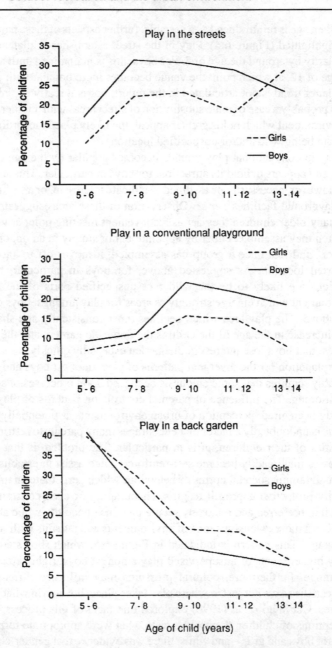

Figure 6.4 Variations in play locations according to age and gender
Source: Parkinson, 1987

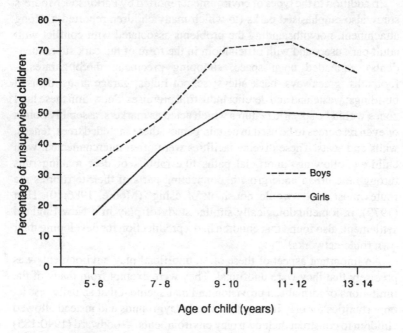

Figure 6.5 Differences in levels of unsupervised play according to age
and gender
Source: Parkinson, 1987

Although useful as an outline précis, Parkinson's (1987) report is
limited both in the variety of play scenarios it addresses and the level of
information gathered from each subject. As a result, some of the more
tantalising aspects of children's play patterns, especially their use of
undesignated play spaces, was not pursued. Moore (1986), however,
explored this aspect of children's behaviour much more fully since not
only did he interview urban children (in London, Stevenage and Stoke-
on-Trent) about where they liked to play and what they did, but also
accompanied them on guided tours of their play environments and even
took part in some events. Such immersion in the actual business of play,
suggests Woodward (1990), exposes more clearly the intrinsic meaning
of activity in a way that cannot be done by simple observation. The insight
gained from this study into how children play and what they need from
an urban environment to form play opportunities is both entertaining and,
from a policy perspective, revealing.

In addition to the types of environment reported by Parkinson, Moore's study also emphasised parks (to which many children reported a strong attachment, notwithstanding the problems associated with conflict with adult park users and with officialdom in the form of the park superintendents); untended open space; shopping precincts; thoroughfares – footpaths, greenways, back alleys; school fields; garage areas; disused buildings; wasteland and derelict industrial premises. Set within these land zones would be specific features which acted as markers, assembly points or even resources to be used in certain games; these included trees, fences, walls and seats. These diverse facilities were often interconnected, with children following 'unofficial paths like rabbits or deer making runs through the urban undergrowth, connecting parts of their territories via routes most adults would not think of using' (Moore, 1986:70). Hart (1979), in a methodologically similar study of play in a New England settlement, also found that children had a predilection for developing their own route networks.

An important aspect of these often unofficial play environments was precisely that they were unofficial. They were exempt from many of the limitations of formalised provision and management that actually restrict opportunities for play in, say, parks and playgrounds and instead allowed children to construct their own play environments. Woodward (1990:185) argues that 'by interacting closely with parts of the environment ignored or not valued by adults, some sense of ownership and control may be achieved'. The need for such child-made places must not be overlooked – places where dens can be built, where collectables such as blackberries, conkers, newts, tadpoles, even items of rubbish may be garnered and put to use in imaginative play, where secrets may be shared, trees climbed, tin cans stoned and fires lit. Manicured spaces and the mown grass that is so beloved of many urban authorities accommodate few, if any, of these interests and activities.

PROVISION FOR PLAY

The play world for many urban children is shrinking and the indications are that play policy has yet to adjust to the changing conditions of modern urban living and provide a range of opportunities to support the play needs of contemporary children. Heseltine and Holborn (1987:11) summarise much of the disquiet that persists amongst child agencies in commenting that 'with the best intentions we have provided playgrounds, play spaces and other physical environments in the UK which are almost valueless in meeting the developmental needs of children'. Children account for more than 20 per cent of the population and are the greatest users of the outdoor urban environment, yet in most contexts their recreational needs are relegated well below those of adults and resource allocations to support play are very limited. Britain lags behind many of its continental neighbours, particularly in Scandinavia and the Netherlands, in the extent to which resources have been committed to innovative provision for children (Play Board, 1985). If this situation is to be remedied, some fundamental reorientation in philosophy and practice will be required: in government policy towards play; in the planned approaches to provision; and in the basic nature of adult–child relationships.

The absence of government policy on play is widely viewed as a major deficiency. Government has in the past flirted with policy guidance in, for example, Circular 79/72 (DoE, 1972) and has concerned itself more recently with matters of playground safety (NCPRU, 1992), but such sporadic and limited intervention falls well short of the type of co-ordinated, strategic initiatives for which calls have been made (CPAC, 1988). Given the substantial benefits which accrue to the development of the child (and by extension to society at large) through exposure to play, there is surely a case for making provision a statutory responsibility of local authorities.

If government at both central and local level needs to rethink its commitment to play, leisure service and land planning units also need to adopt a more enabling stance. Heseltine and Holborn (1987) highlight two basic deficiencies. The first is a tendency in contemporary planning (with its preoccupations with spatial zoning and physical containment) to find a use for every available patch of urban land rather than leave some in an unused state so that it may be utilised by children for their play. Secondly, there is a risk, born of convenience, that provision will be based on relatively easy options – fixed equipment on unsupervised play areas being especially popular with planners though not, unfortunately, with children. Furthermore, Elson (1989) shows how provision that is planned as integral with new housing often fails to materialise as developments take shape on the ground, partly because developers tend to leave such tasks until the end, when they may receive only minimal attention and frequently, it must be said, because of objections from residents fearful of disturbance from play spaces close to their homes. The CPAC (1988) argue that for too long, planning in this area has principally concerned itself with protecting the environment from children, rather than accommodating their needs.

This mismatch in perspectives highlights a third area where, it is argued, fundamental change is necessary – in the relationships between adults and children. A number of studies, including most conspicuously that by Moore (1986), emphasise the need to recognise the special needs of children and to accommodate them on their (the children's) terms. But too often officialdom, in its various guises, seeks to limit where children may play and what they may do. The CPAC (1988:16) again comment that 'children and young people are regarded as a problem to be controlled or removed'. Parks and even ordinary public spaces attract signs declaring 'no ball games' or 'no cycling', ironically often within the types of deprived housing districts (local authority flatted estates, for example) where opportunistic use of areas such as garaging and pedestrian ways is forced upon children by the paucity of proper provision. In fact, in most residential environments, juxtaposition of play space is viewed with dismay by adult residents, fearful of noise, disturbance and vandalism (Chilton, 1985; Play Board, 1985), even though design skills and land-scaping can minimise such interference to a point at which play ought to be acceptable.

These are fundamental obstacles that must be overcome in any quest for a more supportive play policy in urban areas but there are further changes that will strengthen play provision and the utility of play spaces. First, the threat of road traffic needs to be minimised or, preferably, removed in areas where children play extensively. Children will always play in the street outside their homes and those streets require to be made liveable through traffic exclusion, calming or segregation (see Chapter 5).

Secondly it is argued (see for example Coffin and Williams, 1989) that environmental enhancement is important in improving play opportunities, although cleaning up urban neighbourhoods should not be taken to the point at which the scope for play in wild and natural places is lost. But if a child lives amidst blight and decay, he or she will accept those conditions as normal and treat the play environment in the same way. Heseltine and Holborn (1987) draw interesting contrasts between the high levels of vandalism on blighted estates in Britain and the conspicuously low levels of damage in the Finnish new town of Tapiola, where conscious efforts have been made to retain a natural landscape in the city and where children are instilled, in consequence, with a positive attitude to their environment.

Thirdly, there is now almost universal agreement that planning and management of urban play provision is enhanced by involvement of the local communities. Chilton (1985) suggests that community participation in planning and management of play leads to increase in the diversification and quality of the activities provided, reduction in conflict between child and adult, with associated enhancement of experience for both groups, and greater appreciation at the local level of policies and their limitations.

Change along these lines would enhance the climate for urban play provision, but what actual developments should be fostered and how should they be presented and managed? In view of the range of interests that children of differing ages commonly profess, diversity in provision must be a key concept and should be reflected not only in the character of play spaces that are offered but also in their styles of management. Provision should meet the differing environmental requirements for activity and also the way in which children's social needs fluctuate. Children will wish sometimes to play alone, on other occasions with friends and, at other times, even with adults. Several of the studies cited in this chapter promote the benefits of adult-led play quite forcefully, arguing its suitability in contexts such as adventure play or in situations where children's play is constrained by the nature of their home environment or through residence in households where parents find difficulty in supervising their children's play. For this reason, play schemes involving play workers and other adults have been prominent (or at least advocated) in urban areas where physical and social deprivation or environmental deficiencies are apparent, local authority estates, blocks of high-rise apartments or congested older housing areas within the inner cities being typical examples. Where local resources fall short of the level necessary to provide permanent provision, temporary initiatives involving play workers operating from mobile play buses have sometimes proven effective (Fahy, 1988).

However, it is necessary to emphasise the importance of child-managed play too. Places which are not under adult influence or control will exert a strong appeal to many children, especially if they present opportunities to manipulate the environment, to discover things, to construct personalised spaces, to take risks and pursue adventure. In some respects, this private world of child's play may be conceived at the opposite end of the spectrum from the adult-led play schemes and between these poles will, ideally, be a range of play spaces: doorstep play areas, playgrounds at both a neighbourhood and district scale, playing fields, parkland, adventure playgrounds and, as far as it is possible in an urban context, natural areas with trees, rough land and water.

Irrespective of their precise format or character, these play areas require that a number of design attributes or qualities should be considered. For convenience, these are summarised in Table 6.1 and although many aspects of the listing might appear self-evident, inspection of actual play areas reveals just how often providers fail to meet these requirements. Larger play spaces, in particular, benefit from internal variety, whether in fixed apparatus, surface textures or in loose materials that are available on site; diversity in terrain characteristics with slopes, mounds, gullies, flat areas and, if possible, shallow water to enhance play opportunity; and from vegetation in the form of trees to climb and bushes in which to hide. Trees and bushes will also form a means of screening of play space, to protect it from the elements, to reduce interference with adjacent housing and, indeed, to create intimate spaces that afford some privacy for the children at play.

Table 6.1 Design attributes for consideration in creation of play spaces

Terrain characteristics	Flat areas; hollows; slopes; gullies; promontories.
Vegetational characteristics	Short grass; long grass; bushes and undergrowth; trees; wild areas.
Surfaces	Hard – paved areas for wheeled toy and (perhaps) ball play; paths for access.
	Soft – grass; soft fill materials (tree bark, etc.); sand; water; soil; safety surfaces beneath selected apparatus.
	Artificial – either as areas for ball play or as a form of safety surface in equipment areas.
Equipment	Play – fixed and movable apparatus to facilitate a range of movements and creative contexts; loose materials to support creative or constructional play.
	Ancillary – seating (for children and adults); shelter; wind breaks; fencing (to protect from traffic and dog nuisance); bicycle racks; lighting.

The question of safety in play is a vexed one. At one level it commands considerable attention. As noted above, it is almost the only area in play provision where government in Britain has taken an interest, and manufacturers of play equipment are encouraged, though not required, to ensure that their products conform to safety standards (NCPRU, 1992). Yet too strong a focus on safety can become a limitation. It drains the modest play budgets of local authorities and may create play environments which fall short of the challenge which some groups, particularly older children, may require. Preoccupation with safety may also divert attention from the actual quality of the play environment.

The real risk to children at play comes from road traffic and where that is removed from the play area, prospects of serious injury from play diminish significantly. Ball and King (1990) argue that playground injuries are much rarer than assumed and where they do occur, the vast majority are minor. Serious head injury, in particular, is very rare and most falls from height result in injury to limbs rather than the skull. Local authorities spend significant amounts of their play budgets on impact-absorbent play surfaces but Ball and King conclude, unequivocally, that there is very little evidence to support the use of synthetic surfacing as an injury prevention measure.

Too much safety in playgrounds will become self-defeating. If part of the play experience is related to adventure and risk-taking, there must by definition be an element of danger. Where the planned provision fails to provide these periodic challenges which all children need to confront, they will look elsewhere, perhaps to locations which are genuinely dangerous: railway lines, derelict buildings, construction sites and so forth. Playspace design must tread a fine line between the need to create interest, adventure and challenge and the protection of children from the worst outcomes to which their play may lead.

How should play spaces be disposed within an urban environment? A common approach is to adopt a form of hierarchical framework to provision. Table 6.2 sets out a theoretical example as proposed by Coffin and Williams (1989), while Chilton (1985) documents an actual example of an attempt to establish a comprehensive framework for provision within Newcastle upon Tyne. This programme aimed to develop provision across a range of styles: equipped playgrounds, adventure playgrounds, doorstep play, holiday play schemes and events for children with special needs, community play houses and mobile play buses.

But can such ambitious schemes be delivered on a widespread basis and, more fundamentally, are they necessarily appropriate? To implement the structure advocated by Coffin and Williams in even a small British city such as Exeter would, if starting from scratch, necessitate the creation of some 2,100 doorstep play areas, over 60 local play spaces and adventure playgrounds, 15 neighbourhood and 2 district play parks. Even allowing for the fact that existing infrastructure would provide a base for embellishment, and taking into account too the potential for elements lower in the hierarchy to be provided on the same sites as some of the provision at the higher levels, the resourcing and land requirement implications are such that the prospects of achieving such a level of provision would be remote. Comparison with continental experience may indeed demonstrate that significantly higher levels of provision can be achieved (Play Board,

Table 6.2 Theoretical hierarchy for play provision

Level of provision	Location	Purpose	Area	Landscaping and equipment
Doorstep play areas	Within 50 metres of the home	Mainly for under 5s; meeting place for adults; separate sites for older children for social play	small; 50–100 sq. metres	Hard and soft surfacing; protected from wind but receiving plenty of sunlight; planting; on larger sites slopes, mounds, hollows and wild areas to attract birds and butterflies
Local play space	Within 400 metres of the home	Mainly for children over 5, or adults with small children	at least 1 hectare	Favourable micro-climate created by walls and/or planting; slopes and hollows; natural areas with climbable trees, bushes, long grass and water; traditional and adventurous play equipment; sand; flat area for ball games; paths for wheeled toys; seats and benches; lighting
Adventure playgrounds	Within 400 metres of the home	To provide challenging play experience for children of all ages under adult guidance	between 1,000 and 10,000 sq. metres	Fenced site with play hut with electricity, water, toilets and storage space; child-managed landscape with playhuts, dens, gardens, sand, hutches for animals and water
Neighbourhood park/play space	Within 5–600 metres of the home	To provide for all age groups from young children to the elderly	about 4 hectares	Landscaped area with different levels, slopes and mounds; natural areas with trees, water and wild flowers; pitches for formal games; benches; shelter; play equipment
District park/play space	Within 2–3 km of the home	As above	at least 20 hectares	As above but with the addition of formal areas; lakes (with boats); sports facilities – tennis, bowls; cafeterias; pavilions etc.

Source: adapted from Coffin and Williams (1989: 27–30)

1985), but in Britain, with the exception of some of the new towns, such levels have seldom been approached and until such time as there is a fundamental change in the prevailing culture of play provision, such proposals, worthy though they be, will surely founder on the twin rocks of political uninterest and the under-funding of local government.

It is further debatable as to whether a comprehensively structured approach to provision is ideal. Certainly, a base of formal provision in a range of play spaces and in a variety of organisational contexts is an essential starting point, but it cannot expect to meet all the demands that children exert upon the urban environment. It is well understood that children spend only a small part of their play time in playgrounds (Brown and Burger, 1984) and that most forms of individual play apparatus hold the attention of the average child for no more than three or four minutes. Ball game areas are often little used and are rarely used by girls (CPAC, 1988). Playgrounds form a valuable meeting point at which groups of children assemble but then often disperse to other, more alluring attractions and whilst in some contexts children welcome and benefit from the role of adults as play organisers, many children will also seek privacy (Moore, 1986): we have noted how adult recall of childhood experience often places the emphasis upon play that took place away from the adult gaze (Sebba, 1991).

In reviewing the contemporary literature on provision for play there is an evident tension between advocacy of comprehensive, structured and well-resourced approaches to play provision and a tacit recognition that children often get the better play experiences from the places they themselves locate, personalise and manage – the 'found' places, as they are sometimes designated. The problem for providers is that it is very difficult to take 'found' places into account in formulating an overall strategy, not least because of the practical difficulty for adults in actually appreciating what type of casual space would interest a child. But it is argued here that that attempt should be made. Confining children's play to designated spaces, however diverse and interesting they may be, will not ultimately deliver all the benefits in personal development and experience that play should afford. Donnelly (1980:66) talks of 'a *need* [my italics] for ambiguous places, even slightly dangerous places like woods or old disused buildings that can give rise to a range of fantasy play'. He is not mistaken.

The constriction of children's play space that has become evident in the last decade or so has been an evolutionary process but it is surely not an irreversible one. The critical changes necessary to effect such a reversal are, as noted earlier, primarily changes in attitude: a willingness to confront and tame the private car, particularly in the residential areas where children play; a willingness on the part of planners to think more creatively and flexibly about ways in which residential areas are set out and to have the courage to leave some places unused or only lightly managed. If new residential streets were designed for living from the outset rather than reclaimed subsequently from the car at great financial cost, and if in addition to formally designated play space the equivalent of, say, every tenth plot on a development was deliberately left unused or sculpted and planted up as informal play or amenity space, the ambiance of the otherwise tedious modern street would be enhanced for all residents and its utility as a play environment for children transformed. Careful adherence to some of the design principles considered earlier can provide places in which children will wish to play, without it being necessary to equip, surface and manage the space. It is true that a looser pattern of urban land use would threaten to extend the urban area beyond the envelopes that planners prefer to designate as perimeters to growth, but if the gain is a genuine enhancement in the quality of that urban area, this is a price that we should at least consider paying.

We need, too, to rethink some of our managerial attitudes to spaces children use for play. Parks, for example, are a resource with considerable potential for absorbing play, yet many are rule-bound, policed by officious 'parkies' and maintained in a state that is too readily damaged by children at play. But many parks are of a size that could easily accommodate zones of play of different character alongside the managed spaces – a wilder, rougher landscape that is better able to withstand the rigours of playful use and would attract the adventurous child who has limited use for the mown swaths of grass and no use at all for the neat flowerbeds. This is not to argue that such traditional park features should be replaced but rather that they should be supplemented selectively with areas that meet the needs of a different sort of user.

What evidence is there of local authorities moving towards either a more strategic pattern of provision, or indeed, more radical initiatives of the type outlined above? Perhaps predictably for a discretionary area of intervention, the response is variable. Most local authorities now place some form of requirement upon housing developers to provide play spaces as part of a condition of planning permission, or occasionally as an obligation, but strategic development of play is not addressed consistently. A review of current local plans and policy statements from leisure service units reveals, at one extreme, a failure by some to articulate and document any strategy for play whatsoever, whilst others have produced comprehensive proposals for meeting perceived needs for play provision (for examples of the latter, see Cardiff City Council, 1992; Nuneaton and Bedworth Borough Council, undated).

Content analysis of policy statements suggests a widespread preoccupation with a core of common issues, with safety of playgrounds in both design and location, guidelines on proper location for play space relative to housing, adherence to standards of provision and the need for physical maintenance of equipment being typical foci for discussion. Most authorities place the emphasis firmly upon equipped playgrounds as a basis for provision and very few signal the need for public consultation.

This is both encouraging and alarming – encouraging inasmuch as the need to address provision for play is widely recognised, alarming in the extent to which a paternalistic approach to provision based upon equipped playgrounds still prevails. Only one of the authorities studied (Leicester City) gave clear recognition to the role of the street as a play environment and only a small percentage acknowledged that children play in natural areas and unmanaged spaces, as well as designated playgrounds. None of these authorities, however, went so far as to define policy for such provision.

More alarming still are attitudes of the type expressed in a recent article in a professional planning journal, where Sheldon (1990:20) stated quite openly that 'street play is totally unacceptable within the younger population' and that the challenge to planners was 'to keep children off the streets'. The article then went on to enthuse about a new (equipped) play area created along a disused railway embankment to which children should, presumably, be directed. The play area may, indeed, be extremely fine, but one is tempted to ask what play value the old embankment possessed and whether it might have been better retained rather than lost beneath yet another adult-designed space? The author misses completely the point that making streets and public areas more amenable for children's play also makes them amenable for the community at large.

The position may not, in reality, be quite as bleak as these findings imply. The narrow perspectives voiced by Sheldon are not necessarily typical and there is clearly emergent official and public interest in enhancing the environment of towns and cities, a process of which children's play should be a beneficiary, if only an incidental one. Several major urban areas have ambitious strategies for developing natural and wild areas within their boundaries (see, for example, Birmingham City Council, 1989) and children's play will be, *de facto*, one of the uses to emerge in such spaces. But it would be encouraging if policy documents gave explicit recognition to this potential and reassurance that children at play will be welcome in such environments rather than discouraged because of the threat that their play may pose to other policy objectives, especially those of conservation. As always, a balance in policy is the goal at which providers should aim. 'The failure of an urban environment,' writes Ward (1978:87) 'can be measured in direct proportion to the number of playgrounds.' If planners, architects and urban designers have serious intent to improve the play world of the urban child, they would do well to heed this message.

Chapter 7

Fresh air and healthy living – recreation in parks and open spaces

Open space occupies a central place in the provision for outdoor recreation in towns and cities – indeed, without public spaces, outdoor recreation in urban areas would struggle to extend beyond the realm of the domestic garden and the street outside the front door. Formal parks, gardens, recreation grounds, playing fields, playgrounds, urban woodland, commons and untended or disused areas contribute a diversity of spaces and environments that, between them, support and maintain the majority of outdoor activities that engage urban people at leisure. (Since provision for children's play and for sport are considered separately, this chapter is primarily concerned with parks, public gardens and informal or natural open spaces.)

THE ORIGINS OF PUBLIC OPEN SPACE

Open space in towns and cities is probably as old as urbanism itself. From the earliest settlements for which plans are known, space was left within the built-up zone for commercial, civic or military functions and occasionally, recreational purposes too. Such areas were essential to the proper functioning of urban places but their provision, suggests Welch (1991), was also a reflection of the basically gregarious nature of people, and the social dimension to usage of public space has always been a prominent motive in both provision and use.

The creation of a verdant landscape for public use in towns and cities was, however, largely the product of the Victorian era. Green space with varying degrees of public access had existed before this time (in royal parks, private gardens, urban commons, churchyards and on vacant plots), but the widespread provision of public space does not emerge clearly until the second half of the nineteenth century. Although Britain is sometimes seen as a leader in the development of parks, it is probably more accurate to visualise a broadly contemporary development of urban parkland and open space provision across much of Europe, North America and the colonial territories of European powers. By the turn of the twentieth century, not only had parks become an established type of urban land use, but so had public gardens, recreation grounds and, less widely, children's playgrounds too. Only playing fields amongst the major forms of green space were yet to make their appearance, although sports fields attached to public schools had begun to be provided.

The detailed history of this fascinating process will not be reiterated here. For a full account see, for example, Chadwick (1966) or Conway (1991), whilst Nuttgens (1973), Tourism and Recreation Research Unit (TRRU) (1983) and Walker and Duffield (1983) amongst many, offer abbreviated histories. From within these narratives, three primary themes may be discerned: the diversification of space, its popularisation and its physical extension.

Diversification

Initially, the form that public space adopted was limited to parkland (of what would now be recognised as a conventional character) and urban commons, which in Britain survived from the medieval period. The physical character of early parks reflects several prevailing influences which not only shaped the style of the first parks but also set a pattern that has continued to the present in only a slightly modified form. Amongst these diverse influences (which also included the style of old royal parks and the traditions of Georgian private gardens of the type seen in the fashionable squares of Bloomsbury, Bath and Edinburgh), particular emphasis should be placed upon the landscape gardening movement of the eighteenth century. Although past the height of fashion, this was still sufficiently pervasive to have an impact, for example, upon the designs for London's new Regent's Park (1826) and the redesign of the old royal park of St James (1828). Chadwick (1966:20) describes 'the effects of smoothness, roundness, gradual variation and gentle serenity' that typified this style of landscaping, which, he notes, 'became almost a formula' (Figure 7.1). To this comfortable evocation of natural form was soon added a 'gardenesque' style of design, in which floral display came to be a part of public space. This too has become an enduring tradition in official urban horticulture.

A second important influence was the eighteenth-century urban pleasure garden which, although varied in origin and character, was distinguished by the provision of walkways, areas of refreshment and entertainments. These latter took a diversity of popular forms, including

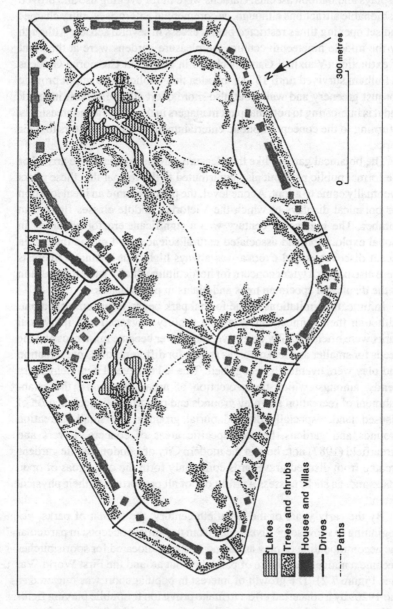

Figure 7.1 The original design by Paxton for Birkenhead Park (1847)

Lakes
Trees and shrubs
Houses and villas
Drives
Paths

300 metres

0

N

circuses and menageries, dances and concerts, *son et lumierè*, firework displays and balloon ascents. Gardens were lit for evening use and proved fashionable attractions although, as commercial enterprises, entry charges and set opening times restricted public access in several senses. Although by the middle nineteenth century the pleasure gardens were at the point of extinction (Vauxhall Gardens closed in 1859, but Cremorne Gardens in Fulham survived until 1877), the idea that public space might provide not just greenery and walks but also more overt attractions left its mark and it is interesting to note that park managers in the 1990s are increasingly returning to the concept of public entertainment to attract visitors to their parks.

The botanical garden, like the pleasure garden, pre-dates the arrival of the formal public park but also contributed to the format that these parks eventually came to adopt. At one level, the parks became an ideal location for botanical displays to which the Victorian middle classes flocked in number. The nineteenth century was a significant era for advances in global exploration and associated natural sciences and public interest in recent discoveries and exotica was always high. But botanical interests were also part of a wider concern for horticulture which fostered a tradition in the display of specimen trees and plants in public parks.

In time, the limitations of the formal park began to become apparent. Although their numbers grew as the century advanced and individual parks were often spatially extensive, they never became numerous and the needs for smaller and less precious spaces for different forms of recreation and play were eventually recognised. This led to several complementary trends, amongst which the protection of urban commons, the establishment of recreation and play grounds and opportunistic reclamation of disused land, especially disused burial grounds, for small recreation grounds and gardens, became specific areas of concern. Rivers and Streatfield (1987) note how in the modern City of London, public gardens created from disused graveyards commonly form the only areas of open space and, as such, possess a utility out of all proportion to their physical extent.

By the early years of the twentieth century, the format of parks was beginning to show some divergence from the initial concepts; in particular the accommodation of play areas and of space allocated for sports pitches became a noticeable feature of parks laid out around the First World War (see Figure 7.2). The growth of interest in popular sport was mirrored in the 1920s by a concerted effort to make provision for public playing fields and sports grounds. This was vigorously promoted by the newly formed National Playing Fields Association (1925) and eventually procedures

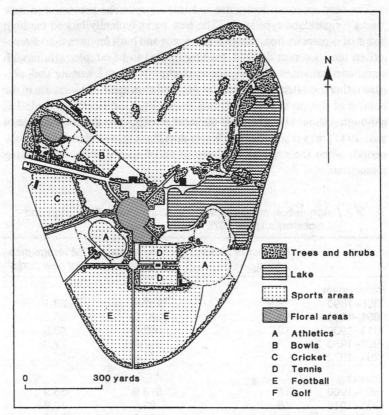

Figure 7.2 The original design by Mawson for Stanley Park, Blackpool (1922)

whereby local authorities might provide playing fields were formally laid down in the Physical Training Act of 1937.

Immediately after the end of the Second World War, provision of land for urban recreation took a significant step forward through its inclusion in the new statutory planning procedures introduced in 1947. Previously, the development of public open space had advanced spasmodically, responding in an *ad hoc* fashion to miscellaneous pieces of legislation or initiatives. The effect of the new planning procedures, although not immediate, was to define new terms of reference for planned provision of space in which standards, hierarchies and open space systems came to be the parlance of provision.

The new approach had a marked impact upon the provision of new 'parks' or parkland-type space. The new parks typically lacked the high levels of ornamentation, use of water space and built features that characterised the Victorian designs, tending instead to be simpler affairs with significant expanses of grass, sports pitches, footpaths, seating and, perhaps rather too often, little else. But this criticism apart, the increase in the number of new parks was sometimes dramatic, as is reflected in Table 7.1, although it should be noted that the total acreages and the average size of post-1945 parks is significantly lower than those provided in the inter-war period, when the expansion of provision of sports fields was gaining momentum.

Table 7.1 Acquisition of open spaces in Birmingham, Edinburgh and Leicester, *c.*1850–1975

	Number of parks added	Total acreage added	Average size of new parks
Birmingham			
1856–1890	8	232.5	29.1
1891–1910	11	387.2	35.2
1911–1930	13	562.2	43.5
1931–1950	4	307.9	77.0
1951–1972	3	71.3	23.8
Edinburgh			
1850–1900	16	573.9	35.9
1901–1918	8	86.4	10.8
1919–1945	23	763.8	33.2
1946–1969	29	669.9	23.1
Leicester			
1850–1900	7	403.0	57.6
1901–1920	6	45.5	7.6
1921–1950	14	454.2	32.4
1951–1975	27	242.6	9.0

Source: adapted from TRRU (1983)

The increase in planned provision owed much to the widespread adoption by local authorities of a standards approach which in many cases highlighted quite marked deficiency. The NPFA standard, in particular, proved a demanding target for many urban authorities seeking to rebuild their towns after the ravages of war and, even where levels were not met, significant increases in the quantity of public space still tended to result. Then, towards the end of the 1960s, more systematic approaches to provision became popular as planners attempted to build open spaces into networks or hierarchies. In this context, the work of the Greater London Council (GLC) was especially influential. Its thoughts on the construction of an open space hierarchy have been quite widely imitated and, even after the demise of the authority, continue to affect official thinking. The most recent advice on open space hierarchies in London (London Planning Advisory Committee, 1988) is set out in Table 7.2, while an example of a planned space hierarchy in Leicester is illustrated in Figure 7.3.

Popularisation

Alongside the increase in diversity of spaces through time, a second key trend has been the popularisation of such space – the diffusion of public access throughout the urban social strata. Although the impetus that led to the creation of the first Victorian public parks was primarily the product of concern for the poor physical and moral state of the urban proletariat, the first parks clearly did not meet popular needs. These were socially exclusive places, laid out to meet the requirements of gentry, not the urban poor. The German landscape gardener, Peter Josef Lenne, who visited England in 1823, commented that to enjoy the London parks 'it is necessary to be a man of fortune, and take exercise on horseback or in a carriage' (quoted in Conway, 1991). He further noted that the parks were fenced, unlike the open parks of Germany. The botanical and zoological gardens (which some parks contained) restricted access to members or to those who could afford an entry charge, while the physical location of parks and gardens in areas of normally high-status residence ensured that ordinary people were largely excluded.

To overcome this problem entailed a conscious effort to locate parks in areas of poor housing and although the Select Committee on Public Walks which reported in 1833 advocated a range of actions to enhance access to green space for the working classes, little was achieved initially, largely due to governmental indifference. However, the report did form a catalyst for local action by municipal authorities, especially in the north of England, which began thereafter to provide genuinely public parks. Victoria Park in the East End of London (opened 1845) was partly funded by the government but the first parks in Manchester (1846–48) were financed entirely by public subscription. Elsewhere, for example in Sheffield, Liverpool and Derby, public parks were provided by the generosity of wealthy benefactors, as well as through the process of linking park

Table 7.2 Hierarchical pattern of public open space

Type and main function	Approximate size and distance from home	Characteristics
Regional park Weekend and occasional visits by car or public transport	400 hectares 3.2–8 km	Large areas of natural heathland, common woodland and parkland. Primarily providing for informal recreation with some non-intensive active recreations. Car parking at strategic locations
Metropolitan park Weekend and occasional visits by car or public transport	60 hectares 3.2 km but more when park is larger than 60 hectares	Either natural heath, common, woods or formal parks providing for active and passive recreation. May contain playing fields, provided at least 40 hectares remain for other pursuits. Adequate car parking
District parks Weekend and occasional visits on foot, by cycle, car or short bus trip	20 hectares 1.2 km	Landscaped settings with a variety of natural features providing for a range of activities, including outdoor sports, children's play and informal pursuits. Some car parking
Local parks For pedestrian visitors	2 hectares 0.4 km	Providing for court games, children's play, sitting out etc. in a landscaped environment. Playing fields if the park is large enough
Small local parks Pedestrian visits especially by old people and children, particularly valuable in high-density areas	2 hectares 0.4 km	Gardens, sitting-out areas, children's playgrounds, etc.
Linear open space Pedestrian visits	Variable Where feasible	Canal towpaths, footpaths, disused rail lines etc., providing opportunities for informal recreation

Source: London Planning Advisory Committee (1988)

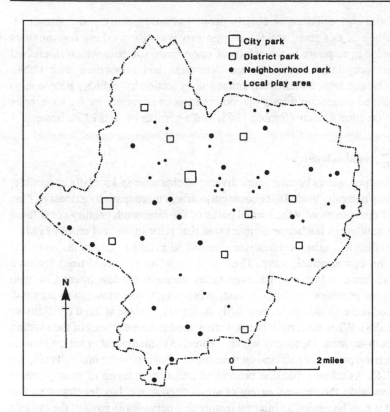

City park
District park
Neighbourhood park
Local play area

N

0   2 miles

Figure 7.3 An example of a planned hierarchy of public open spaces,
                Leicester
Source: Leicester City Council, 1991

provision with property speculation, the potential for which had been
shown at Regent's Park and also in Birkenhead. After the passage of the
Public Improvement Act of 1860, local authorities were permitted to use
moneys raised through rates to acquire and manage open space, provided
equal amounts came from public subscription. A substantial increase in
provision of open space followed the Public Health Act of 1875, which
for the first time allowed local authorities to borrow money for such
purposes.

Earlier, the Recreation Grounds Act (1859) had recognised the need
for smaller spaces that would complement major parks in being more
locally accessible and able to meet some of the needs of poorer families,

those with children, or elderly people whose mobility was constrained. Much of this small scale, localised provision for working communities arose in response to the efforts of open space societies which flourished in many cities during the late Victorian and Edwardian eras. Urban common land, a traditional venue for recreation by ordinary people, also gained protection through a combination of advocacy by the Commons Protection Society (formed 1865) and a number of Acts of Parliament.

Physical extension

As open spaces became more diverse in character and socially accessible, they naturally tended to become collectively more spatially extensive. One of the reasons why the formal parks of the nineteenth century constituted a new urban landscape element was that prior to the real onset of industrialisation, urban centres were small and access to commons and rural land comparatively easy. There was, thus, no perceived need for such provision, a factor which even today accounts for low interest in open space provision in countries such as Norway, where most towns are small and recreational space, especially in forests, is close at hand (Wilkinson, 1988). When new, most parks were placed at the periphery of the existing built-up area, a tendency which creates, in contemporary cities, a characteristic pattern of parkland on the edge of what is now the inner city (Figure 7.4). As urban expansion proceeded and as new forms of space became available, the physical extent of urban open spaces has developed so that it is now becoming an integral feature that pervades all parts of the modern urban fabric, except perhaps the commercial core. In most countries, planning regulations now impose varying requirements upon developers to set aside amenity spaces as a normal part of their developments; urban renewal typically sees public space as a primary beneficiary and, occasionally, truly extensive tracts of recreational land have been consciously planned in order to enhance a city's recreational opportunities. Examples include London's Lea Valley, the Amsterdam Bos (forest park) and Helsinki's Central Park (Chadwick, 1966; Friberg, 1979). Such large-scale provision of public space represents a marked contrast to the very limited responses that, inevitably, characterised the formative years of the open space movement.

If diversification, popularisation and physical extension provide the vertical strands of the open space 'fabric' (its 'warp'), then it may be perceived that there is a 'weft' of related changes that have bound the process of open space development together. Amongst these should be highlighted on-going legal and social reform and the activities of pressure

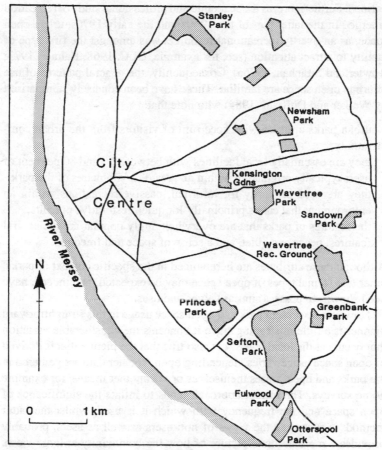

Figure 7.4 An example of parkland fringing an inner city, Liverpool

groups and advocates of change, both of which reflect and are a part of the wider changes in cultural values and expectations that have redefined successively the benchmarks against which levels and styles of open space provision have been assessed.

THE USE OF PUBLIC OPEN SPACE

The established position of parks and other forms of conventional public open space means that patterns of associated use are similarly well defined. Furthermore, as the academic and professional study of recreation emerged in the latter part of the 1960s and the early 1970s, urban open space, as an overtly recreational resource, was amongst the first type of facility to attract attention (see, for example, GLC, 1968; Balmer, 1973; Bowler and Strachan, 1976a). Consequently, the general patterns of use of urban open space are familiar. These have been concisely summarised by Walker and Duffield (1983) who note that:

- urban parks attract a wide spectrum of visitors from the urban community;
- they are essentially local facilities with between 60 and 80 per cent of users typically originating within an area of 2 kilometres of the park;
- they are used primarily for informal, passive recreations within an environment that caters principally for quiet, restorative pursuits;
- the features of parks that are overwhelmingly popular are the natural features, peace and quiet, and a sense of space and freedom.

Although these attributes are here voiced in the specific context of parks, other less formal types of open space may be expected (and indeed, have been shown) to possess similar values and uses.

However, to present park and open space usage in this straightforward manner is a little misleading since it conceals the considerable variation that occurs at the local level. It is also true that the picture that is derived of open space usage varies, depending upon whether data are gathered in the parks and open spaces themselves or via another means, for example home surveys. The former approach tends to inflate the significance of open space and the frequency with which it is used, whilst the latter method, in recording the views of non-users as well as users, probably provides a more accurate picture of how the community at large views these resources.

It may be noted that although it is true that public open space draws use from a wide spectrum of the community, it does not draw evenly according to age, gender or economic status. For example, a survey of parks in Leicester (LCC, 1985) established that the main user group according to age was young people between 10 and 19 years, followed by people between 25 and 34 years and then those aged over 65 (Table 7.3). This finding accords with studies of parks in Edinburgh and Nottingham reported by the TRRU (1983), which also noted high proportions of children using parks. However, a study of use by adults of parks and informal open spaces in the Potteries conurbation in Staffordshire (Williams and Jackson, 1985) found that those showing above-average levels of use were young adults between 22 and 30 years (24 per cent of sample) and, at the other extreme, those over 65 years (13 per cent of sample). The survey of the Potteries did not cover children below the age of 16, so may not be directly compared in detail with the position in Leicester, but older teenagers who were interviewed showed quite low levels of interest in parks and open spaces. However, both studies concur in emphasising the value of open space to young adult groups and the elderly.

Table 7.3 Age distribution of park users – Leicester 1984

	Age						
	10–19	*20–24*	*25–34*	*35–44*	*45–54*	*55–64*	*65-plus*
Percentage	28.7	10.8	19.3	10.8	8.2	9.2	12.9

Source: Leicester City Council (1985)

Explanation for the appeal of parks to adults under the age of 30 may lie in the opportunities to play sport that many parks afford and the attraction of these areas as somewhere to take young family groups. Amongst older people, the peaceful atmosphere of parks is often valued and these spaces are sometimes perceived to be safer places in which to relax, although the study of open spaces in Greenwich by Burgess *et al.* (1988) reveals that fear of open spaces is becoming a significant constraint in some situations. The fall-off in usage of parks and open space amongst middle-aged people was a striking feature in both the Potteries and Leicester and perhaps tells us something about personal motives for visiting parks. Respondents in the Potteries survey signalled a clear loss of interest in parks during mid-life. Some stated they were too busy, middle age often coinciding with periods in which commitments to work and work-associated responsibility were at their peak, whilst a number stated that as their children had grown up, the perceived need to go to parks and open space had dissipated.

Gender contrasts in open space usage are apparent too, though not necessarily consistent. In the Potteries, Williams and Jackson (1985) found women to be in the majority (62 per cent of identified park users), especially mothers escorting young children, female students in groups and older women exercising dogs, whereas the study of park users in Leicester (LCC, 1985) found an opposite position in which men accounted for 58 per cent of visits. However, in an interesting refinement, the data for Leicester were recast according to whether the spaces in question possessed neighbourhood, district or city-wide catchments: when so treated, usage of neighbourhood facilities by men and women came out as equal. The largest difference was in use of district facilities where sports provision was prominent: these attracted large numbers of men.

We have seen how, historically, parks and urban open spaces were partly provided for the recourse of the disadvantaged and whilst contemporary urban conditions no longer generate that need in quite the same manner, studies suggest that parks still remain important resources for the outdoor recreation of people of poorer status, especially those whose homes lack a private garden or who lack the means to travel more widely. TRRU (1983) note disproportionately high levels of park use by people in 'blue collar' occupations, people who are economically inactive (housewives, the retired, the unemployed, etc.) and people without access to a car, whilst 59 per cent of visitors to Leicester's parks were 'unwaged' (LCC, 1985).

The behavioural patterns associated with parks and open space reflect a distinctive pattern of informality and engagement in casual activity, although the precise blend will be governed by the facilities that different spaces afford, and where sports fields form part of the provision, activity patterns will show less emphasis upon passivity. Table 7.4 draws together findings from several studies, not all of which are directly comparable but which taken together confirm the tendency for parks and open space activity to be dominated by walking, sitting, watching people or events and general relaxation. Parks and open spaces may further form links in route networks: most studies record people simply walking through parks

Table 7.4 Activity patterns in parks – the Potteries, Leicester and London (%)

	Potteries	Leicester	London
Sitting	7.5	12.0	—
Sitting and walking	—	—	86.0
Walking	61.0	50.0	—
Picnicking	1.0	1.0	—
Playing sport	15.5	9.0	6.0
Informal games	2.0	9.0	—
Spectating	3.0	5.0	—
Activities with children	—	—	12.0
Entertainments	—	—	3.0

Sources: GLC (1968); Bowler and Strachan (1976a, 1976b); Williams and Jackson (1985)

in order to get to another destination, the open space forming either a short cut or a more agreeable routeway than might be afforded along a busy street. A study of open spaces in Islington, Birmingham and Warrington (Millward and Mostyn, 1989) found that an average of 16 per cent of users were simply passing through, while the study of parks in Leicester found almost a quarter of 'users' of neighbourhood parks were of this type, although the larger parks attracted significantly less of this incidental usage (LCC, 1985).

The social value of open space is variable. It is well understood that a significant number of users go to parks, gardens and informal spaces for solitude and for temporary escape from the pressures of contemporary urban life. But Burgess *et al.* (1988) emphasise too the social dimension to usage of public open space: the opportunities for children to play, for adults and youths to engage in sport, for mothers or the elderly to meet and chat, for families to make outings. In the Potteries, for example, whilst nearly 15 per cent of park users visited alone, almost 70 per cent were accompanied by a spouse, or by children or other relatives in what was clearly a sociable use of public space (Williams and Jackson, 1985).

The frequency with which people visit parks and open space often shows a duality, a divide between groups of regular users who come often and those for whom the park is an occasional resource. In Leicester 78 per cent of users of neighbourhood parks claimed they visited at least once a week, and even for the major city parks the figure was 63 per cent (LCC, 1985). These high values probably reflect the fact that data were gathered in the parks and were therefore more likely to reveal the patterns of people who used the areas regularly. In contrast, the study of the Potteries by Williams and Jackson (1985) was conducted via home-based interviews and here the majority of park users (57 per cent) said they visited parks less than once a week.

Duration of visits varies somewhat according to the nature of the park, small neighbourhood facilities in Leicester showing most visits as being of less than 30 minutes whereas the average length of stay in a major city park was over two hours (LCC, 1985). In general, however, comparative study reveals visits of less than an hour to be the norm (Table 7.5). Timing of visits typically reveals a marked focus upon weekend as opposed to weekday use but within these periods there are variations too. For exam- ple, Bowler and Strachan (1976b) noted significant weekday usage of parks after school hours whilst at the weekend, patterns of sporting activity produced concentrations of activity in the middle of Saturday afternoons and again on Sunday mornings in those parks and spaces that provided for sports. These patterns are, of course, subject to a seasonal effect, although

Table 7.5 Length of visits to parks – London, Liverpool and Leicester (%)

	London	Liverpool	Leicester (1976)	Leicester (1984)
Under 1 hour	54	68	48	47
1–2 hours	23	17	37	26
Over 2 hours	20	15	15	27

Sources: GLC (1968); Balmer (1973); Bowler and Strachan (1976a, 1976b); Leicester City Council (1985)

even in the depths of winter parks will still attract usage, especially from habitual users for whom such visits are an established and routine feature of their recreational lifestyles.

The characteristic pattern of localised, often regular, and typically informal use extends also to other forms of open space. Examination of reclaimed land in Stoke-on-Trent by Bush *et al.* (1981b) and Williams and Jackson (1985) found little difference in the manner of usage of these spaces when compared with formal parks and gardens. Perhaps more surprisingly, Harrison (1983), in a study of 16 semi-rural sites in London's urban fringe, also concluded that usage was very like that seen in parks – localised, informal and limited in duration.

Proximity to parks and other spaces appears to be an especially important factor in determining how those areas are used, since all studies tend to indicate that open space is typically a localised resource and unless there is a special purpose, the distance travelled to parks will not normally exceed a mile, or thereabouts. The common means of reaching a park or open space is to walk (Strachan and Bowler, 1978). Studies which have looked at a range of spaces and not just formal parks (e.g. Williams and Jackson, 1985; Burgess *et al.*, 1988) confirm the significance of small areas of unofficial local space which residents use in a quite incidental way. If the motives are simply to walk, relax, take the air, exercise the dog or play, then in selecting a location most people do not appear to draw significant distinctions between parks and informal spaces: they simply visit the space that is nearest, provided it is suited to their current need. It has also been shown that people value more highly those spaces in which they themselves have a managerial role (Francis, 1987b). Recreational providers have perhaps been guilty of overlooking too readily the value of both incidental, informal spaces and those in which the local community itself has a direct interest. The provision of well-tended, formal space that lies at a distance from people's homes will not necessarily meet the needs for open space throughout the urban community as a whole.

THE NEED FOR INNOVATION

The preceding remark hints at a measure of dissatisfaction with established modes of provision of urban open space and, indeed, over the course of the last ten years or so, a debate has developed over the viability of conventional forms of space and the needs for a more innovatory approach that matches more effectively provision to needs. The utility of parks and open spaces has come into question for a variety of reasons. For some writers, the fact that formal parks have changed so little since their formation in the closing decades of the nineteenth century reflects a lack of creativity on the part of modern recreational providers. Walker and Duffield (1983) suggest that Victorian attitudes continue to prevail inasmuch as providers still view the role of open space as to provide relief from problems of urban life and even as part of a wider approach to social control through provision of recreation facilities aimed at countering boredom and tendencies to crime, especially by the young. The philosophical environment in which the original parks emerged and which Newby (1990:6) describes as an 'intellectual reaction to many of the tenets of economic liberalism [and] a growing disenchantment with the *accoutrements* of urban industrialisation' still has apparent currency.

Parks were originally designed to provide an experience of the countryside in the city. The fact that it was a tamed and sanitised version of rural landscape was, for a period, unimportant since the direct experience of countryside recreation for the majority of the urban population was limited. However, increases in mobility and disposable income in the post-1945 era has prompted significant growth in the use made of countryside areas by people at leisure, to the extent of an estimated 900 million day visits in 1993 (Anon., 1994). Furthermore, the range and sophistication of outdoor activities in which people engage has taken many patterns of demand well beyond the capabilities of traditional forms of urban space. The rise of environmentalism in the public conscience since the end of the 1970s, allied with direct experience of more natural environments, has prompted a growing desire to incorporate natural areas into the fabric of modern cities, not necessarily as replacement spaces but as additional forms of public space that differ significantly from the conventional, closely managed and often unnatural environment of the town park or recreation ground (Laurie, 1979a; Nicholson-Lord, 1987).

The evident decline in interest in conventional parks and open spaces has not been confined to users but extends now to providers too. Welch (1991) argues that under-resourcing is a major contemporary problem that now prevents adequate maintenance and precludes significant development. Parks and open spaces typically absorb anything up to 40 per cent of local authority recreation budgets, but since the 1970s attention of both public and providers has tended to shift to other types of urban resource, especially the sports and leisure centre. As a result, many parks and public spaces have become the subject of relative neglect, as Rendel (1983:13) comments, 'embarrassing commitments rather than outstanding assets'. Burgess *et al.* (1988:467) are more forceful in their criticisms, stating that, 'people's aspirations for open space provision and use contrast strongly with the realities of their local parks' and that 'the poverty of the environmental experiences afforded by these areas is further aggravated by dog-fouling, unsympathetic staff, the lack of facilities and absence of social areas and events'.

Criticism has also been directed at the styles of formula-based planning of open space which came into fashion in the 1970s and 1980s. Detractors point to several shortcomings in such approaches. For example, Walker and Duffield (1983) argue that standardised approaches tend to view open space purely as a land use to be provided in given quantities, rather than a facility to match local needs. The value of open space can be appraised from a range of perspectives – its visual and landscape qualities, its natural characteristics, its capacity to support wildlife, its ability to accommodate a range of recreations (Bradley and Millward, 1986) – yet these key facets are seldom recognised in simple space plans. Burgess *et al.* (1988) take the argument a step further in suggesting that parks and open spaces have a significant socio-cultural value that is far more than the physical measurement of space and that, for many people, the truly valuable spaces are those incidental areas that fall outside the planned hierarchy or standardised open space plan. Welch (1991) agrees and adds that such structured approaches tend to produce inert management that is unresponsive to changing conditions of demand and recreational behaviours.

What should be done to try to ensure that public needs are matched by public provision? Three broad approaches are currently evident in the plans and strategies of local providers in Britain. The first is based upon reinvigorating established forms of space, especially the park; the second approach is concerned with reintroduction to the urban environment of natural or semi-natural green areas, particularly woodland; while the third seeks to introduce new types of informal spaces which perhaps are suited to activities that are incompatible with conventional parks or natural areas.

NEW DIRECTIONS

Reviving the park

The process of rethinking the format of the town park is not, of course, a new one and any historical survey of park development will show change in form and, to a lesser degree, function through time. However, most of the historic changes took place when a healthy demand for access to formal parks still prevailed – a point of significant contrast to more recent experience in which the appeal and value of parks has tended to decline. Innovation has, therefore, been more prominent in the recent development or redevelopment of town parks.

There are a number of studies of new or rejuvenated urban parks (see, for example, Bellamy, 1976; McCance, 1983; Nice, 1983; Rendel, 1983) which, although varying in detail, reflect certain common themes. These may be concisely stated as:

* extending the appeal of parks, for example through provision of new forms of facility such as cycle tracks and fitness trails; through improvement to support services (toilets, refreshments, information); and by the organisation and promotion of events and entertainments;
* extending access to parks, by removal of perimeter fencing, provision of lighting and, where feasible, provision of all-weather/all-season facilities such as artificial sports surfaces;
* extending public involvement in design and operation of parks, through public consultation or even public participation on local parks management boards. Public involvement has been advocated in a variety of contexts including, at one end of the scale, small inner city community gardens (Stamp, 1987) and at the other, metropolitan parks (Grocott, 1990a, 1990b);
* extending the diversity of park environments by movement away from an emphasis upon mown swaths of grass or ornamental horticulture to a more variable parkscape that includes a range of natural and semi-natural areas too.

An example of a new park development that reflects most of these attributes is the Town Park at Telford new town in Shropshire, which has been studied by Williams (1991). This extensive project, which covers a tract of some 463 acres, has been developed from scratch since 1974 to form the principal element in a planned open space hierarchy. The site constraints (see Figure 7.5) were considerable, the area featuring extensive zones of derelict land and water space associated with mining and other heavy industries. This had been further exacerbated by dumping of constructional spoil from initial phases of the new town development. Mineshafts and land liable to subsidence were an additional hazard.

The design for the new park submitted to the Secretary of State (Telford Development Corporation, 1973) reflected both ambition in the scale of the venture and innovation in several aspects of design and although not all elements in the initial plans have been realised, the format of the finished park (Figure 7.6) shows a number of interesting ideas.

The scheme was conceived as parkland with two distinct but linked forms. In the northern zone is located the modern equivalent of the formal park. This is a high-capacity area centred on ornamental, water and play spaces, each of which enjoys a measure of physical separation though juxtaposed to permit ease of movement between the contrasting areas. Direct pedestrian access from the main shopping centre, proximity to other amenities (the main library, an ice rink and a racquet centre) and the availability of extensive free car parking ensures heavy usage, but by concentrating usage into a relatively compact space, the main tasks of park maintenance are also focused and thus rendered more cost-efficient. The floral displays, for example, are principally confined to two small themed gardens which, because of their limited extent, can be maintained to a high standard. Lakeside areas that include refreshment and toilet facilities, public information services, covered seating and illuminated walkways are also prominent features of the formal zone. The lighted walks reflect the fact that most areas of this park have 24-hour access, the main exceptions being the floral gardens and 'Wonderland', a children's theme park. Close to this formal zone is an extensive grass amphitheatre which is the location for a range of planned events and entertainments, including, in recent years, laser shows, circuses and funfairs, parachute drops and hot-air balloon ascents. Such events not only bring people into the park in large number but, as commercial activities, provide a source of revenue generation within a facility that is traditionally regarded as free from entry charges and from which it is difficult to raise significant revenue.

The main area of the park is dominated by the second form of space. There is some provision of playing fields alongside the residential land which bounds the park on its southern perimeter, but most of the central and southern section is left in a natural or semi-natural state. Disused mineral railways have been turned into walkways, lanes which pre-dated the designation of the park have been retained, along with areas of established and planted woodland and unmown grass. Water spaces such as the Randlay and Blue Pools are accorded only minimal management, the overriding approach being to let nature look after these spaces. This

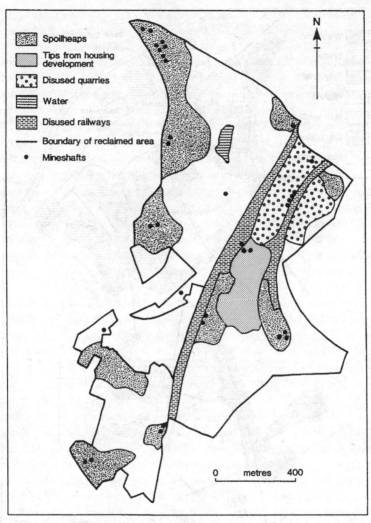

Figure 7.5 Site constraints prior to development of Telford Town Park
Source: Telford Development Corporation, 1973

may, of course, be viewed as a pragmatic response to the impossible task
of maintaining such a large area, but the resulting effect is to produce a
genuine feeling of the countryside in the heart of the new town: the area
supports a substantial wildlife population which is freely and regularly

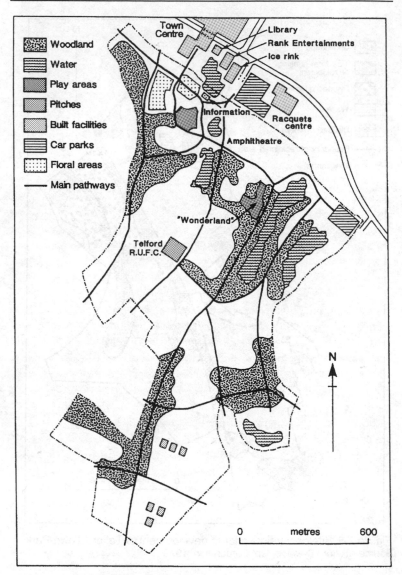

Figure 7.6 Telford Town Park, 1994

encountered in a manner that is quite untypical of the conventional town park.

The re-establishment of nature in urban areas

The success and undoubted popularity of the Telford Town Park demonstrates that a range of open spaces can be combined effectively to meet the different types of need that users will express, and that natural areas can be readily re-established in urban places, even on land that has suffered the worst forms of industrial blight.

The re-establishment of natural spaces in urban environments has become a prominent theme within urban open space planning since the end of the 1960s. At that time, conventional thinking tended to view urban nature as being rightly consigned to urban fringe areas and designated green belts or, if special circumstances prevailed, at dedicated sites. However, several related trends have prompted reappraisal and new approaches to the integration of nature into the urban fabric.

First, Harrison *et al.* (1987) argue, there has been a shift within the urban conservation movement in which the enjoyment of nature as a recreational/aesthetic experience has become more significant than conventional scientific/educational rationales for conservation. It is argued that only by comprehending the popular values that urban people place upon direct experience of nature can the decline in the appeal of traditional parks be fully appreciated and new forms of space that reflect needs be created.

Secondly, the aesthetic value of natural space, particularly woodland, has come to be more widely appreciated by planners and urban designers. Nicholson-Lord (1987) asserts that this is a partial reaction to the urban experience of the 1960s in which featureless public housing schemes and bland suburban landscapes became the vogue; he emphasises the emergence of ecology as a paradigm for the development of landscape design in the 1970s. But there is a simpler reason too, and it is that people enjoy observing natural areas and often the mere presence of woods or other forms of natural space is all that is needed to enhance the quality of individual environments. Tartaglia-Kershaw (1982) and Croke *et al.* (1986) agree that the values of such spaces are not reflected in direct usage but in a wider appreciation of intrinsic qualities of natural space, perhaps as a view from a window or a habitat from which birds and other wildlife may periodically invade the suburban garden. In Tartaglia-Kershaw's study of public response to an area of local urban woodland in Sheffield, he found that only a small fraction of residents actually used the woods, but 72 per cent valued their visual quality and 86 per cent thought the woods generally important to the quality of the area. Such hidden appreciation has often misled urban authorities to undervalue natural areas by relying too heavily upon indicators of use.

Reappraisal has been prompted, thirdly, by the realisation of the shortcomings of urban fringe and green belt locations in providing natural experiences. The notion that urban fringe locations act as an accessible form of countryside was questioned by Elson (1979) and the types of popular perception of rural space exposed in the study of Greenwich by Harrison *et al.* (1986) served to support Elson's view and reinforce the limitations of urban fringe and green belts as natural areas.

Fourthly, there was a clear opportunity to rethink open space strategies in major urban conurbations in the 1970s, arising from efforts initiated at that time to clear up urban dereliction. Some of these programmes progressed on a grand scale. Manchester, for example, reclaimed over 4,200 acres of derelict land between 1974 and 1982, on which more than 9 million trees were planted, mostly within and around the ten new country or water parks. In Liverpool, Stoke-on-Trent, Glasgow, Gateshead and Ebbw Vale, national garden festivals provided an additional catalyst for land recovery in which public open space was commonly a major beneficiary (Holden, 1989). These large-scale civic projects were complemented by a plethora of much smaller-scale reclamations, typically in areas of inner city decay, in which individual and volunteer groups opportunistically sought to reclaim small patches of wasteland and abandoned sites. Nicholson-Lord (1987) applauds these individual initiatives and the pocket parks, community and nature gardens that they created, noting how they occurred in some of the very worst areas of urban decay and how, within communities that habitually took little pride in their surroundings, these popular attempts at greening the city were highly valued by their creators. Although such voluntary projects were often only temporary, they have a significance in highlighting changing public perspectives on the desirability of nature in cities and are part of a wider growth in voluntary urban conservation that has become more firmly established, for example in urban environmental trusts such as Groundwork, which was set up in 1981 in the Greater Manchester area. Groundwork projects seek to involve public bodies, industry and local people in land restoration projects (Elson, 1986) and the success of the initial scheme is reflected in its subsequent extension to other major conurbations; for example the Black Country Groundwork Trust was formed in 1988.

Natural or semi-natural areas may be restored to cities and towns in a number of ways, both in terms of the types of space and its pattern or disposition. The value of urban woodland as a visual element has already been noted but Tregay (1979) launches a wider argument for trees in cities, stressing their diversity of roles: as a natural habitat, as a recreational resource with strong interactive capabilities (unlike a conventional park), as a structural device for physical zoning and segregation of urban land use and even, potentially, as an economically productive resource. Laurie (1979b), in contrast, advocates wider attention to urban commons which, he claims, possess unique qualities of visual diversity and contrast, both in vegetation and physical character, while supporting a wide range of casual and structured outdoor recreations. Handley (1983) argues a broader theme of increasing the biological diversity of urban land by conservation of remaining fragments of primary habitats, encouragement of natural plant succession on damaged or neglected sites and promotion of ecological diversity on a range of managed spaces, for example roadside verges, through changes in management practice. All these writers emphasise the relatively low cost of managing natural areas of this type, a factor that ought to appeal to local authorities in an era of tight control on public spending.

Implicit in most of these approaches is that natural green space should be a pervasive element in the urban fabric rather than something that is contained within designated and separate areas. To a degree, the latter is unavoidable given the history and pattern of urban development. Only perhaps in new towns is it possible to infuse woodland and other natural areas alongside housing, shops and industry in a way that was achieved, for instance, in Tapiola (Finland). But, argues Cook (1991), if natural areas are to be sustainable and make a positive contribution to the quality of urban life, they must be integrated, wherever possible, with other land uses.

This approach is reflected in the current popularity of designating green wedges or corridors of green spaces. This is not a novel approach as the inter-war development of, for example, Copenhagen (Friberg, 1979) or Abercrombie's 1944 plan for London reveal (Turner, 1991), but the concept has certainly enjoyed a recent revival. Figure 7.7 illustrates a typical example from the open space strategy for Dudley Metropolitan District in the West Midlands. Here there is a visible attempt to protect largely agricultural land at the fringes of the built-up area, while designating corridors of penetration to the heart of the urban zone. These link local parks, playing fields, woodland areas, water and open space in a concerted effort to introduce the countryside, and the amenity opportunities that such land presents, to the conurbation (Dudley Metropolitan Borough Council, 1993). Dudley's larger neighbour Birmingham likewise has a major programme for nature conservation in the city, in which designated green corridors and wedges form integral parts of the strategy by providing routeways for nature (and people) that penetrate deep into the inner city space (Birmingham City Council, 1989) as does another Midlands city, Leicester (LCC, 1989).

Green corridors may be visualised as an introduction of urban fringe land use into linear zones within the built-up area and, as such, are perhaps

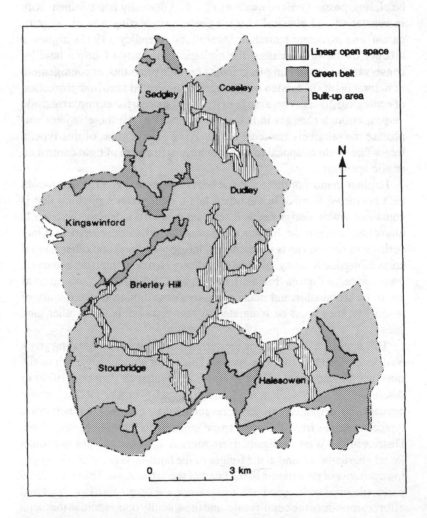

Figure 7.7 Major green areas within the Dudley Open Space Strategy
Source: Dudley Metropolitan Borough Council, 1993

indicative of changing attitudes to the relationship between town and country. For much of the post-1945 period, major cities have attempted to contain their expansion by throwing green belts around their outer fringes. In time this created pressures which, through development, saw significant reductions in public open space in the cities and development leap-frogging the green belt to more distant rural areas. Many planners remain committed to the concept of green belts (Haslam, 1990) but other observers are less convinced of their merits in an era of dispersed cities and are willing to countenance more flexible patterns in which development and green space are merged in what some have termed 'green areas' (Herington,1991). Urban green corridors may be one manifestation of this view, and more recent initiatives to develop community forests as an additional form of natural space at the edges of major urban areas may perhaps be viewed as another reflection of changing ideas in how we should view the urban shoreline.

The community forest is a joint initiative of the Forestry Commission and the Countryside Commission to create major areas of woodland on the fringes of towns and cities. Started in 1989, three 'lead' projects and nine secondary schemes have so far been designated. The concept is not to create dense expanses of forest, but rather a blend of woods, open space and productive farmland that will provide major amenity areas for casual recreation for urban residents. As is characteristic of current political thinking, the scheme is seen as being advanced largely via co-operative action on the part of landowners, with only minimal financial inducements and without significant transfers of land into public ownership. The recreational utility of such spaces, once matured, would no doubt be high, but commentators are already debating whether the voluntary character of the enterprise, the modesty of the prevailing grant structure and the complexity of land ownership patterns at the urban fringe is actually a recipe for success (Bishop, 1991). Figure 7.8 illustrates the proposals for one of the 'lead' projects, the Forest of Mercia which lies on the northern fringe of the West Midlands conurbation.

An alternative and perhaps more attainable goal is to use selective areas of reclaimed or vacated land to create woodland within city boundaries. Examples of this approach are rarer but authorities in Stoke-on-Trent, which has seen a major programme of land reclamation since the mid-1970s, have shown a commendable degree of vision in their attempts to establish Hanley Forest Park. Here reclaimed land lying immediately to the north of the city centre has been laid out with grassland, trees and water space as a planned exercise in forming a natural park at the heart of the city.

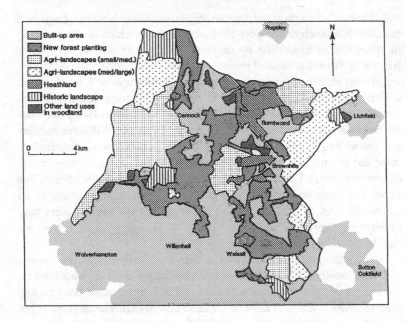

Figure 7.8 Major land use zones within the proposed Forest of Mercia
Source: Forest of Mercia, 1993

New forms of open space

Not all restored space is being devoted to natural areas, of course, and it
will be many years before the distinctive, dislocated landscape of reclamation matures and blends with other elements in the urban fabric. In the
meantime, there is an evident opportunity to use such spaces to extend
provision to cover activities that have always tended to be excluded from
parks, gardens and recreation grounds and which are incompatible with
natural areas. Noisy activities such as motor scrambling or go-karting;
uses which degrade surfaces such as mountain biking or horse riding;
adventurous forms of play – these are all potential uses of new spaces
within urban environments.

The planned response to these demands has followed a number of
courses.

1   Greenways and linear parks (often an elegant sobriquet for the course
    of former urban railways) that facilitate walking, cycling, horse riding
    and, less officially, motor scrambling are one example. (Leicester, for

instance, is developing a network of cycling routes which follow restored rail routes and other green corridors.)

2   New forms of water space created from disused gravel pits or industrial reservoirs and ponds have afforded opportunity for provision for water sports, particularly sailing, water skiing and power boating, as well as bank-side fishing, picnicking or bird watching. (Westport Lakes in Stoke-on-Trent are an example of such a land use conversion; a more prestigious example is the development of the National Water Sports Centre at Holmepierpoint, Nottingham.)

3   Activity sites, too, have taken advantage of changing patterns of land use. Skateboard and BMX cycle parks developed in number in the late 1980s, especially in inner city sites such as the Wheels Adventure Park in Birmingham. At the nearby Ackers Trust scheme, another derelict site now provides a range of facilities including a dry-ski slope, climbing wall, orienteering and trim trails, mountain bike areas and water for canoeing (Pack and Glyptis, 1989). Although such spaces are not necessarily green in a conventional sense, they serve a potentially valuable role in attracting bona fide activity that might otherwise seek to use open spaces where their presence would not be so easily accommodated or readily welcomed.

Open space provision has come a long way since the first tentative steps to form public parks at the beginning of the nineteenth century. Almost unnoticed, green areas have come to form a major urban land use but, significant though that space has become, Morphet (1990) argues that co-ordinated provision of open space remains limited – by a lack of funding, by uncertainty over its status in the planning system, by the absence of statutory protection – hence its continued vulnerability to the many forms of urban development. So despite the welcome advances in the level and diversity of provision that have been charted in this chapter, there still remains much to be done to maintain public open space in towns and cities and the opportunities for outdoor recreation that it affords.

Chapter 8

A sporting life – participation in and provision for outdoor sport

Towns and cities are ideal venues for many sporting activities, their concentrations of population ensuring the necessary thresholds to provide users for sporting facilities, local taxes to help finance their provision and people to spectate at sporting events. But there is also a more pervasive association between sport and urbanism that goes beyond simple provision and participation. Sport has been identified as a major contributor to the national economy and a significant generator of employment, much of which is concentrated in urban areas (Sports Council, 1988). At a local level, sports-related development has contributed to urban regeneration (Page, 1990) and it is routine for extensive tracts of urban land to be devoted to playing fields, sports pitches, golf courses and sports stadia. This, in turn, reflects a lengthy history of sport in urban places and the central role that sport plays within popular urban culture and many individual lifestyles. Karp and Yoels (1990) have shown how sporting participation is an important mechanism through which individuality may be projected in an otherwise impersonal and anonymous urban world. For disadvantaged groups, in particular, sport is widely perceived as one route to social mobility and within communities it may help to instil a sense of belonging and a common identity. Such an identity is further advanced by the professional teams that concentrate in urban places and which afford not just a focus for collective popular support but also become ambassadors for their town or city in both the national and, increasingly, the international community. A team photograph of, say, Manchester United AFC is almost as likely to adorn a bar in Hong Kong or Adelaide as one in Manchester itself. The links between sport and the urban environment are both extensive and well forged.

This chapter explores the place of sport in cities through a consideration of patterns of participation, the changing balance between indoor and outdoor activity and the role of providers in meeting the diverse demands that sporting participation can create. It must be acknowledged, though, that the study of sport in urban places is constrained by several factors, some of which are general in their application, others specific to the case of Britain. There is, for example, a definitional problem of what actually constitutes sport. Sport may be construed as a sub-set of recreation inasmuch as participation normally makes use of uncommitted periods of time, and activity reflects at least a degree of free choice on the part of the participant. It may also be helpful if sport is recognised as active recreation, typically involving physical effort and acquired skills and normally codified and competitive in nature.

However, not all would agree with definitions which place the emphasis upon physical effort within a competitive, rule-bound context. The Centre for Leisure Research (CLR)(1991:2), for example, is happy to talk of sport as being no more than 'recreational activities that require a measure of physical effort and skill'. Such a definition is perhaps rather too slack since it could cover a whole range of activities in which participants exercise skills and work up a good sweat in the process, but which are difficult to visualise as sports in the conventional sense. These could include, for example, gardening, certain types of DIY, or even walking, the latter being an activity which both the Centre for Leisure Research and the General Household Survey are willing to admit as a 'sport'. But what these uncertainties do highlight is that in discussing sport, it is helpful to distinguish between the 'pure sports' which conform to the more restrictive definitional criteria given above, and the 'recreational sports' in which exercise and skills may be apparent, but which do not necessarily have the competition and codification of the 'pure sports'. This permits two useful extensions to the discussion; first to include, where appropriate, traditional sporting activities (such as shooting and fishing) and modern outdoor pursuits (such as canoeing or sailing). Secondly, it permits recognition that individual sports themselves may be enjoyed in either a 'pure' or a 'recreational' fashion and that the context will vary according to individual taste and to the occasion. Different people will engage in sports in a variable manner, and in some circumstances participants will place little or no emphasis upon exercise or competition elements that may be a normal part of the game. Badminton, for example, may have rules, a scoring system and all the accoutrements of a 'pure' sport, but not everyone attending the local sports centre to play will enjoy the game in this way. Similarly, activities such as swimming or cycling, which can be undertaken in a competitive, sporting fashion, will more normally witness purely recreational participation. Likewise, a round of golf may on one occasion be played competitively, but on another might be a gentle means of relaxation and enjoyment of fresh air. The definition of sport owes as much to the context in which the activity is conducted as it does to its intrinsic qualities.

In Britain, there is an additional problem relating to the quality of official statistics on sporting participation. The plethora of individual agencies that govern sport in Britain, and their often idiosyncratic methods of enumerating participants, means that many scholars and practitioners rely upon the General Household Survey (GHS) for indicative measurement of sporting participation. However, the GHS suffers from three major shortcomings. The first is that its enumeration of recreation includes incidence of activity which is not always recreational in character. This occurs in the case of both walking and cycling, where journeys for other than recreational purposes (for example to work) are included as engagement with the activity. Secondly, alterations in the manner in which the survey work is conducted mean that figures after 1987 are not directly comparable with those gathered before that date. It therefore becomes impossible to construct accurate time-series to illustrate how sporting participation has changed through time, both in aggregate terms and in relation to individual sports. Finally, the survey does not distinguish where sporting participation takes place so that although we might assume a measure of concentration upon urban environments, the precise nature of the balance between urban and rural sport remains unclear.

The net effect of these uncertainties and ambiguities, together with the deficiencies in official data, is probably to over-estimate the incidence of pure sporting participation in urban communities at large. The CLR (1991:3), taking its cue from the 1987 GHS, asserts quite boldly that in 1987, 61 per cent of the adult population participated in at least one sporting activity, a figure that had apparently risen to 65 per cent in 1990 (OPCS, 1992). This is misleading, since not only are these figures based upon the most generous of definitions of what constitutes sport, but they also include journeys made on foot or on a bicycle that may have nothing to do with recreation, and may have been undertaken out of necessity rather than choice. Williams and Jackson (1986) in a survey of sporting habits amongst some 450 adults in Stoke-on-Trent found that only around 26 per cent participated in what are here termed as the 'pure sports', although a higher proportion took physical exercise as recreational swimmers, cyclists, joggers and keep-fit enthusiasts. This is not to say that sport is unimportant in urban areas since, as the introduction to this chapter has already suggested, it is prominent in contemporary urban life. However its participatory significance should not be inflated in the way that some statistics permit.

THE LEGACY OF THE PAST AND CONTEMPORARY THEMES

Sport in urban society has a very lengthy history and although many modern sports can trace their formal organisation to nineteenth-century Britain, contemporary patterns should be considered as being derived from a combination of Victorian innovation and much more deep-seated traditions in sports and games.

Sports history is a specialised field and a detailed précis is out of place in this current work. Readers who would like to know more are encouraged, as a starting point, to look at the work of Holt (1989) who provides a very thorough analysis of the social context for development of sport in Britain. Mason (1989) affords a similar perspective, with a more structured focus on individual sports. In brief, an outline summary of the early developmental process would need to recognise the following:

1 The nineteenth century was a period in which sport underwent a remarkable social transformation. Decline in the public acceptability of many older popular sports, especially those which tended towards rowdyness (e.g. street football), or those which inflicted suffering on animals (e.g. cock-fighting), was paralleled by a cultural shift in which the urban middle classes became appreciative of the benefits of sporting participation, particularly the capacity for enhancement of physical and mental health, endurance, courage, discipline and teamwork. The self-evident virtues of these attributes led to a vigorous uptake of sport in public schools and universities and sporting prowess often became a better guarantee of social advancement than intellectual achievement.

2 As sports became socially acceptable, formal codification and organisation became widespread. It is no accident that most of the ruling bodies in modern sport can trace their foundation to the middle years of the nineteenth century and they reflect, to the present, the pattern of middle- and upper middle-class governance that was established at that time.

3 Participation in sport was encouraged only selectively. Whilst public schools and universities facilitated sport, ordinary elementary schools stuck to traditional practices of military-style drill to inculcate discipline and exercise young bodies. Women, too, were discouraged from participation. Lenskyj (1986) describes how the medical profession argued the dangers to female physiology of exercise patterns associated with sport, clergy advanced theological reasons why women should not play games, and politicians, businessmen and civic leaders

agreed that sport in general was, as Park (1987) describes it, the 'natural' province of the male. Men feared displacement in the social order and that they would suffer a loss of identity if women were permitted access to activities which were seen as the male preserve (Mrozek, 1987).

4 Exclusion of social and gender groups from middle-class, male sport led inexorably to the creation of distinctive and separate sporting traditions within the urban working classes and amongst women. Fletcher (1987) and McCrone (1987) both show how, by the turn of the twentieth century, a separate tradition in sport for middle-class women had developed in female public schools (based upon team games and gymnastics) and this extended later to suburban tennis and golf clubs. In working-class areas, especially in the urban-industrial north of England, a strong, largely male popular culture also had evolved, with sport at its very heart, reinforced by the continuance of traditional activities but supplemented by newly popular mass events, particularly spectating at association and rugby football matches (Holt, 1989).

These historic processes are important because they created a legacy that still exists today. Thus, at the general level, modern urban society has acquired a preoccupation with sport and it has become central to popular culture, especially amongst men. Estimated annual expenditures within the ten sports with the highest levels of spending came to over £1,000 million in 1990 (Mintel, 1991b), while media coverage of sport on British terrestrial television in 1989 amounted to over 1,600 hours (Research Services Ltd, 1989). Although this accounted for less than 10 per cent of total broadcasting time, sports coverage figures prominently within programming of core viewing hours, and during premier events can dominate transmissions in a manner which applies to virtually no other area of coverage.

There are more specific effects too. First, the association between sport and education remains significant. Most people are introduced to sport through schools and colleges and departure from education is often linked with significant falls in sporting participation. Secondly, the parallel sporting traditions of the middle and working classes are still very apparent. In England, for example, the middle-class image of rugby union contrasts strikingly with the hard, working-class persona of rugby league; tennis and golf retain much of their exclusivity, whilst the champions in the world of snooker or darts originate, very obviously, in a different social background. Social divides, thirdly, may also generate spatial divides.

Attachment to some sports occasionally had a pronounced spatial focus –
the strength of rugby league in Lancashire and Yorkshire, of rugby union
in south Wales, or of soccer and cricket in the large industrial conurbations
– and although subsequent development in sport has blurred some of these
geographical divides, many remain discernible and of local importance.
Finally, despite the social advances towards the emancipation of women,
there are still marked imbalances between the sexes in their interest and
participation in sport.

PATTERNS OF PARTICIPATION IN SPORT

The post-1945 period has seen significant increases in participation in
sport, especially if one deploys a broad definition of activity to include
the popular outdoor pursuits and informal physical recreations. The GHS
estimated in 1983 that, excluding walking, some 44 per cent of the British
population engaged in at least one sport or physical recreation (CLR,
1991). The 1990 survey, whilst not precisely comparable, suggests that
the figure had risen to 48 per cent (OPCS, 1992). Data deficiencies
prohibit a longer perspective on change but in West Germany, for example, Brettschneider (1992) reports how sporting participation amongst
15–24-year-olds increased from 47 per cent of the group in 1954 to 72 per
cent in 1984 and how the range of activities in which these young Germans
engaged more than doubled over the same period through uptake of new
or imported sports.

Explanations for the increased attraction of sport lie in several areas.
First, there has been a conscious and concerted effort to promote sport in
society, the Sports Council (which was formally incorporated in 1972)
being prominent in direct advocation of sport and its benefits. 'Sport for
All' campaigns and low-interest groups – older people, housewives,
ethnic minorities and disabled people – have been accorded particular
attention, notably during the 1980s.

Part of this drive reflected a belief in the intrinsic value of sport for
sport's sake, but a wider public awareness of the benefits of health-related
fitness has been a significant factor too. This is mirrored most visibly in
the growth in popularity of jogging as an aid to fitness but also has much
to do with the revival of cycling as a recreational activity and the attraction
of other 'lifetime' activities such as swimming and golf.

Public interest in sport and exercise has prompted further provision.
All three sectors, the public, private and voluntary, have contributed to the
expansion of the resource base for urban sport, but the role of local
authorities has been central. Capital investment in new provision by local

government averaged more than £100 million annually throughout the 1980s (Audit Commission, 1989). Estimated local authority expenditure on leisure in 1992–93 stood at £1,781 million, of which some £601 million was expended on outdoor provision for sport (including golf courses), urban parks and open space. It should be conceded that the major share of this sum (£538 million) went to parks and urban open spaces, although many of these do provide for outdoor sport as well as passive recreations (CIPFA, 1992). Investment in new sports and leisure centres has seen their numbers in England and Wales rise from just a couple of dozen in 1970 to over 1,200 at the start of the 1990s (CLR, 1991).

The media have played a significant role. The level of exposure of sport on television has already been noted and this, together with radio and newspaper coverage, ensures that sport is given prominence, whether it is welcomed or not. Media exposure serves several purposes. It affords demonstrations of sports and, in so doing, encourages new participation by placing particular sports in the spotlight. The dramatic growth in popularity of snooker, for example, was almost entirely driven by television coverage, a fact that is illustrated by the manner in which interest declined in the early 1990s, as television coverage of the sport reduced from its peak levels in the mid-1980s. American football was unknown in the UK prior to the commencement of television coverage on Channel 4 in 1982. By 1988, however, nearly 200 senior teams and over 15,000 registered players were active in the sport (Little, 1990; Maguire, 1990, 1991). As a second effect, through their handling of sporting heroes the media create and sustain role models, especially for the young. The gradual socialisation of women into sport which occurred in the inter-war years owed much to the influential effect and media coverage of several prominent sporting women, especially in North America (Lenskyj, 1986).

So, what are the popular contemporary sports and physical recreations? Table 8.1 sets out a listing derived from the 1990 GHS, subdivided according to the likelihood of activity being indoor or outdoor. The data suggest several tentative conclusions concerning the significance of sports in general and the relative attractiveness of indoor and outdoor environments. For example, although the range of outdoor activities is more extensive, the indoor pursuits tend to attract higher levels of interest, particularly when measured over a 12-month period. If the problematic areas of walking and cycling are temporarily withdrawn from the list of outdoor events, together with outdoor swimming, which is usually a holiday activity rather than an element of routine engagement, then the most widely practised outdoor sport is golf, which some 12 per cent of adults stated they had played in the previous year. In comparison, indoor swimming, snooker, pool and billiards, keep fit and aerobics and darts were all ahead of this level and ten-pin bowling only marginally behind. Similarly, more people played badminton than the national outdoor team game, soccer, and, although often advanced as one of the most popular outdoor sports in the UK (Lowerson, 1989), angling appears to be no more attractive than middle-ranking indoor sports such as squash or table tennis.

Table 8.1 Percentage of adults over 16 years participating at least once in named sports (a) in the 4 weeks or (b) in the 12 months prior to survey, 1990

	Outdoors			Indoors	
	a	b		a	b
Walking	40.7	65.3	Cue sports	13.6	21.7
Cycling	9.3	17.0	Swimming	12.2	35.6
Golf	5.0	12.2	Keep fit	11.6	18.8
Jogging	5.0	9.5	Darts	7.1	13.1
Swimming	3.9	21.8	Weight lifting	4.8	9.1
Soccer	3.8	7.3	Ten-pin bowling	3.8	11.4
Tennis	2.0	7.4	Badminton	3.3	8.5
Fishing	2.0	6.1	Squash	2.5	6.2
Bowls	1.2	3.8	Table tennis	2.0	5.4
Water sport	1.2	5.0	Soccer	1.8	4.4
Cricket	1.1	3.8	Bowls	1.1	2.9
Horse riding	1.0	3.1	Ice skating	0.7	3.6
Sailing	0.8	2.8	Basketball	0.6	1.7
Hockey	0.6	1.6	Netball	0.4	1.4
Athletics	0.5	1.7	Gymnastics	0.2	0.5
Rugby	0.5	1.1			
Motor sport	0.4	1.2			
Skiing	0.4	3.0			

Source: OPCS (1992)

The second feature is that although the 1990 GHS found that 48 per cent of adults had done at least one of these sports (excluding walking) during the survey periods, at the level of the individual sport, interest is embodied in an often comparatively small minority. This is most apparent in those traditional sports on which the sporting interest of the nation so often focuses – soccer, tennis, cricket, athletics and rugby – all of which show participation percentages in single figures, although it should be noted that the 3.8 per cent who play cricket, for example, translate into some 1.7 million participants. Only golf appears to command a healthy level in percentage terms of both interest and participation. In contrast, 'recreational sports' where the emphasis falls upon activity rather than competition appear much more attractive.

Although sport in general has seen increased interest, the growth has not been consistent across all areas of sporting participation. Some activities have grown spectacularly, others have displayed a relative decline in fortunes. Accurate charting of the shifts in individual sports is difficult, held hostage to the uncertainties of sample surveys and the varying fashion in which data are derived. However, Table 8.2 sets out change in participation in 29 common sports, as reflected in the two most recent GHS which have included questioning on this area of activity (1987 and 1990).

The data show a simple net change and by placement of sports in rank order according to change, and by the further addition of (admittedly arbitrary) dividing lines, the listing may be subdivided into varying categories of apparent growth, stability or relative decline. The list is also annotated according to whether the sport is an indoor or outdoor pursuit, or one which may be enjoyed in either environment. Several points are worthy of emphasis.

First, the attraction of lifetime sports is readily evident. Of the eight sports or activities appearing at the head of the listing, only hockey and perhaps ten-pin bowling lie outside the normal realms of the lifetime activities. Secondly, the emphasis within the areas of present growth is very clearly upon individual as opposed to team-based pursuits. Only hockey reveals evidence of expanding interest, whilst basketball, rugby and netball show a static position and soccer and cricket even suggest some relative decline in popularity, although not necessarily an absolute decline. Thirdly, there is some evidence of a small shift towards the outdoor sports, though not to conventional team games. Nineteen sports in the list show a positive shift in their share of participants and of these, only five are normally conducted indoors, although as Table 8.1 reveals, most swimming is done at indoor pools too. Amongst the ten activities showing a negative shift, six are conventionally indoor sports.

So far the discussion has focused upon participation, but it should not be forgotten that for many people the interest in sport lies in spectating. The business of spectating at outdoor sport has enjoyed mixed fortunes, although the overall effect has been one of decline in numbers paying to attend a sporting fixture. Table 8.3 sets out some sample figures for attendance at five traditionally popular spectator sports and reveals that whilst the smaller spectator sports of horse racing and rugby have apparently become more popular, major spectator sports such as greyhound

Table 8.2 Recent growth and decline in popular sports, 1987–90

Activity	Net change (%)	Indoor/outdoor	Growth category
Swimming	7.8	I	
Ten-pin bowling	5.7	I	
Walking	5.2	O	
Keep fit	4.5	I	Pronounced
Golf	3.0	O	growth
Cycling	2.2	O	
Bowls	1.6	Both	
Hockey	1.3	O	
Weight training	0.9	I	
Tennis	0.8	O	
Horse riding	0.5	O	Modest
Badminton	0.3	I	growth
Water sports	0.3	O	
Sailing	0.3	O	
Fishing	0.3	O	
Motor sports	0.1	O	
Basketball	0.1	I	
Rugby	0.0	O	Essentially
Netball	0.0	I	static
Ice skating	−0.1	I	
Gymnastics	−0.1	I	
Athletics	−0.3	O	
Soccer	−0.4	O	Modest
Cricket	−0.4	O	decline
Squash	−0.5	I	
Table tennis	−0.9	I	
Jogging	−1.0	O	Pronounced
Cue sports	−1.2	I	decline
Darts	−2.3	I	

Source: OPCS (1989, 1992)

racing and, especially, soccer have become significantly less so. Explanations for such trends are a little elusive. Amongst the bodies that control football it has been fashionable to lay blame at the door of television coverage, but since the other named sports (with the exception of greyhound racing) receive extensive television coverage too, the validity of that particular line of reasoning is suspect. The expense of admissions, the modest achievements of national teams and the unattractive association

Table 8.3 Changes in levels of spectating at major sports, 1972–91

Sport	Spectators (000s) 1971–72	Spectators (000s) 1990–91	Net change (%)
Football (England and Wales)	28,700	18,828	−34.4
Football (Scotland)	4,521	3,377	−25.3
Greyhound racing	8,800	5,121	−141.8
Horse racing	4,200	4,698	+11.9
Rugby union (England)	700	1,250	+78.5
Rugby league	1,170	1,539	+31.5

Source: Central Statistical Office (1992)

of football with crime and hooliganism are other factors which might account for the loss of spectators at the national game.

Spectating might be expected to have a broad base of appeal (depending upon the sport), but actual participation is more selective. Normally, explanation for the conspicuous variations in sporting participation within communities is made with reference to a range of demographic and socio-economic variables, including age and gender, position in the life cycle, educational and employment history and social class. Glyptis (1992:526) summarises the conventional wisdom succinctly in noting that those most likely to take part in sport are male, young, white, car owners and in white-collar occupations, whilst non-participants are characteristically women, older people, ethnic minorities, non-car owners and in blue-collar occupations.

Since most sporting activities make certain demands upon the physical fitness and abilities of participants, it is not surprising that there should be associations between sporting participation and youth. When data are cast in terms of the proportion of an age group that participates in sport, it is always the young who exhibit the highest levels of involvement, and within the urban community at large, the proportion of participants declines fairly persistently thereafter. In 1990, 82 per cent of people aged between 16 and 19 engaged in at least one sporting activity but for those over 70 years the comparable figure was just 12 per cent (OPCS, 1992).

However, the release of time associated with later middle age and retirement can sometimes bring about a small up-turn in interest amongst older groups.

It is a little misleading to form a simple association between youth and sporting participation since, in practice, there are more participants over the age of 30 than below it. This is a consequence of the age distribution of the urban population: although the proportion of participants amongst people between 15 and 24 years is high, this group accounts for only around 14 per cent of the population. They are outnumbered in absolute terms by older people who, although participating at a lower per capita rate, are drawn from a larger population base. Roberts *et al.* (1991:263) also make the critical observation that it is a 'mistake to infer from the well-known decline in participation with age that this is an across-the-board disengagement and weakening of sports interest'. They continue that 'it is more accurate to talk of a progressive polarisation between an active minority of diminishing size but whose mean loyalty to sport actually increases . . . and . . . a growing number of adults whose separation from all sport grows longer and longer'. The older player may be every bit as committed to his or her sport as their young counterparts, perhaps even more so if increased age has also been associated with more free time and the resources to make use of it. The individual sports may differ, the young participant being more typically associated with vigorous team sports for example, but the attachment to sport in general may be no less strong. Kay (1991), in his study of the urban population of Broxtowe, Nottinghamshire, found that the proportion of respondents who expressed positive perceptions of outdoor sports and recreations actually increased in mid-life and that people in the 16 to 19 year group were unique (in that study) in expressing a significant aversion to these activities.

Once sport is discarded as an area of leisure activity, it is unlikely to be resumed later in life (Roberts *et al.*, 1991). Continuance of participation is therefore central to developing a wider base of participation within the urban community at large. It is for this reason that a recent observable decline in youthful interest in sport has raised concerns (Sports Council, 1988; Sleap and Walker, 1992): if young people relinquish sporting participation, the evidence suggests that most will not be encouraged back. The desertion of sport by young people has been particularly pronounced in the case of outdoor activity. Figure 8.1 shows the changes in participation between 1983 and 1988 for both indoor and outdoor activity and according to gender. The figure shows first how it is the 13–24 age group, almost in isolation, that is displaying a loss of interest overall and that where interest continues and is flourishing, it is in indoor pursuits. This is especially striking amongst young women. Explanation for this decline in interest may lie in a number of areas but is likely to be associated with the shift towards individual participation and away from the conventional team games that tends to dominate outdoor sport; the erosion of sport at school, especially as an extra-curricular activity; the fact that many children have unsatisfactory or unpleasant experiences of sport in schools; the seductive appeal of other facets of youth culture; and the fact that, amongst girls in particular, sport and physical education readily appear to be at odds with images and expectations of femininity (Sleap and Walker, 1992). There are substantial peer group pressures to which many succumb. Sport may remain a feature of young urban lifestyles, especially in the use of sporting goods as fashionable leisurewear, but it seems that fewer young people are keen to be active and to retain involvement in sport on leaving education. (Analysis of trends from 1987 to 1990 – Sports Council, 1993 – suggests that all age groups have increased their participation, but the generous definition of 'sport' in this case should sound a note of caution in any interpretation.)

In contrast to the uncertainty surrounding youthful interest in sport, Figure 8.1 shows that amongst older people, active interest in sport is on the increase, although in outdoor activity, growth is more pronounced amongst men than women. The increased popularity of personal fitness activity such as jogging and cycling and lifetime sports such as fishing, bowls and golf (which appeal disproportionately to men), will partly explain this pattern, whilst increased incidence of early retirement will have a positive influence in liberating time to pursue sports.

Alongside age, gender is a primary discriminating factor in determining sporting participation. The GHS documents that 73 per cent of men partake in at least one sporting activity (including walking), while for women the equivalent figure is 57 per cent (OPCS, 1992). Furthermore, not only do fewer women than men play sport, but amongst those women that do, the tendency is to possess fewer sports in their repertoire, to engage in activity on a less regular basis and to play for shorter time periods (Boothby *et al.*, 1981; Roberts *et al.*, 1991; Williams and Jackson, 1986). However, the GHS suggests that actual sporting interests do not differ as greatly between the sexes as might be anticipated. Although the list of popular male sports includes soccer and the women's list gives prominence to keep fit, the other most popular activities are common to both, being walking, swimming, cue sports, cycling and darts (OPCS, 1992).

Much has been written in explanation of the lower profile of women in sport (see for example Deem, 1986; Talbot, 1988). As discussed earlier, there is an historic legacy which has fostered and perpetuated an image of

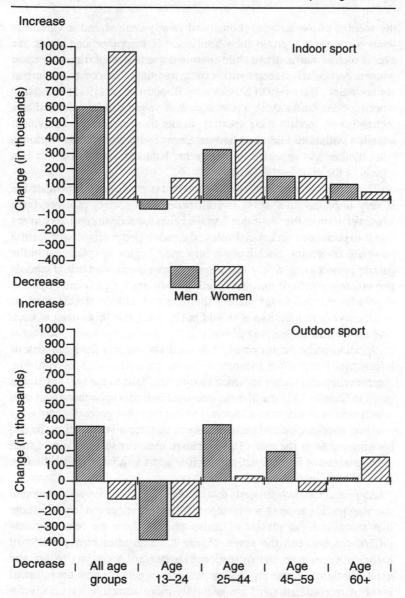

Figure 8.1 Changes in participation in indoor and outdoor sport
according to age and gender, 1983–88
Source: Sports Council, 1988

the woman's role as being home and family-centred and a view that women comprise a group for whom sport is inappropriate. Major life events such as marriage and child-rearing impact disproportionately upon women, particularly it seems within more traditional, working-class urban communities. The study of Stockton by Boothby *et al.* (1981) noted that working-class husbands in a marriage with young children showed less inclination to modify their sporting habits than men in an equivalent situation within middle-class homes. Conversely, though, the working-class mother was expected to change her habits in a way that was less typical of the middle-class wife.

The process of socialisation into sport that is implicit in this perspective is very important in shaping overall patterns. If society projects, from whatever source, the view that certain behaviours compromise conventional expectations and social roles, then such perspectives will form a powerful constraint. Socialisation into sport begins in childhood but if parents project a negative image of sport or are uninterested in it, if schools perpetuate separate or unequal sporting traditions for girls and boys and if popular cultural forms present the lean and athletic female form as unattractive or unfeminine, it should not be a surprise that young women take up sport in a selective fashion.

Sporting participation amongst women also suffers from the lack of leisure time that is often a feature of contemporary female lifestyles. The disproportionate manner in which leisure time falls to the two sexes was noted in Chapter 2 but it will make a particular impact upon those activities which require blocks of time. Sport is of that type: it is generally necessary to travel to a facility and perhaps also to stay for a set duration, be it a booking period or the span of an organised match or session. Where time is fragmented or limited, activity such as sport will be amongst the first areas of participation to suffer.

Empirical research suggests that the divergence of men and women in sporting participation is narrowing and there is further evidence to show that amongst older groups of active players there are relatively few differences between the sexes. Figure 8.2 illustrates how patterns of participation in pure and recreational sports vary according to age and gender within a sample city region. Readers might note how the informal areas of recreational sport are generally more attractive, especially for young women, and that activities such as aerobics are currently very popular. But it should also be observed how the lines on the graph converge in the older age categories, no doubt reflecting the way in which, as Roberts *et al.* (1991) have suggested, sporting participation becomes focused upon a core of keen participants who may be of either gender. The

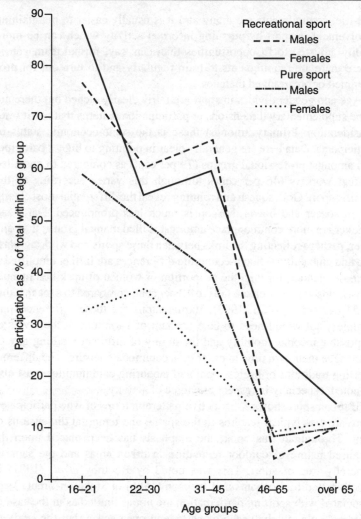

Figure 8.2 Participation in 'recreational' and 'pure' sports according to age and gender, Stoke-on-Trent
Source: Williams and Jackson, 1986

up-turn in mid-life of participation in recreational sports is interesting and may perhaps be explained as a result of a transference of activity from the more demanding regimes of the pure sports to the more flexible and accommodating domain of recreational sport. For people of both sexes in mid-life, commitments are many and it is usually easier to maintain an involvement in sport by pursuing informal activity which can be more readily adjusted to fit opportunities than can, say, formal team games where there are requirements to train regularly and to turn out for programmed or prearranged matches.

Age and gender divides in sport are fairly clearly etched but there are some supplementary dimensions to participation patterns that merit brief consideration. Primary amongst these is the socio-economic status of participants. Data here are generally clear in pointing to higher participation amongst professional groups (79 per cent) as compared to unskilled manual workers (46 per cent), although this varies according to the specific sport. Golf, squash and running reveal the differential most clearly but in soccer and bowls the gap is much less pronounced. Darts and snooker are more commonplace amongst skilled manual groups than any other, perhaps reflecting the links between these sports and working-class pub and club culture. Socio-economic differences are further amplified if linked to gender, for then the proportion of women of unskilled manual households who participate falls to 40 per cent, compared to a mean value of 57 per cent (OPCS, 1992). Explanations for these differences are complex, but would need to take account of variations in the levels of disposable income, mobility and the ability of different working groups to manage their own time in order to accommodate leisure. The different sporting traditions of professional and labouring communities must also be noted, especially in respect of choice of activity.

If urban sport shows a distinctive pattern in terms of who participates, there are also typical features to the spatial and temporal dimensions of play. Throughout this book, the emphasis has been placed upon the localised nature of outdoor recreation in urban areas and the same is generally true of sport. This was noted by Boothby et al. (1981) in Stockton and by Williams and Jackson (1986) in Stoke-on-Trent. Trips associated with sporting participation are not as limited as in the case of children's play or the usage of parks and open space, but the study of Stoke-on-Trent, for example, established that 58 per cent of sport-related journeys were of less than two miles and 88 per cent of events took place within five miles of respondents' homes. Generally speaking, the longer journeys were associated with trips to use more specialised facilities (such as golf courses) or in places where there was a degree of local under-provision, but where pitches, greens or courts were freely available, journeys to play were characteristically short.

Frequency and timing of participation reveal fairly clear patterns too. Figure 8.3 shows participation frequencies for 'pure' and 'recreational'

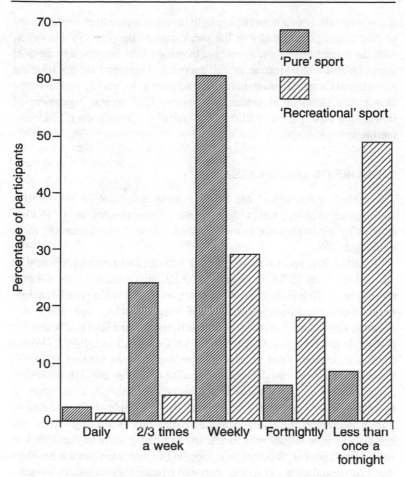

Figure 8.3 Frequency of participation in 'recreational' and 'pure' sports,
Stoke-on-Trent
Source: Williams and Jackson, 1986

sports in Stoke and reflects, quite distinctly, the types of regular commitment that formalised sports such as soccer, rugby or cricket tend to bring
forth. In contrast, the recreational participants in this survey performed
less frequently, reflecting the different personal circumstances in which
such participation often occurs. There is, of course, a seasonality to many
sports but within the confines of the season, particular times are especially
important. Weekends are widely used for winter games such as soccer and

rugby while the longer hours of daylight in summer permit more flexibility so that evenings, especially in the week, come into play too. However, with the exception of Sunday mornings, which have become a traditional time of play for local league soccer, mornings in general are not sporting periods and the pattern elsewhere is for activity to be heavily concentrated into a small number of preferred sessions. This creates a problem of shortage at peak periods and direct physical pressure upon pitches and facilities.

INDOORS OR OUTDOORS?

The preceding discussion has made passing comment on the relative significance of indoor and outdoor sporting environments, but this theme is of sufficient importance to merit a brief, but separate discussion, in its own right.

Traditionally, sport was an outdoor activity and up to as recently as perhaps the early 1970s, most activity in Britain continued to be pursued out of doors. That pattern has been changed by the widespread development of urban multi-purpose sports and leisure centres. From a low base of around 30 indoor centres in 1972, the figure for England and Wales has risen to in excess of 1,600 in 1991 (Sports Council, 1982, 1993). Growth on this scale cannot fail to have had an impact upon outdoor sport and although data to provide detailed and precise measurement of the changing balance is once again elusive and sometimes outwardly contradictory, there are several indicators of trends. These include the popularity of indoor swimming, the emergence of activities such as aerobics and ten-pin bowling as new indoor attractions, the marked growth in the 1980s of squash and snooker, the continuing appeal of badminton and the development and popularising of indoor versions of established outdoor games – soccer, hockey and bowls, for example. These all reflect the attraction of the indoor game, whilst apparent stagnation or decline in participation in outdoor team games is perhaps indicative of shifts within outdoor activity, where less formalised pursuits such as jogging and cycling have become more popular. Although earlier it was noted that for some participant groups, recent short-term trends might be interpreted as favouring outdoor activity, a longer-term perspective tends to provide a different view.

The attraction of indoor sport is readily appreciated. The modern leisure centre affords several direct advantages. First it is a controlled environment in which the participant is protected from the vagaries of weather and can play under conditions of physical comfort and on surfaces that are normally reliable and consistent. Secondly, the indoor centre provides opportunity for experiencing a range of sports in the same visit and within the same building. Users may elect, for example, to take an aerobics class, enjoy a swim and then adjourn to the bar for a drink and a game of pool, and such diversity of opportunity permits participants to optimise the use of their leisure time in a way that is not so easy when outdoor provision is being used. Thirdly, it may be argued that the indoor centre is often a more sociable context in which to pursue sport. The physical comfort that the players enjoy also extends to spectators and thus encourages formation of social groups that include non-participants. The bars and restaurants that are often integral to the sporting facilities allow for extension of socialisation around the sporting event. Many leisure centres also enhance their social dimension by periodic leasing of their undedicated space to non-sporting activities – dances, parties, exhibitions and displays, for example. Flexible management in this way helps to reinforce the place of leisure centres within both the context of urban recreation and the wider social life of the community.

PROVIDING FOR URBAN SPORT

In considering provision for sport, it is important to appreciate that the ability of providers to respond to definable needs in a co-ordinated fashion is partly constrained by the diverse range of organisations that oversee or manage different facilities or sports. Elvin (1990) has charted the organisational context for sport in which central and local government, the Sports Council, independent voluntary bodies (such as the Central Council for Physical Recreation and the National Playing Fields Association: NPFA), the many governing bodies of sport and the commercial sector are required to interact. Amongst the various areas of provision for recreation in urban areas, sport is probably unique in the degree to which it involves all three sectors of provision, but it is a distinction that is not especially welcome because of the complexities it creates and because of the loose nature of the linkages between the different agencies. For example the Sports Council, which strives to be influential in setting an agenda for sporting development, has direct influence over neither central government in the matter of finance provision for sport, nor the major providers of outdoor facilities (particularly the local authorities) who are not bound, nor even necessarily guided, by the targets that the Council sets for new provision or the encouragement of participation. Local authorities receive separate direction on priorities for development in the form of planning policy guidance, and in practice the PPGs (and, indeed, the views of locally elected council members) are more often influential on the character and extent of local provision for sport than are Sports Council strategies. The private and voluntary sectors, except where they are subject to certain legal requirements (for example planning permissions for physical development), are essentially autonomous.

Local authorities have suffered some criticism over their performance as providers of sporting opportunity. The Minister for Sport's Review Group (1990), in appraising the specific context of Britain's inner cities, found that many authorities lacked accurate and comprehensive data on sporting needs and the performance of existing provision, and so had only a limited basis on which to develop future strategy. Furthermore, the group noted a tendency to invest in provision without always engaging in proper consultation with intended users, with attendant risks of resources being wasted on unwanted facilities.

The patterns of participation that have been outlined are sufficiently clear, however, to guide policy on provision in several distinct directions. The attraction of indoor play may be expected to be reflected in continuing development of such opportunity, while in the outdoor sector, the appeal of golf, running, cycling, walking and, less widely, traditional team games such as soccer, points to the types of facilities which should be receiving attention from providers: new courses, pitches to support popular team games and routes suited to jogging, cycling or walking. Most of these needs have been reflected in the most recent statements of objectives by the Sports Council (Tables 8.4 and 8.5). The provision of routeways for activity such as walking and cycling has already been outlined in chapter

Table 8.4 Summary of Sports Council policies for the increase in mass participation between 1988 and 1993

- Increase participation by young people and women.
- Increase provision of indoor dry sports facilities by an additional 500 halls, particularly in inner cities, urban resorts and rural areas.
- Further the development of dual-use provision, especially at schools.
- Increase provision of indoor swimming pools by 150.
- Improve the quality of existing stocks of outdoor sports pitches.
- Identify where new artificial surfaces can help enhance sporting experience.
- Encourage development of linear and circular routes for jogging and cycling.

Source: Sports Council (1988)

Table 8.5 Summary of Sports Council strategies for the period between 1993 and 1997

- Continue advocacy of the principles of 'Sport for All'.
- Emphasise education and training as a means of introducing people to sport and nurturing their development.
- Improve the co-ordination between education and sport.
- Continue the provision of quality facilities.
- Improve levels of awareness and information.
- Consider increased selectivity in resource allocation and identification and support for sporting talent.
- Emphasise the supporting role of sports science and sports medicine.

Source: Sports Council (1993)

five. Here we will examine current approaches to playing field and golf course provision.

Playing fields and pitches

These form the basis of much of the outdoor sporting activity that takes place in urban areas and their provision and maintenance should be central to any strategy for sporting provision. This significance is signalled in the production in 1991 of a strategy for playing pitches (Sports Council, 1991), and similar concerns have been expressed in a number of regional and local strategies too (see, for example, London Council for Sport and Recreation, 1987). These reports echo common sentiments in noting shortages caused by the loss of public playing fields and company sports grounds to urban development and as a result of school closures, a geographical drift in provision towards peripheral urban areas and the problems of maintaining grass pitches in a state that can withstand pressures of use from large numbers of players.

However, although the problem is readily defined, effective solutions are made elusive by several practical difficulties. First, playing fields are by definition extensive and where space is in short supply, as is often the case within developed urban land, finding sufficient room to accommodate sports such as cricket, soccer and rugby can be problematic. This accounts for an observed tendency for provision to become more focused upon a smaller number of large sites at or near urban peripheries, where land is cheaper and more widely available (Sports Council, 1991).

Secondly, orthodox grass fields have a rather low carrying capacity, especially in winter when the surface is readily damaged and is slow to recover. Estimates suggest that for undrained and pipe-drained pitches the effective capacity when local ground conditions are poor may be less than one game per week and seldom more than three (Sports Council, 1991). This, in itself, is a limitation but it should be further noted that the quality of provision is every bit as important as the quantity; this applies not just to the playing surface but to the ancillary facilities such as changing rooms.

Thirdly, it is often difficult to gauge accurately the demand for sports fields, which is one reason why provision based upon population standards is such a popular approach with local authorities. The NPFA recommended standard is widely followed as a means for providing guidance to local authorities on deficiencies in provision, whilst more recently some authorities have begun to apply the techniques advocated in the Sports Council's *Playing Pitch Strategy*. This permits a more sensitive assessment of local needs by relating actual expressed demand to the number of pitches available and the temporal patterns of activity of teams. It may also be used in conjunction with population projections of participant populations to provide forecasts of future needs. Winchester City Council (1992), for example, using this technique, estimated a shortfall of some 26 pitches (nine each for soccer and rugby, four each for hockey and cricket) by the year 2001 and were able, in consequence, to identify a range of options through which this deficit might be addressed.

The types of approach recommended to remedy deficiencies in provision may follow one of several courses. For some years it has been a popular strategy to spread the loading on public pitches by bringing into play facilities under the control of local education authorities. These account for about one-third of all senior pitches and if junior pitches are included too, the proportion rises to around a half. The Sports Council, since the early 1980s, has been advocating recourse to dual use schemes to make these types of facility more widely available (Sports Council, 1981), but the Minister for Sport's Review Group (1990:23) was still able to observe that the commitment of local education authorities to dual use remained 'less than whole-hearted'. The potential for dual use schemes to affect significantly the level of provision is demonstrated in Table 8.6. This contains data relating to Stevenage where, without use of school fields, a deficit of some 74 hectares, spread over all districts, is experienced, while if existing school fields were to become available for public use there is an aggregate surplus in provision.

Emphasis has also fallen upon upgrading existing facilities, through better drainage of pitches and new or improved changing accommodation. Table 8.4 shows that in the period up to 1993, the Sports Council viewed

Table 8.6 Example of the potential impact of dual use schemes on
sporting provision – Stevenage New Town

District	Population (1986)	Hectares required*	Existing provision	Deficit	Position if school fields used
Bedwell	8394	15.11	4.73	–10.38	–4.92
Broadwater	12,410	22.34	20.10	–2.24	+3.57
Chells	8704	15.67	2.22	–13.45	+14.48
Old Stevenage	6516	11.73	8.04	–3.69	+11.60
Pin Green	10,696	19.25	6.53	–12.72	+0.34
Shephall	12,497	22.49	10.95	–11.54	+8.69
St Nicholas	7904	14.23	5.07	–9.16	–5.87
Symonds Green	7661	13.78	2.24	–11.54	–1.40
Total	74,782	134.60	59.88	–74.72	+26.49

* assumes NPFA standards
Source: Stevenage Borough Council (1991)

remedial work of this character as being a more productive approach than new provision, where costs are higher and problems of location a more significant constraint.

As an alternative to provision of new grass pitches, attention has been directed towards artificial turf. Although synthetic surfaces suffer from a high capital cost of installation (which may be at least £500,000 at current prices: Sports Council, 1991) they enjoy lower maintenance costs and, especially where floodlit, extend the capacity of a space to support games well beyond the limitations of turf playing fields. Monitoring of artificial pitches in Nottingham showed that they carried almost four times as many hours of play as compared to natural grass areas (Nottinghamshire County Council/Sports Council, 1989). The apparent 'shortage' of urban sports pitches does not always stem from a numerical deficiency but rather from a shortfall at peak times. At other times of the week, many pitches stand idle for long periods. However, the floodlit, artificial surface is able not only to withstand better the pressure of constant use but can also help disperse usage by permitting play late into the evenings, providing neighbouring areas are not likely to be adversely affected, in which case local planning authorities may impose some limitations on hours of use. The numbers of artificial pitches in England have increased from fewer than

30 in 1982 to over 280 in 1993 (Sports Council, 1988, 1993) and most current local plans acknowledge the scope for such development, especially where there is a shortage of land, where land values are high or where there is a concentration of local demand for sports pitches. In addition to providing artificial surfaces for field games such as soccer, hockey or American football, artificial cricket wickets and synthetic tennis courts have also begun to appear, funded both by local authorities and by some of the more prosperous private clubs (London Council for Sport and Recreation, 1987). In absolute terms, however, their number still remains low.

Golf courses

The increasing attraction of the game of golf has fuelled significant demands for new provision. Although there are over 1,250 18-hole equivalent courses in England and Wales (Sports Council, 1993) and a further 450 courses in Scotland (Scottish Sports Council, 1991), estimates suggest that these match only 70 per cent of existing demand (Jenkins, 1991), leaving a significant requirement for new courses. Provision for golf is not, of course, necessarily an urban function, but the fact that the majority of players will reside in towns and cities, allied with the spatial variations in existing course provision, shows that courses in, or very close to, urban areas are a key requirement. The Scottish Sports Council study (1991), for example, revealed that in rural areas such as the Borders there is an average of one 18-hole course per 9,300 people, whereas in urban Glasgow the equivalent figure is one per 77,000 people. Apart from aggregate deficits of this type, there are also shortages that affect specific sectors of the golfing market: the Sports Council (Southern Region) (1989) noted, for example, that affordable provision for the needs of casual players and beginners is an area of pronounced deficiency.

But meeting such needs is not a simple matter as there are complex and interrelated problems associated with securing land and adequate funding for course development, locating suitable sites for new courses and resolving potential conflicts with other land uses. Golf courses are extensive facilities by definition, a typical 18-hole course requiring between 125 and 150 acres and in congested urban environments, land in such quantity is neither readily available nor cheap to purchase.

The Scottish Sports Council (1991) suggests that provision of new courses may originate potentially in one of three broad categories: course-owning private clubs, municipal or proprietary courses. The prospect for significant expansion in course-owning clubs is thought to be remote, reflecting the fact that the needs of the comparatively small numbers of individuals or groups capable of financing such projects are already well met. Municipal authorities, too, beset with the uncertainties surrounding CCT and constrained in areas of expenditure, are not seen as major providers at this time, although pay-as-you-play courses may afford one approach through which wider public provision might be advanced. Proprietary courses, however, are considered as an area of potential expansion. These are courses constructed as part of a wider business investment, typically in association with hotel developments, prestige housing or sometimes leisure centres and where the conditions of course access, pricing structures and so forth are a matter for the owner of the business.

Proprietary forms of development are not, though, a total answer for several reasons. First, although there has been some development of cheap, basic golfing provision on 'rough courses' on farmland around the peripheries of towns and cities, many courses linked to hotels or housing schemes are being developed as exclusive ventures which do little to address identified needs for facilities for new or occasional players. Secondly, there have been problems associated with land developments, especially when the provision of a course has been used as a vehicle for introducing physical development to areas under nominal protection. Historically, the conventional placement of courses on the edge of built-up areas aided planners in the creation of buffer zones of green space between adjacent urban places, but the move towards proprietary forms of provision has made such locations strategically less acceptable to local planning authorities. The edges of most major urban areas are designated green belts in which golf courses are often an accepted or conforming use but where the hotels, executive homes or leisure complexes that developers of proprietary courses might favour are not. Since the EC introduced the 'Set Aside' scheme to encourage the release of former farmland to alternative use (such as leisure), the difficulty in converting farmland to new uses such as golf provision has eased somewhat. But planning regulations aimed at protecting the edges of cities from encroachment by physical development have not relaxed to the same degree and it is partly for this reason that doubts have been voiced over whether many of the new course developments that have been proposed are actually desirable additions to the peri-urban land mosaic that will come to fruition.

The risks of physical development associated with golf courses in urban fringe areas have sometimes been exacerbated by potential conflicts with nature conservation objectives. Superficially, golf courses provide a convenient form of provision for nature and there is no doubt that many support significant populations of flora and fauna. But golf courses also attract people, road traffic and physical development that may compromise conservation goals and render golf provision an unsuitable use of fragile or special environments. Jenkins (1991) shows too how through time, many courses succumb to housing development as they are engulfed by urban growth, so long-term protection of special sites is not necessarily advanced through their use for golf.

In the light of such uncertainties, it is unclear how far and by what means the growing demand for golf may be met. Urban land shortage and a lack of investment capital suggests that the least productive pathway would appear to be through development of orthodox, large-scale provision of club-based golf. Instead, cheaper and more flexible forms of provision will need to have a higher emphasis within policy statements. For example, the Sports Council (1988, 1993) has been keen to promote the benefits of pay-as-you-play courses whilst Jenkins (1991) argues that in the short term, 'rough' courses carved out of redundant farmland may meet part of the demand and may be returned more readily to productive use were agricultural policy to change. Land reclamation programmes also provide opportunities to set out new urban courses on land that may be relatively cheap, and floodlit driving ranges have been proven to be attractive, high-capacity facilities that at least serve one facet of the game. Nine hole and 'par 3' courses provide alternative formats where land or financial resources are constraints. However, the key to the expansion of opportunities for golf in urban areas probably lies in the attitudes and approaches of urban planning authorities, for whilst planning policy continues to place the emphasis upon physical containment of urban land, the prospects for significant expansion of golf provision are limited.

SPORT FOR ALL?

The challenge to sporting provision is not, however, purely a question of facilities and the Sports Council (1993), in articulating its vision of sport, places emphasis upon interrelationships within a shared task. Golf, perhaps more than most sports, illustrates how the different sectors of voluntary, private and public provision can come together to realise opportunities for participation, but involvement of people in sport depends, too, upon other factors. From the user's perspective that means not just access to facilities but education in training in how to use them and awareness of pathways through which participation in sport may be developed. For the providers, improvement in the co-ordination between the diverse agencies that govern and provide for sport is now being accorded the emphasis that it merits, as is the notion that the way forward may lie in increased selectivity in resource allocations, rather than the type of widespread support that has tended to be encouraged to date.

In a perceptive analysis, Roberts (1992) argues that urban sport is breaking up, not in a sense of decline but in the sense that there is now visible separation between top professional sport, amateur club sport and mass participation. This has developed, Roberts argues, through media coverage and commercialisation of professional sport and the erosion of the basis of amateur club sport by widespread and affordable public facilities that permit individuals to arrange their own participation without ever needing recourse to traditional club facilities. 'Sport,' writes Roberts, 'has become a less coherent entity' (p. 589) and as well as having implications for the study of sport (which Roberts highlights), it surely has more profound implications for sports policy. Policy requires an element of balance: between the different sectors of provision; between the interests of the keen sportsperson and the dabbler; between the novice and the expert; and between investment in the newer forms of (often indoor) activity and the continuing needs of (typically outdoor) established sports. If sport is a less coherent entity, then provision for sport must be flexible in its recognition of local demands and conditions and scarce resources must be targeted to meet those needs. 'Sport for all' may be a rallying call but whether it is an adequate definition of appropriate approaches to urban sporting development is open to debate.

Chapter 9

Retrospect and prospect

Urban areas are dynamic environments, and although the rate and character of change inevitably fluctuates there are few phases in history in which the progress of urban evolution has stood still. Indeed, it has been suggested that 'one of the fundamental strengths of cities has been an ability to respond, by a process of adaptation and renewal, to changing pressures – economic, technological, cultural and political' (Wilson, 1991:10). Retrospective evaluation of the period since around 1945 suggests that this era has been one of the more active phases in which the nature of urban places has altered significantly so the expansion of outdoor recreation in urban areas over much the same period has taken place against a background of a rapidly shifting physical, economic and social landscape.

URBAN LEISURE AT A CROSSROADS?

This text opened with the proposition that the development of urban recreation had reached a crossroads and this is the theme to which we now return. The analysis of recreational patterns and resources in earlier chapters highlights the point that the modern urban lifestyle affords many opportunities for outdoor leisure but that the further development of opportunity may be regulated by potentially powerful forces of constraint. The pathways that may be followed from this crossroads depend very much upon how the tensions between opportunity and constraint are evaluated and addressed.

A general analysis of recent and contemporary urban change suggests that the development of outdoor recreation in towns and cities is potentially facilitated by three broad processes: the emergence of so-called post-industrial cities, the spread of environmentalism as a paradigm guiding urban design and management, and growing concerns over the sustainability of urban life.

Post-industrialism is a generic term of convenience which attempts to summarise and describe the significant changes experienced by western cities in the latter half of the twentieth century (Herbert and Thomas, 1990). In summary, post-industrial cities display:

- a shift away from a rationale for urbanism based upon traditional heavy and manufacturing industry to one based upon services, i.e. a move from a production-based to a consumption-based economy. Office employment, administration, business, commerce and finance, communications, tourism and leisure provide the economic rationale for the post-industrial city;
- development of new areas of production, usually based upon high technology industry and associated research, or services such as retailing and leisure, and increasingly located at urban peripheries or along corridors of communications. Control of new technology is central to economic development and production is typically becoming concentrated in a smaller number of large, dominant companies;
- dispersal of urban functions as the frictional effect of distance is reduced by developments in the technology of communications and information transfer;
- erosion in size and significance of industrial working-class groups as occupational structures have changed to accommodate the expansion in professional and technical classes;
- blurring of conventional socio-economic divides through convergence in income levels amongst skilled production workers and certain professional groups; in levels of personal mobility; in levels of general affluence and disposable income; and the gentrification of poorer housing areas. Zones of low social status become fragmented but do not disappear, becoming spatially concentrated into pockets of deprivation in otherwise affluent urban areas.

Implicit in several of these observations is the tendency for older, central areas of cities to decay as expired industry closes and the population previously dependent upon such employment becomes redundant. These locations often become areas for high-profile redevelopment of offices, high-quality housing and leisure facilities. 'The high density central city with its low density, residential suburban ring has been replaced by a multi-nodal, sprawling built environment with the central city less and less distinguishable from its competitive 'outer cities'' (Beauregard, 1991:91). (For more detailed discussion of post-industrialism and its impact upon urban systems see, amongst many, Bell, 1974; Savitch, 1988; Soja, 1989; Beauregard, 1991; Keil, 1994; Keil and Ronneberger, 1994).

The implications of these changes for development of leisure are significant. First, space for recreation has been created in areas of the city where previously it was scarce. In particular, the removal of older areas of high-density housing and of Victorian industry from inner cities has afforded opportunity for implantation of new leisure facilities in more central locations. The development of Festival Park in Stoke-on-Trent (illustrated in Chapter 3) is an example.

Secondly, conventional patterns of land value have changed. The shift away from an emphasis upon the primacy of central areas towards a more flexible pattern has had several effects, on the one hand affording the prospect of significant growth of recreation, especially tourism, as major industries in the central city (Perloff, 1985), on the other promoting fashionable development of out-of-town retailing and leisure facilities.

Thirdly, changes in socio-economic conditions associated with post-industrialism also facilitate increased participation in recreation. Reductions in the incidence of shift working create a more amenable pattern of time availability, while improvement in levels of affluence, particularly mobility, are essential in permitting recreational travel. The ability to travel is especially important in the post-industrial city where facilities are likely to be scattered, in keeping with the dispersed nature that is characteristic of such urban places.

Fourthly, new forms of post-industrial urban recreation have developed, especially that associated with tourism and heritage. It is one of the ironies of development that once it is redundant, the mundane often takes on a new interest. Expired urban industry has thus come to provide a source of interest to the post-industrial population at leisure and there has been significant development of recreational facilities in areas which have an industrial heritage. The Black Country Museum in the West Midlands, Albert Dock Liverpool, South Dock Swansea, Wigan Pier and the Beamish Museum near Newcastle upon Tyne are all examples of tourist destinations that are flourishing by purveying the recent past to contemporary urban populations.

Environmentalism, as reflected in the idea of a green city, is not new, as the emergence of a garden city movement in the late nineteenth century bears witness. What is new is the extent to which urban authorities and populations have turned to the concept of a green city as an alternative to the conventional city in which green space was a minor feature and often confined to designated zones such as formal parks. The precise origins of the rise of urban environmentalism are not easy to locate in time or explain in concise terms. The evident collapse of Victorian industry and its legacy of dereliction was one factor that contributed to many urban improvement schemes of the 1970s. That decade also saw reorganisation of local government in Britain which, argues Nicholson-Lord (1987), provided opportunities to incorporate new professional skills in ecology and landscape design into the framework of local authority work, a move that perhaps reflected a wider development of green politics and the influence of environmental pressure groups. Urban authorities also became more conscious of image as a factor in promoting (or inhibiting) the further economic growth of their cities. Many forms of subsequent urban development were embellished with an environmentally friendly patina, mirrored in a new vocabulary of urban development that recognises greenways, linear parks, business parks, science parks, green wedges and natural corridors.

There are reciprocal benefits in the greening of cities and the development of opportunity for outdoor recreation. This operates on several planes. The overt provision of green spaces of varying styles and formats, which implicitly play a major role in supporting a diversity of active and passive forms of outdoor recreation, represents one such level but, as was argued in Chapter 5, the incidental improvement of the urban environment through the planting of street trees and other forms of urban horticulture also benefits outdoor recreation by providing a more amenable environment in which to socialise, play or take exercise.

Ultimately, environmental enhancement becomes a part of wider concerns for the sustainability of urban life. Discussions of sustainability rightly concern themselves with a wider portfolio of issues that threaten the long-term health and vitality of settlements, including proper management of natural resources, regulation of land development and associated transportation systems, efficiency in urban energy consumption, management of waste and regulation of urban pollution (Breheny and Rookwood, 1993). Discussions of strategies for urban sustainability seldom place much emphasis upon the role of outdoor recreation, although issues that do command attention – for example urban greening, the creation and protection of more diverse natural habitats in towns and cities, promotion of public transport and reduction in dependency upon private forms of travel – clearly have implications for the capacity of towns and cities to accommodate a wide range of outdoor activities. Furthermore, it would be unwise to overlook the contribution that high-quality provision for outdoor recreation makes to the often intangible, but nevertheless significant, element of quality of life. This text has noted a number of instances in which local authorities have consciously sought to project a positive and attractive image for their urban areas through investment in recreation provision, especially within the new towns.

OBSTACLES IN THE PATH?

Set against these changes, which have a broadly positive effect upon provision for outdoor recreation (or at least afford the prospect of improvement), is a set of factors the effects of which are either uncertain or potentially negative. Two are especially important: the uncertainty surrounding the political climate of urban leisure provision and the scope for unfavourable images and perceptions of urban life to undermine the viability and attractiveness of outdoor forms of leisure.

The political context is especially relevant to outdoor recreation because, by tradition, so much of the provision for such activity has been the responsibility of the public sector. The experience of the 1980s has shifted significantly the basis upon which such public provision has been founded. Mellor (1989) argues for what she terms 'transitions' – decisive phases which mark a shift in state–society relationships. Much of the post-1945 development in recreation provision occurred under a philosophy guided by concerns for urban welfare, reflected, *inter alia*, in strategies for provision of decent housing, fiscal incentives to home ownership, state investment (especially via local authorities) in roads, public open space, community facilities etc., and a delegation of many powers to the local level. The 1970s marked a 'transition' in Britain, out of which emerged a new political agenda based upon a return to right-wing values. Benington and White (1988b) note how the re-emergence of right-wing central government challenged not only the fiscal burden of public services but more fundamentally the whole post-war consensus in support for a welfare state based upon collective solutions to needs. The emphasis has fallen instead upon meeting of individual needs through personal purchases of goods and services, rather than dependence on publicly provided services that have been required to become not just more efficient in service delivery, but more accountable for their actions. Contraction of central resources available to support local services and the introduction of CCT are but two indications of the manner in which central government has been able to assert its will over local authorities.

The implications of these changes for provision of outdoor recreation are potentially profound and have led a number of authors to speculate upon the future of publicly provided urban leisure. Henry (1988), for example, maps out five possible scenarios. At one extreme, he locates a situation in which strong right-wing Conservative central government prevails and where provision becomes largely a matter for the free market, where public services are privatised and government becomes the provider of last resort. At the other end of the scale, a left-wing Labour government holds power and a high level of local autonomy is reflected in significant levels of public intervention, guided by principles of equality of opportunity.

Where, between these extremes, policy will actually be located remains uncertain but there is an emerging consensus amongst academics and practitioners, if not amongst politicians, that there ought to be a role for local-level public provision of recreation. Veal (1987) argues that the role of the public sector is central to the continued provision of parks, pools, sports centres, libraries, museums and 'the arts' in general, and states quite simply that the private and voluntary sectors possess neither the inclination nor the resources to fill the void that would be created by withdrawal of public provision. Benington and White (1988b) concur, noting that whilst competitive markets are good at producing innovation and achieving cost-efficiency, they are poorly placed for developing overall strategies for meeting diverse but often interrelated leisure needs. The challenge to the public sector, they conclude, is to help identify and articulate the basic values that ought to inform the wider development of leisure services.

Political approaches will also be important in addressing the problems of social malaise within cities. Mellor (1989:573), in her study of urban 'transitions', comments that 'cities have become less habitable . . . and conventions of everyday life – the use of public places, relationships with neighbours, the basis of consent for policing are being reassessed'. 'The UK,' she asserts, 'has become a less comfortable and a less happy society.' For outdoor recreation, these are worrying views, for at many junctures in the preceding chapters the importance of safe and attractive public places (as a spatial context for activity) and of well-developed relationships with friends and neighbours (as a social context for recreation) has been stressed. The onset of post-industrialism has not removed what Hall (1988) has characterised as 'the city of the permanent underclass'. Indeed, there is evidence that exaggeration in the differential prosperity within modern cities, particularly during the 1980s, served only to highlight the plurality of social groups, especially those at disadvantage. Keil and Ronneberger (1994:153) describe an increasingly familiar element in urban life in noting that 'in the commercialised postmodern core of Frankfurt . . . homeless people and substance abusers are part and parcel of the daily shopping experience' and that 'violent youth gangs "hanging out" in shopping areas and subway trains, as well as drug dealers and an increase in common street crime are the most visible signs that the dream of becoming a world city has come at a price'. Frankfurt, of course, is atypical and the majority of urban people probably reside in 'small town' situations in which such problems (and indeed problems of serious traffic congestion, pollution, slum housing or ethnic tensions) seldom surface. But the image of urbanism as associated with such problems is certainly becoming a powerful one and there is no doubt that discretionary areas of personal behaviour, including outdoor recreation, are widely affected by perceptions of such risks.

The tensions between the opportunities and constraints embodied in many contemporary urban places are reflected in some of the evident trends in urban leisure behaviour, in particular the privatisation of leisure consumption, the increasing trend towards commodification and associated changes in the balance between formality and informality.

The privatisation of leisure was noted in Chapter 4, where the growing dominance of the home as a recreational environment was recorded. This trend reflects a number of processes, some positive, others less so. The increasing popularity of home-based forms of entertainment, including a burgeoning market in hobby-related interests, is a part of the process and reflects the expansion in the availability of leisure goods and disposable income necessary for their purchase. Less positively, the apparent reduction in the appeal of recreation sites away from home, either because they are perceived to be less interesting or, as discussed above, less attractive or safe, is also a factor affecting patterns, particularly amongst children, women and the elderly. But other forms of recreation are also showing evidence of increased privatisation, for example sports participation (Chapter 8) and whilst an increasing willingness to pay for outdoor recreations is to be welcomed inasmuch as it takes some pressure off hard-pressed local authorities, there is an attendant risk that the role of public provision becomes one of meeting the needs of those disadvantaged groups who cannot afford the luxury of privately purchased recreation. To the extent that this is a potentially divisive development, there is a case for a measure of resistance against its full potential impact.

Similar concerns have been expressed about the commodification of leisure, a practice that is now so widespread that it is commonly overlooked. Veal (1987:157) notes several examples: the dominance of the British holiday market by the package and the associated tendency of the press to report on 'shortages' or 'availability' of holidays, clearly as if the holiday were only available as a product and not something capable of being fashioned by individuals to suit their needs. More tellingly, perhaps, he cites a second and less obvious example in noting that 'children used once to play in relatively safe, stimulating environments near their homes, watched over by grandparents and neighbours: now play schemes and play centres with trained staff and expensive equipment are required'. The packaging of leisure in this manner is one approach and it is not necessarily inappropriate for some circumstances and some experiences. But it should not become the norm and it should not have escaped the reader's notice that throughout this book the prevailing argument has been that approaches which define and demarcate recreation in this manner do not form a suitable basis for the development of the full potential for outdoor urban leisure.

The formalised basis for provision of opportunity is a third area of potential concern. In view of the prevalence of planning as a mechanism for shaping contemporary urban development and the primary role played by public agencies in the provision to date of much of the infrastructure for outdoor recreation, it is no surprise that a great deal of that provision is structured within formal frameworks. Space is allocated according to formalised planning procedures, while management of resources is, as we saw in Chapter 3, shaped by committee structures and corporate decision-making procedures. In the chapters dealing with, for example, the street, open space and provision for children's play, the thrust of the argument was for more informality in provision, yet many of the trends in provision continue to emphasise an opposite tendency towards formality and commodification.

AN AGENDA FOR THE FUTURE?

So, which path do we take from the crossroads? We should start by reasserting the significance of the urban environment as a venue for outdoor recreations and the special value of locally based policy for provision. Despite trends towards counter-urbanisation, in countries such as Britain most people will continue to reside in urban environments and expend most of their leisure time locally. There is much in the contemporary literature on changing urban systems that emphasises globalisation as a process and the emergence of networks of world cities. But this has little to do with the day-to-day activities of people at leisure (except perhaps where their lives are touched by the international tourist and where their choice of what to do in their spare time is influenced by incidental media exposure of trends and habits within a national or international context). Fundamentally, people shape their recreational habits according to the opportunities they see around them, so a local dimension to development of recreational policy should remain central.

Existing practices and beliefs have so far delivered only a set of partial opportunities for a leisured urban lifestyle. Provision in the form of dedicated recreational facilities has increased but there has been a marked erosion of the incidental opportunity for play or for casual and sociable forms of recreation and exercise that in Britain characterised urban recreation up to as recently as the 1960s. Reclamation of such opportunity, if it is thought to be worthwhile, demands radical alternatives to present custom and practice in urban development, design and management.

This text has attempted to articulate some of the ways in which we might think differently about creation of opportunity for urban recreation. To establish residential areas in which residents will enjoy recreation close to home and association with their neighbours needs a clear rejection of the unimaginative and predictable manner in which housing developments, guided by planning norms, are set out and endowed with private gardens and communal spaces. To reclaim the street as a prime venue for socialisation, walking, cycling and children's play we need to tame the car and regulate more directly how it may be used. To get the best for our children out of their experience of play, we need more than the designated playgrounds that tend to dominate the planner's thinking. To establish open space systems that bring nature back into cities and provide residents with a diversity of experiences that they will value requires a shift in emphasis away from formally managed, conventional spaces to a much wider range of formal and informal spaces that meet better the diversity of needs and interests latent within any modern urban population.

To achieve these objectives requires a different approach to that which currently prevails. It requires a political commitment to support local public provision of recreational opportunity. It requires a fundamental change in planning philosophy with much less emphasis upon conventional spatial zoning strategies and a willingness to countenance mixed patterns of land use in which recreational spaces infuse the built-up area. It requires a will to experiment, to be flexible, to learn from experience elsewhere and to commit resources where the long-term benefits suggest that such investment is worthwhile. It requires that the views and needs of the ordinary people who live, work and play in towns and cities be understood and taken into account. Then, perhaps, we will begin to create an urban environment that will be truly supportive of outdoor recreation. Wilson (1991:11) summarises these sentiments succinctly. 'Cities,' he writes, 'are for people to live and work in. We have only ourselves to blame if we do not play a part in deciding their future shape and purpose.'

Bibliography

Anon. (1994) 'The 1993 UK day visits survey'. *Countryside Recreation Network News* Vol. 2 No. 1: 7–12.

Audit Commission (1989) *Sport for Whom? Clarifying the Local Authority Role in Sport and Recreation*, London: HMSO.

Ball, D. and King, K. (1990) 'Play right'. *Leisure Management* Vol. 10 No. 3: 54–57.

Balmer, K. (1973) *The Use of Open Space in Liverpool*, Liverpool: Liverpool City Corporation.

Barnett, L.A. (1990) 'Developmental benefits of play for children'. *Journal of Leisure Research* Vol. 22 No. 2: 138–153.

BBC: British Broadcasting Corporation (1978) *The People's Activities and Use of Time*, London: BBC.

Beauregard, R.A. (1991) 'Capital restructuring and the new built environment of global cities: New York and Los Angeles'. *International Journal of Urban and Regional Research* Vol. 15 No. 1: 90–105.

Bell, D. (1974) *The Coming of Post-industrial Society*, London: Heinemann.

Bellamy, J. (1976) 'Burgess Park: the history of a new metropolitan park'. *Greater London Intelligence Quarterly* Vol. 34: 5–16.

Benington, J. and White, J. (eds) (1988a) *The Future of Leisure Services*, Harlow: Longman.

—— (1988b) 'The need for a new strategic vision for leisure services'. In Benington, J. and White, J. (1988a): 245–252.

Bernard, M. (1988) 'Leisure-rich and leisure-poor: leisure lifestyles among young adults'. *Leisure Sciences* Vol. 10 No. 2: 131–149.

Birmingham City Council (1989) *Birmingham – a Greener Future: a Nature Conservation Strategy for the 1990s*, Birmingham: Birmingham Council Department of Recreation and Community Services.

Bishop, K. (1991) 'Community forests: implementing the concept'. *The Planner* Vol. 77 No. 18: 6–10.

Blowers, A. (ed.) (1993) *Planning for a Sustainable Environment*, London: Earthscan.

Boothby, J., Tungatt, M., Townsend, A. and Collins, M.F. (1981) *A Sporting Chance? Family, School and Environmental Influences on Taking Part in Sport*, Sports Council Study No. 22, London: Sports Council.

Bowler, I.R. and Strachan, A.J. (1976a) *Parks and Gardens in Leicester*, Leicester: Leicester City Council Recreation and Cultural Services Department.

—— (1976b) 'Visitor behaviour in urban parks'. *Parks and Recreation* Vol. 41 No. 9: 18–25.

Bradley, C. and Millward, A. (1986) 'Successful green space – do we know it when we see it?' *Landscape Research* Vol. 11 No. 2: 2–8.

Brahman, P., Hendry, I., Mommaas, H., and van der Peol, H. (eds) (1989) *Leisure and Urban Processes. Critical Studies of Leisure Policy in Western European Cities*, London: Routledge.

Breheny, M. and Rookwood, R. (1993) 'Planning the sustainable city region'. In Blowers (1993): 150–189.

Brettschneider, W.D. (1992) 'Adolescents, leisure, sport and lifestyle'. In Williams, *et al.* (1992): 536–550.

Bromley, R.D.F. and Thomas, C.J. (eds) (1992) *Retail Change: Contemporary Issues*, London: UCL.

Brown, J.G. and Burger, C. (1984) 'Playground design and pre-school children's behaviors'. *Environment and Behavior* Vol. 16 No. 5: 599–626.

Bruton, M.J. (ed.) (1984) *The Spirit and Purpose of Planning*, London: Hutchinson.

Bryan, H. and Stuebling, S. (1987) 'Natural light and the urban environment'. In Moudon (1987): 299–309.

Buchanan, C. (1963) *Traffic in Towns*, Harmondsworth: Penguin.

Burgess, J., Harrison, C.M. and Limb, M. (1988) 'People, parks and the urban green: a study of popular meanings and values for open spaces in the city'. *Urban Studies* Vol. 25 No. 6: 455–473.

Burns, L.S. and Friedmann, J. (1985) *The Art of Planning: Selected Essays of Harvey S. Perloff*, London: Plenum.

Burton, T.L. (1967) *The Classification of Recreation Demands and Supplies*, Research Memorandum No. 1, Birmingham: University of Birmingham Centre for Urban and Regional Studies.

Bush, P.W., Kivell, P.T., Fenn, M.H.M. and Bannell, A.B. (1981a) *Derelict Land and Restored Derelict Land in North Staffordshire*, Evaluation of Land Reclamation Policies in North Staffordshire Working Paper No. 2, Stoke-on-Trent: University of Keele/North Staffordshire Polytechnic Departments of Geography.

—— (1981b) *A Site-based Survey of Recreation Facilities in North Staffordshire*, Evaluation of Land Reclamation Policies in North Staffordshire Working Paper No. 4, Stoke-on-Trent: University of Keele/North Staffordshire Polytechnic Departments of Geography.

Bussey, K. (1987) 'Leisure and shopping'. *Leisure Management* Vol. 7 No. 9: 22–24/26.

Cardiff City Council (1992) *City of Cardiff Playground Strategy*, Cardiff: Council Leisure and Amenities Department.

Carter, H. (1981) *The Study of Urban Geography*, London: Edward Arnold.

Carvalho, A.M.A., Smith, P.K., Hunter, H. and Costabile, A. (1990) 'Playground activities for boys and girls: developmental and cultural trends in children's perceptions of gender differences'. *Play and Culture* Vol. 3 No. 4: 343–347.

Central Statistical Office (1992) *Social Trends 22*, London: HMSO.

—— (1993) *Regional Trends 28*, London: HMSO.

—— (1994) *Annual Abstract of Statistics 1994*, London: HMSO.

Chadwick, G.F. (1966) *The Park and the Town*, London: Architectural Press.

Chambers, D.A. (1986) 'The constraints of work and domestic schedules on women's leisure'. *Leisure Studies* Vol. 5 No. 3: 309–325.

Cherry, G.E. (1982) *Leisure and the Home*, London: Sports Council / SSRC.

—— (1984a) 'Town planning: an overview'. In Bruton (1984): 170–188.

—— (1984b) 'Leisure and the home: a review of changing relationships'. *Leisure Studies* Vol. 3 No. 1: 35–52.

Child, E. (1985) *General Theories of Play*, Birmingham: Play Board.

Chilton, A. (1985) *Children's Play in Newcastle upon Tyne*, Birmingham: Play Board/NPFA.

CIPFA: Chartered Institute of Public Finance and Accountancy (1992) *Leisure and Recreation Statistics 1992–93*, London: CIPFA.

Clawson, M. and Knetsch, J. (1966) *Economics of Outdoor Recreation*, Baltimore: Johns Hopkins University Press.

CLR: Centre for Leisure Research (1991) *Digest of Sports Statistics*, London: Sports Council.

Coalter, F. (1985) 'The defence of public sector services'. *Leisure Management* Vol. 5 No. 5: 12–15.

Coffin, G. and Williams, M. (1989) *Children's Outdoor Play in the Built Environment*, London: National Children's Play and Recreation Unit.

Conway, H. (1991) *People's Parks: the Design and Development of Victorian Parks in Britain*, Cambridge: Cambridge University Press.

Cook, E.A. (1991) 'Urban landscape networks: an ecological planning framework'. *Landscape Research* Vol. 16 No. 3: 7–16.

Cook, J.A. (1968) 'Gardens on housing estates: a survey of users' attitudes and behaviour on seven layouts'. *Town Planning Review* Vol. 39: 217–234.

Cooke, P. (1990) *Back to the Future: Modernity, Post-modernity and Locality*, London: Unwin Hyman.

Coppock, J.T. (1993) 'Government, conservation, outdoor recreation and tourism: a British–Australian perspective'. In Glyptis (1993): 71–84.

Coulson, N. (1980) 'Space around the home'. *Architects Journal* 24/31 December: 1245–1260.

Countryside Commission (1986) *A Step in the Right Direction: the Marketing of Circular Walks*, Cheltenham: Countryside Commission.

—— (1988) *Paths, Routes and Trails*, Cheltenham: Countryside Commission.

—— (1993) *National Target for Rights of Way: the Milestones Approach*, Cheltenham: Countryside Commission.

Coupland, A. (1992) 'Docklands; dream or disaster?'. In Thornley (1992): 149–162.

CPAC: Crime Prevention Advisory Committee (1988) *Growing up on Housing Estates: a Review of the Play and Recreational Needs of Young People*, London: National Association for the Care and Resettlement of Offenders.

Crawford, D.W. and Godbey, G. (1987) 'Reconceptualizing barriers to family leisure'. *Leisure Sciences*, Vol. 9: 119–127.

Crawford, D.W., Jackson, E.L. and Godbey, G. (1991) 'A hierarchical model of leisure constraints'. *Leisure Sciences* Vol. 13 No. 4: 309–320.

Croke, K., Fabian, R. and Brenniman, G. (1986) 'Estimating the value of open space preservation in an urban area'. *Journal of Environmental Management* Vol. 23 No. 4: 317–324.

Crouch, D. (1989a) 'The allotment, landscape and locality'. *Area* Vol. 21 No. 3: 261–267.

—— (1989b) 'Patterns of co-operation in the cultures of outdoor leisure – the case of allotments'. *Leisure Studies* Vol. 8 No. 2: 189–199.

—— (1991) 'Local land, local culture'. *Town and Country Planning* Vol. 60 No. 11/12: 325–327.

Crouch, D. and Ward, C. (1988) *The Allotment: its Landscape and Culture*, London: Faber and Faber.

Cullingworth, J.B. and Nadin, V. (1994) *Town and Country Planning in Britain*, London: Routledge.

Davies, W.K. and Herbert, D.T. (1993) *Communities within Cities: an Urban Social Geography*. London: Belhaven.

Deem, R. (1986) *All Work and No Play? The Sociology of Women and Leisure*, Milton Keynes: Open University Press.

Department of Transport (1992) *Transport Statistics Great Britain 1992*, London: HMSO.

District of the Wrekin (1990) *Telford Local Plan*, Telford: District of the Wrekin Planning and Environmental Services Department.

Dixey, R. (1983) 'The playing of bingo: industry, market and working class culture'. In Tomlinson (1983): 52–67.

DoE: Department of the Environment (1972) *Children's Playspace*, Circular 79/72, London: HMSO.

—— (1975) *Sport and Recreation*, Cmnd 6200, London: HMSO.

—— (1991) *Sport and Recreation*, Planning Policy Guidance No. 17, London: HMSO.

—— (1994) *Transport*, Planning Policy Guidance No. 13, London: HMSO.

Donnelly, D. (1980) 'The child in the environment'. *Built Environment* Vol. 6 No. 1: 62–67.

Dower, M. (1965) *Fourth Wave: the Challenge of Leisure*, London: Civic Trust.

—— (1993) '"Fourth Wave" revisited'. In Glyptis (1993): 15–21.

Dudley Metropolitan Borough Council (1993) *Dudley Countryside Strategy*, Dudley: Dudley Council.

Edwards, A.M. (1981) *The Design of Suburbia: a Critical Study in Environmental History*, London: Pembridge.

Elson, M.J. (1979) *The Leisure Use of Green Belts and Urban Fringe*, London: Sports Council/SSRC.

—— (1986) *Green Belts: Conflict Mediation in the Urban Fringe*. London: Heinemann.

—— (1989) *Recreation and Community Provision in Areas of New Private Housing*, London: Housing Research Foundation.

—— (1993) 'Negotiating for sport and recreation using planning obligations'. *The Planner* Vol. 79 No. 8: 17–18.

Elson, M.J. and Payne, D. (1993) *Planning Obligations for Sport and Recreation. A Guide for Negotiation and Action*, London: Sports Council.

Elvin, I.T. (1990) *Sport and Physical Recreation*, Harlow: Longman.

Eubank-Ahrens, B. (1987) 'A closer look at the users of woonerfen'. In Moudon (1987): 63–79.

Euromonitor (1991) 'Garden leisure'. *Market Research Great Britain* Vol. 32 December: 83–94.

—— (1993) 'Gardening profiles'. *Market Research Great Britain* Vol. 34 September: 123–133.

Fahy, S. (1988) *Mobilising for Play*, Bristol: National Playbus Association.

Fazey, D. and Ballington, N. (1992) 'Adult female participation in physical activity: perception of competence and attitude towards the participation motives of other women'. *Physical Education Review* Vol. 15 No. 1: 53–60.

Fletcher, S. (1987) 'The making and breaking of a female tradition: women's physical education in England 1880–1980'. In Mangan and Park (1987): 145–157.

Forest of Mercia (1993) *The Forest of Mercia, Executive Summary*, Cannock: Forest of Mercia.

Francis, M. (1987a) 'The making of democratic streets'. In Moudon (1987): 23–39.

—— (1987b) 'Meanings attached to a city park and a community garden in Sacramento'. *Landscape Research* Vol. 12 No. 1: 8–12.

Francis, M. and Hester, R.T. (eds) (1990) *The Meaning of Gardens: Idea, Place and Action*, Cambridge Mass.: MIT.

Franklin, A. (1985) *Pub Drinking and the Licensed Trade. A Study of Drinking Cultures and Local Community in Two Areas of South West England*, Bristol: University of Bristol School for Advanced Urban Studies Occasional Paper No. 21.

Friberg, P. (1979) 'The parkland of Scandinavian cities'. In Laurie (1979a): 327–349.

Gaskell, S.M. (1980) 'Gardens for the working class: Victorian practical pleasure'. *Victorian Studies* Summer: 479–501.

Gaster, S. (1991) 'Urban children's access to their neighbourhood. Change over three generations'. *Environment and Behavior* Vol. 23 No. 1: 70–85.

Gehl, J. (1980) 'The residential street environment' *Built Environment* Vol. 6 No. 1: 51–61.

Gershuny, J. and Jones, S. (1987) 'The changing work/leisure balance in Britain, 1961–1984'. In Horne *et al.* (1987): 9–50.

GLC: Greater London Council (1968) *Surveys of the Use of Open Space*, London: Council Planning Department.

Glyptis, S. (1981) 'Leisure lifestyles'. *Regional Studies* Vol. 15 No. 5: 311–326.

—— (1992) 'Access to sport and leisure: the winners and losers'. In Williams *et al.* (1992): 525–535.

Glyptis, S. (ed.) (1993) *Leisure and the Environment: Essays in Honour of Professor J.A. Patmore*, London: Belhaven.

Glyptis, S. and Chambers, D. (1982) 'No place like home'. *Leisure Studies* Vol. 1 No. 3: 247–262.

Glyptis, S., McInnes, H. and Patmore, J.A. (1987) *Leisure and the Home*, London: Sports Council / ESRC.

Grahn, P. (1991) 'Landscapes in our minds: people's choice of recreative places in towns'. *Landscape Research* Vol. 16 No. 1: 11–19.

Green, E., Hebron, S. and Woodward, D. (1990) *Women's Leisure: What Leisure?* Basingstoke: Macmillan.

Grocott, A. (1990a) 'Design your own park'. *Leisure Manager* Vol. 8 No. 6: 4–5.

—— (1990b) 'Parks for the people'. *Leisure Manager* Vol. 8 No. 7: 6–7.

Grove, A.B. and Cresswell, R.W. (1983) *City Landscapes*, London: Butterworth.

Halkett, I.P.B. (1978) 'The recreational use of private gardens'. *Journal of Leisure Research* Vol. 10 No. 1: 13–20.

Hall, A.C. (1987) 'The provision of private open space for dwellings: an assessment of policies of local planning authorities'. *Town Planning Review* Vol. 58 No. 2: 183–198.

—— (1990) 'Design control: a call for a new approach' *The Planner* Vol. 76 No. 39: 14–18.

Hall, P. (1988) *Cities of Tomorrow: an Intellectual History of Urban Planning and Design in the Twentieth Century*, Oxford: Blackwell.

Handley, J. (1983) 'Nature in the urban environment'. In Grove and Cresswell (1983): 47–59.

Harrison, C.M. (1983) 'Countryside recreation and London's urban fringe'. *Transactions of the Institute of British Geographers* (New Series) Vol. 8 No. 3: 295–313.

Harrison, C.M., Limb, M. and Burgess, J. (1986) 'Recreation 2000: views of the country from the city'. *Landscape Research* Vol. 11 No. 2: 19–24.

—— (1987) 'Nature in the city: popular values for a living world'. *Journal of Environmental Management* Vol. 25 No. 4: 347–362.

Hart, R. (1979) *Children's Experience of Place*, New York: Irvington.

Hartman, J. (1990) 'The Delft bicycle network'. In Tolley (1990): 193–200.

Haslam, M. (1990) 'Green belts and the future – a view from the districts'. *The Planner* Vol. 76 No. 34: 14–16.

Hass-Klau, C. (1990) *The Pedestrian and City Traffic*, London: Belhaven.

Haworth, J.T. (1986) 'Meaningful activity and psychological models of non-employment'. *Leisure Studies* Vol. 5 No. 3: 281–298.

Hendry, L.B. (1981) *Adolescents and Leisure*, London: Sports Council/ESRC.

Henry, I. (1988) 'Alternative futures for the public leisure service'. In Benington and White (1988a): 207–243.

Herbert, D.T. and Johnston, R.J. (1981) *Geography and the Urban Environment: Progress in Research and Applications, Vol. 4*, Chichester: John Wiley.

Herbert, D.T. and Raine, J.W. (1976) 'Defining communities within urban areas'. *Town Planning Review* Vol. 47: 325–338.

Herbert, D.T. and Thomas, C.J. (1990) *Cities in Space: City as Place*, London: David Fulton.

Herington, J. (1991) 'How to deal with urban shorelines?' *Town and Country Planning* Vol. 60 No. 4: 124–126.

Heseltine, P. and Holborn, J. (1987) *Playgrounds: the Planning, Design and Construction of Play Environments*, London: Mitchell.

Hillman, M. (1990) 'Planning for the green modes: a critique of public policy'. In Tolley (1990): 64–74.

Holden, R. (1989) 'British garden festivals: the first eight years'. *Landscape and Urban Planning* Vol. 18 No. 1: 17–35.

Holme, A. and Massie, P. (1970) *Children's Play: a Study of Needs and Opportunities*, London: Michael Joseph.

Holt, R. (1989) *Sport and the British: a Modern History*, Oxford: Oxford University Press.

Horne, J., Jary, D. and Tomlinson, A. (eds) (1987) *Sport, Leisure and Social Relations*, London: Routledge.

Hudson, M. (1982) *Bicycle Planning: Policy and Practice*, London: Architectural Press.

Imrie, R. and Thomas, H. (eds) (1993) *British Urban Policy and the Urban Development Corporations*, London: Paul Chapman.

Jackson, A.A. (1991) *Semi-detached London: Suburban Development, Life and Transport*, Didcot: Wild Swan.

Jackson, G.A.M. (1991) 'Recreation constraint in an urban context', Staffordshire Polytechnic, unpublished Ph.D. thesis.

Jackson, G.A.M. and Kay, T. (1992) 'Leisure constraints'. In Williams *et al.* (1992): 551–562.

Jacobs, J. (1961) *The Death and Life of Great American Cities*, New York: Random House.

Jansen, A.C.M. (1989) 'Fun shopping as a geographical notion, or the attraction of inner city Amsterdam as a shopping area'. *Tijdschrift voor economische en sociale geografie* Vol. 80 No. 3: 171–183.

—— (1993) 'Economic activity and the quality of public space in inner cities'. *Tijdschrift voor economische en sociale geografie* Vol. 84 No. 1: 13–26.

Jansen-Verbeke, M. (1988) *Leisure, Recreation and Tourism in Inner Cities: Explorative Case Studies*, Netherlands Geographical Studies No. 58, Amsterdam.

Jenkins, R.O.J. (1991) *Golf Course Development in the UK*, Sunningdale: Sunningdale Publications.

Johnson, J.H. (1972) *Urban Geography*, Oxford: Pergamon.

Kaplan, M. (1975) *Leisure: Theory and Policy*, Chichester: John Wiley.

Karp, D.A. and Yoels, W.C. (1990) 'Sport and urban life'. *Journal of Sport and Social Issues* Vol. 14 No. 2: 77–102.

Kay, G. (1988) *Allotment Gardens in Stoke-on-Trent*, Occasional Papers in Geography No. 11, Stoke-on-Trent: Staffordshire Polytechnic.

—— (1991) *Outdoor Sport and Recreation in Broxtowe, Nottinghamshire*, Unpublished report to Broxtowe Borough Council, Staffordshire Polytechnic, Department of Geography and Recreation Studies.

Kay, T. and Jackson, G.A.M. (1991) 'Leisure despite constraint'. *Journal of Leisure Sciences* Vol. 23 No. 4: 301–313.

Keil, R. (1994) 'Global sprawl: urban form after Fordism'. *Environment & Planning D: Society and Space* Vol. 12 No. 2: 131–136.

Keil, R. and Ronneberger, K. (1994) 'Going up the country: internationalization and urbanization of Frankfurt's northern fringe'. *Environment and Planning D: Society & Space* Vol. 12 No. 2: 137–166.

Kellett, J.E. (1982) 'The private garden in England and Wales'. *Landscape Planning* Vol. 9: 105–123.

Kelly, J.R. (1983) *Leisure Identities and Interactions*, London: George Allen and Unwin.

Kerten, V. (1988) 'Play development: relating provision to needs. Part 2'. *Leisure Management* Vol. 8 No. 9: 85–87.

Kivell, P.T. (1993) *Land and the City: Patterns and Processes of Urban Change*, London: Routledge.

Kroon, M. (1990) 'Traffic and environmental policy in the Netherlands'. In Tolley (1990): 113–133.

Laurie, I.C. (ed.) (1979a) *Nature in Cities: the Natural Environment in the Design and Development of Urban Green Space*, Chichester: John Wiley.
—— (1979b) 'Urban commons'. In Laurie (1979a): 231–266.
Lawless, P. and Brown, F. (1986) *Urban Growth and Change in Britain*, London: Harper and Row.
LCC: Leicester City Council (1985) *Leicester Parks: 1984 Survey*, Leicester: Leicester Council Recreation and Arts Department.
—— (1989) *Leicester Ecology Strategy*, Leicester: Leicester Council Planning Department.
—— (1991) *Open Space Standards*, Leicester: Leicester Council Planning Department.
Leeds City Council (1980) *Space about Dwellings*, Leeds: Leeds Council Department of Planning.
Leisure Consultants (1990a) *Leisure Trends: the Thatcher Years*, Sudbury: Leisure Consultants.
—— (1990b) *Leisure Forecasts: 1991–1995*, Sudbury: Leisure Consultants.
Lenskyj, H. (1986) *Out of Bounds: Women, Sport and Sexuality*, Toronto: The Women's Press.
Little, A. (1990) 'The grid-iron invasion: American football in Britain'. *Sport Place* Vol. 4 No. 2: 20–25.
London Council for Sport and Recreation (1987) *A Capital Prospect – a Strategy for London Sport*, London: London Council.
London Planning Advisory Committee (1988) *Strategic Planning Advice for London*, London: LPAC.
Long, J. and Wimbush, E. (1979) *Leisure and the Over 50s*, London: Sports Council/ESRC.
Lowerson, J. (1989) 'Angling'. In Mason (1989): 12–43.
McCance, M. (1983) 'New park development in Glasgow's inner area'. *Landscape Research* Vol. 8 No. 2: 19–25.
McClintock, H. (1987) 'On the right track? An assessment of recent English experience of innovations in urban bicycle planning'. *Town Planning Review* Vol. 58 No. 3: 267–292.
—— (1990) 'Planning for the bicycle in urban Britain: an assessment of experience and issues'. In Tolley (1990): 201–217.
—— (ed.) (1992) *The Bicycle and City Traffic*, London: Belhaven.
McClintock, H. and Cleary, J. (1993) 'English urban cycle route network experiments: the experience of the Greater Nottingham network'. *Town Planning Review* Vol. 64 No. 2: 169–192.
McCrone, K.E. (1987) 'Play up! play up! And play the game! Sport at the late Victorian girls' public school'. In Mangan and Park (1987): 97–129.
McKenna, M. (1989) 'Municipal suburbia in Liverpool'. *Town Planning Review* Vol. 60 No. 3: 287–318.
Maguire, J. (1990) 'American football: an emergent sport form in English society'. *Sport Place* Vol. 4 No. 2: 2–13.
—— (1991) 'American football in English society'. *Physical Education Review* Vol. 14 No. 2: 135–142.
Mangan, J.A. and Park, R.J. (eds) (1987) *From 'Fair Sex' to Feminism: Sport and the Socialization of Women in the Industrial and Post-industrial Eras*, London: Frank Cass.

Mann, P. (1990) 'Planning and management of local authority leisure strategies'. *The Planner* Vol. 76 No.12: 11–14.

Mason, A. (ed.) (1989) *Sport in Britain: a Social History*, Cambridge: Cambridge University Press.

Mellor, R. (1989) 'Transitions in urbanization: twentieth century Britain'. *International Journal of Urban and Regional Research* Vol. 13 No. 4: 573–596.

Mercer, D. (1980) *In Pursuit of Leisure*, Melbourne: Sorrett.

Michels, T. (ed.) (1992) *Still More Bikes behind the Dikes*, Netherlands: Centre for Research and Contract Standardisation in Civil and Traffic Engineering.

Miles, C. and Seabrooke, W. (1977) *Recreational Land Management*, London: E. and F.N. Spon.

Miller, M. (1992) *Raymond Unwin, Garden Cities and Town Planning*. Leicester: Leicester University Press.

Millward, A. and Mostyn, B. (1989) *People and Nature in Cities. The Social Aspects of Planning and Managing Natural Parks in Urban Areas*, London: Nature Conservancy Council.

Minister for Sport's Review Group (1990) *Sport and Active Recreation Provision in the Inner Cities*, London: DoE.

Ministry of Housing and Local Government (1961) *Homes for Today and Tomorrow* (the Parker Morris Report), London: HMSO.

Mintel UK (1991a) 'Leisure time – age and leisure' *Leisure Intelligence* Vol. 2: 1–27.

—— (1991b) *The Sports Market*, London: Mintel.

Monheim, R. (1990) 'The evolution and impact of pedestrian areas in the Federal Republic of Germany'. In Tolley (1990): 244–254.

Moore, R.C. (1986) *Childhood's Domain: Play and Place in Child Development*, London: Croom Helm.

—— (1987) 'Streets as playgrounds'. In Moudon (1987): 45–62.

Morphet, J. (1990) 'Urban green space – an issue for the 1990s'. *Town and Country Planning* Vol. 59 No. 7/8: 198–199.

Moudon, A.V. (ed.) (1987) *Public Streets for Public Use*, New York: Van Nostrand Reinhold.

Moughtin, C. (1991a) 'The European city street. Part 1 – paths and places'. *Town Planning Review* Vol. 62 No. 1: 51–77.

—— (1991b) 'The European city street. Part 2 – relating form and function'. *Town Planning Review* Vol. 62 No. 2: 153–199.

Mrozek, D.J. (1987) 'The "Amazon" and the American "Lady" – sexual fears of women as athletes'. In Mangan and Park (1987): 282–298.

Munton, R. (1983) *London's Green Belt*, London: George Allen and Unwin.

NCPRU: National Children's Play and Recreation Unit (1992) *Playground Safety Guidelines*, London: Department of Education and Science.

Newby, H. (1990) 'Ecology, amenity and society: social science and environmental change'. *Town Planning Review* Vol. 61 No. 1: 3–20.

Newman, O. (1972) *Defensible Space: Crime Prevention through Urban Design*, London: Macmillan.

Nice, S. (1983) 'A masterplan for the rejuvenation of Battersea Park'. *Landscape Research* Vol. 8 No. 2: 16–18.

Nicholson-Lord, D. (1987) *The Greening of the Cities*, London: Routledge and Kegan Paul.

Nottinghamshire County Council/Sports Council (1989) *The Costs in Pitch Use*, Nottingham and London: Nottingham and London Councils.

Nuneaton and Bedworth Borough Council (undated) *Standards of Play and Open Space Provision*, Nuneaton: Council Planning and Development Department.

Nuttgens, P. (1973) 'The people and the park'. *Parks and Sports Grounds* Vol. 38 No. 2: 512–518.

Oc, T. (1991) 'Planning natural surveillance back into city centres'. *Town and Country Planning* Vol. 60 No. 8: 237–239.

OPCS: Office of Population Censuses and Surveys (1989) *General Household Survey 1987*, London: HMSO.

—— (1992) *General Household Survey 1990*, London: HMSO.

—— (1993) *Mortality Statistics 1991*, London: HMSO.

Olszewska, A. and Roberts, K. (eds) (1989) *Leisure and Life Style: a Comparative Analysis of Free Time*, London: Sage.

Oosterman, J. (1992) 'Welcome to the pleasure dome. Play and entertainment in urban public space: the example of the sidewalk café'. *Built Environment* Vol. 18 No. 2: 155–164.

Osborn, F. J. and Whittick, A. (1977) *New Towns: their Origins, Achievements and Progress*, London: Leonard Hill.

Pack, C. and Glyptis, S. (1989) *Developing Sport and Leisure: Case Studies of Good Practice in Urban Regeneration*, London: HMSO.

Page, S. (1990) 'Sports arena development in the UK – its role in urban regeneration in London Docklands'. *Sport Place* Vol. 4 No. 1: 3–15.

Park, R.J. (1987) 'Sport, gender and society in a transatlantic Victorian perspective'. In Mangan and Park (1987) : 58–93.

Parkinson, C.E. (1987) *Where Children Play: an Analysis of Interviews about Where Children Aged 5–14 Normally Play and Their Preferences for Out-of-school Activities*, Birmingham: Association for Children's Play and Recreation.

Patmore, J.A. (1970) *Land and Leisure*, Newton Abbot: David and Charles.

—— (1983) *Recreation and Resources: Leisure Patterns and Leisure Places*, Oxford: Blackwell.

Perloff, H.S. (1985) 'The central city in the post-industrial age'. In Burns and Friedmann (1985): 29–46.

Piche, D. (1981) 'The spontaneous geography of the urban child'. In Herbert and Johnston (1981): 229–256.

Pigram, J. (1983) *Outdoor Recreation and Resource Management*, London: Croom Helm.

Play Board (1985) *Make Way for Children's Play: a Discussion Document on a Play Policy for the Future*, Birmingham: Play Board.

Pooley, C.G. (1977) 'The residential segregation of migrant communities in mid-Victorian Liverpool'. *Transactions of the Institute of British Geographers*, New Series, Vol. 2 No. 3: 364–382.

Punter, J. (1990) 'The ten commandments of architecture and urban design'. *The Planner* Vol. 76 No. 39: 10–14.

Ramsay, A. (1990) 'A systematic approach to the planning of urban networks for walking'. In Tolley (1990): 159–171.

Rapoport, A. (1990) *History and Precedent in Environmental Design*, New York: Plenum.

Rapoport, R. and Rapoport, R.N. (1975) *Leisure and the Family Life Cycle*, London: Routledge and Kegan Paul.

Relph, E. (1987) *The Modern Urban Landscape*, London: Croom Helm.

Rendel, S. (1983) 'Renewal of parks in inner London'. *Landscape Research* Vol. 8 No. 2: 13–15.

Research Services Ltd (1989) *Sportscan*, London: Research Services.

Reynolds, J. (1992) 'The proliferation of planned shopping centres'. In Bromley and Thomas (1992): 70–87.

Richardson, M. and Parkinson, C.E. (undated) *Children's Range Behaviour in Inner City Birmingham*, Birmingham: Play Board.

Rivers, R. and Streatfield, D. (1987) 'Graveyards into gardens: public open spaces in nineteenth and twentieth century London'. In Moudon (1987): 241–252.

Roberts, K. (1977) 'Leisure and lifestyles under welfare capitalism'. In Smith (1977): 2.1–2.18.

—— (1989) 'Great Britain: socio-economic polarisation and the implications for leisure'. In Olszewska and Roberts (1989): 47–61.

—— (1992) 'The disintegration of sport'. In Williams *et al.* (1992): 585–590.

Roberts, K., Minten, J.H., Chadwick, C., Lamb, K.L. and Brodie, D.A. (1991) 'Sport lives: a case study of leisure choices'. *Loisir et Société* Vol. 14 No. 1: 261–284.

Rodgers, H.B. (1993) 'Estimating local leisure demand in the context of a regional planning strategy'. In Glyptis (1993): 116–130.

Rose, E.A. (1984) 'Philosophy and purpose of planning'. In Bruton (1984): 31–65.

Russell, J. (1990) 'Traffic calming and town planning'. *Town Planning Review* Vol. 61 No. 2: iii–vi.

Savitch, H.V. (1988) *Post-industrial cities – Politics and Planning in New York, Paris and London*, Princeton: Princeton University Press.

Scott, D. and Willets, F.K. (1989) 'Adolescent and adult leisure patterns: a 37 year follow-up study'. *Leisure Sciences* Vol. 11 No. 4: 323–335.

Scott, M. (1990) 'A blooming business'. *Leisure Management* Vol. 10 No. 4: 42–45.

Scottish Sports Council (1991) *Study of Golf in Scotland*, Research Report No. 19, Edinburgh: Scottish Sports Council.

Seabrook, J. (1988) *The Leisure Society*, Oxford: Blackwell.

Sebba, R. (1991) 'The landscapes of childhood: the reflection of childhood's environment in adult memories and in children's attitudes'. *Environment and Behavior* Vol. 23 No. 4: 395–422.

Shaw, S.M. (1991) 'Women's leisure time'. *Leisure Studies* Vol. 10 No. 2: 171–181.

Sheets, V.L. and Manzer, C.D. (1991) 'Affect, cognition and urban vegetation'. *Environment and Behavior* Vol. 23 No. 3: 285–304.

Sheldon, T. (1990) 'Children's play and recreation'. *The Planner* Vol. 76 No. 13: 20–21.

Sleap, M. and Walker, L. (1992) 'Usage of community sports centres by adolescents: a case study of a secondary school'. *Physical Education Review* Vol. 15 No. 1: 61–71.

Smith, J. (1987) 'Men and women at play: gender, life cycle and leisure'. In Horne *et al.* (1987): 51–85.

Smith, M.A. (1977) *Leisure and Urban Society*, Leisure Studies Association Conference Papers No. 6.

Smith, S.J. (1987) 'Fear of crime: beyond a geography of deviance'. *Progress in Human Geography* Vol. 11 No. 1: 1–23.

Soja, E.J. (1989) *Postmodern Geographies: the Re-assertion of Space in Critical Social Theory*, London: Verso.

Spink, J. (1989) 'Urban development, leisure facilities, and the inner city: a case study on inner Leeds and Bradford'. In Brahman *et al.* (1989): 195–215.

Spirn, A.W. (1987) 'Better air quality at street level: strategies for urban design'. In Moudon (1987): 310–320.

Sports Council (1981) *Sharing Does Work. Economic and Social Benefits and Costs of Direct and Joint Sports Provision*. Sports Council Study No. 21, London: Sports Council.

—— (1982) *Sport in the Community: the Next Ten Years*, London: Sports Council.

—— (1988) *Sport in the Community: into the 90s*, London: Sports Council.

—— (1991) *The Playing Pitch Strategy*, London: Sports Council.

—— (1992a) *Women and Sport: a Consultation Document*, London: Sports Council.

—— (1992b) *Young People and Sport: a Consultation Document*, London: Sports Council.

—— (1993) *Sport in the Nineties: New Horizons*, London: Sports Council.

Sports Council (Southern Region) (1989) *Providing for Golf in the Southern Region*, Reading: Sports Council.

Stamp, D. (1987) 'Inner city community gardens'. *Landscape Research* Vol. 12 No. 1: 5–8.

Stevenage Borough Council (1991) *Open Space Survey Technical Note*, Stevenage: Stevenage Council.

Stokowski, P.A. and Lee, R.G. (1991) 'The influence of social network ties on recreation and leisure'. *Journal of Leisure Research*, Vol. 23 No. 2: 95–113.

Strachan, A.J. and Bowler, I.R. (1978) 'Urban open space for recreation'. *Parks and Recreation* Vol. 43 No. 10: 32–39.

Talbot, M. (1988) 'Beating them at our own game? Women's sports involvement'. In Wimbush and Talbot (1988): 102–114.

Tartaglia-Kershaw, M. (1982) 'The recreational and aesthetic significance of urban woodland'. *Landscape Research* Vol. 7 No. 3: 22–25.

Telford Development Corporation (1973) *Town Park*, unpublished submission to the Secretary of State for Environment.

Thornley, A. (ed.) (1992) *The Crisis of London*, London: Routledge.

Thorpe, H. (1975) 'The homely allotment: from rural dole to urban amenity'. *Geography* Vol. 60 No. 3: 169–183.

Tolley, R.S. (1989) *Calming Traffic in Residential Areas*, Tregaron: Brefi Press.

—— (ed) (1990) *The Greening of Urban Transport: Planning for Walking and Cycling in Western Cities*, London: Belhaven.

Tomlinson, A. (ed.) (1983) *Leisure and Popular Cultural Forms*, Brighton Polytechnic: Chelsea School of Human Movement.

Tregay, R. (1979) 'Urban woodland'. In Laurie (1979a): 267–295.

TRRU: Tourism and Recreation Research Unit (1983) *Urban Parks and Open Spaces: A Review*, London: Sports Council/SSRC.

Turner, T. (1991) 'Updating Abercrombie's open space plan'. *Town and Country Planning* Vol. 60 No. 5: 143–144.

Ullrich, O. (1990) 'The pedestrian town as an environmentally tolerable alternative to motorised travel'. In Tolley (1990): 97–110.

Untermann, R.K. (1984) *Accommodating the Pedestrian. Adapting Towns and Neighborhoods for Walking and Bicycling*, New York: Van Nostrand Reinhold.

Unwin, R. (1909) *Town Planning in Practice: an Introduction to the Art of Designing Cities and Suburbs*, London: Fisher Unwin.

Valentine, G. (1990) 'Women's fear and the design of public space'. *Built Environment* Vol. 16 No. 4: 288–303.

—— (1992) 'London's streets of fear'. In Thornley (1992): 90–102.

Veal, A.J. (1982) *Planning for Leisure: Alternative Approaches*, Papers in Leisure Studies No. 5, London: Polytechnic of North London.

—— (1987) *Leisure and the Future*, London: Allen and Unwin.

—— (1993a) 'The concept of leisure lifestyle: a review'. *Leisure Studies* Vol. 12 No. 4: 233–252.

—— (1993b) 'Planning for leisure: past, present and future'. In Glyptis (1993): 85–95.

Vidal, J. (1994) 'Darkness on the edge of town'. *The Guardian*, 17 March.

Walker, S.E. and Duffield, B.S. (1983) 'Urban parks and open spaces – an overview'. *Landscape Research* Vol. 8 No. 2: 2–12.

Walmsley, D.J. and Lewis, G.J. (1989) 'The pace of pedestrian flows in cities'. *Environment and Behavior* Vol. 21 No. 2: 123–150.

Ward, C. (1978) *The Child in the City*, New York: Pantheon.

Ward, D. (1980) 'Environs and neighbours in the "Two Nations": residential differentiation in mid-nineteenth century Leeds'. *Journal of Historical Geography*, Vol.6 No. 2: 133–162.

Ward, S. (1992) *The Garden City: Past, Present and Future*, London: E. and F.N. Spon.

Welch, D. (1991) *The Management of Urban Parks*, Harlow: Longman.

Whitehand, J.W.R. (1991) *The Making of the Urban Landscape*, Oxford: Blackwell.

Whitelegg, J. (1990) 'The principle of environmental traffic management'. In Tolley (1990): 75–87.

Wilkinson, P.F. (1988) 'Urban open space planning in Finland, Norway and Sweden'. *Leisure Studies* Vol. 7 No. 3: 267–285.

Williams, S. (1991) *Recreation Planning in the Public Sector: a Case Study of Telford New Town*, Occasional Papers in Geography, No. 15. Stoke-on-Trent: Staffordshire Polytechnic.

Williams, S. and Jackson, G.A.M. (1985) *Recreational Use of Public Open Space in the Potteries Conurbation*, Occasional Papers in Geography, No. 5. Stoke-on-Trent: North Staffordshire Polytechnic.

—— (1986) *Participation in Sport and Physical Recreation in the Potteries Conurbation*, Occasional Papers in Geography, No. 6. Stoke-on-Trent: North Staffordshire Polytechnic.

—— (1987) *Entertainments and Social Recreation in the Potteries Conurbation*, Occasional Papers in Geography, No. 9. Stoke-on-Trent: North Staffordshire Polytechnic.

Williams, T., Almond, L. and Sparkes, A. (eds) (1992) *Sport and Physical Activity: Moving towards Excellence*, London: E. and F.N. Spon.

Willis, P. (1990) *Moving Culture: an Enquiry into the Cultural Activities of Young People*, London: Calouste Gulbenkian Foundation.

Wilson, J.B. (1991) 'The future city: where is the city going?'. *The Planner* Vol. 77 No. 3: 9–11.

Wimbush, E. (1986) *Women, Leisure and Well-being*, Edinburgh: Dunfermline College of Physical Education, Centre for Leisure Research.

Wimbush, E. and Talbot, M. (eds) (1988) *Relative Freedoms: Women and Leisure*, Milton Keynes: Open University Press.

Winchester City Council (1992) *Sport and Recreation Strategy 1993–1996*, Winchester: Winchester Council.

Winter, J., Coombes, T. and Farthing, S. (1993) 'Satisfaction with space around the home on large private sector estates. Lessons from surveys in southern England and south Wales'. *Town Planning Review* Vol. 64 No. 1: 65–88.

Woodward, S.C. (1990) 'The phenomenon of vacant land in Stoke-on-Trent', Staffordshire Polytechnic, unpublished Ph.D. thesis.

Wynne, D. (1990) 'Leisure, lifestyle and the construction of social position'. *Leisure Studies* Vol. 9 No. 1: 21–34.

York City Council (1993) *The Pedestrian Strategy and Pedestrian Route Network*, York: Council Directorate of Development Services.

Young, M. and Wilmott, P. (1973) *The Symmetrical Family*, London: Routledge and Kegan Paul.

Index